Želimir Dj. Mikić

Ever Yours Sincerely

The Life and Work of Dr. Katherine S. MacPhail

Translated by

Dr. Muriel Heppell

Perfect Publishers Ltd

ISBN 978-1-905399-27-7

Cover Design – Duncan Bamford
www.insightillustration.co.uk

This is a Perfect Publishers Book

Perfect Publishers Ltd
23 Maitland Avenue
Cambridge
CB4 1TA
England
www.perfectpublishers.co.uk

Original Serbian text first published by
"Matica Srpska", Novi Sad (Republic of Serbia), 1998, under the title

Uvek Vaša, Život i delo Dr. Ketrin Makfejl

* * *

The original Serbian text has been dedicated to the memory of
Dr. Katherine S. MacPhail, Mrs. Elspeth Biggs and other members of the
MacPhail family

* * *

This translation is affectionately dedicated
to
Peter Beckley, MBE
and
Diana Beckley, MBE

and all other members of the Norfolk & Norwich Novi Sad Association

All proceeds from the sale of the book will be donated to a charity set up to restore the "English Hospital" in Sremska Kamenica, as a memorial to Dr. Katherine MacPhail

Contents

Author's Biography

Prof. Želimir Mikić was born in 1936, and since 1965 has lived and worked in Novi Sad. He graduated in medicine in Belgrade in 1961, completed specialist study in orthopaedic surgery in Novi Sad in 1969, and was awarded a doctorate in the University of Novi Sad in 1975. He has engaged in specialist study in Great Britain, Denmark and Canada. In Novi Sad he has been head of department in the Clinic for Orthopaedic Surgery and Traumatology, and professor in the Medical Faculty. He is a member of several Serbian and foreign specialist organisations, and on the editorial board of a number of Serbian and foreign journals. He has been president of the Vojvodina Medical Association, and of the Society of Orthopaedic Specialists and Traumatologists in Yugoslavia. He has also been engaged in various aspects of publicity, and published several articles in Yugoslav and international journals, and books on orthopaedic and experimental surgery, and on the History of Medicine.

Translator's Biography

Muriel Heppell is Emeritus Reader in the Medieval History of Orthodox Eastern Europe in the University of London, where she worked from 1968 to 1983. Before that she worked as English Lector in the universities of Novi Sad and Belgrade. She has written a number of works on the medieval history of southeast Europe, and also translated those of Yugoslav writers, including the epic novel, *Vreme Smrti* (A Time of Death) by Dobrica Cosić. Her latest work is *George Bell and Nikolai Velimirović: The Story of a Friendship* (Lazarica Press, 2001).

Author's Preface

It was early in the summer of 1965, when I was a young doctor accepted for specialisation in orthopaedic surgery in the Surgical Clinic in Novi Sad, that I first visited the so-called "English Hospital" in Sremska Kamenica, which was an integral part of that Clinic; and it was then that I first heard of Dr. Katherine MacPhail and her hospital, though I had studied medicine in Belgrade. I was greatly surprised by this discovery, and very anxious to learn more; unfortunately I could rarely discover anything further about the fate of this, to me, mysterious doctor, and even less about her work and activities. Clearly the dust of oblivion had covered the whole story.

As the hospital in Sremska Kamenica was in fact part of the Orthopaedic and Traumatologic Department, I often went and worked there in the course of my own job; and since my interest in the founder of the hospital increased over the years, I gradually discovered more about Dr. Katherine MacPhail herself and her humanitarian activities. The more I learnt, the more fascinated I became by this exciting story, by her nobility and by all that she had achieved; however I must admit that I also felt very sad, most of all by the fact that such a person, who had done so much for this country and its people, should towards the end of her life, have had the experience of actually being driven out of her hospital, and out of the country which she regarded as her second homeland; and then because she had so easily been forgotten. I felt that this was a great injustice, I even felt in some way personally offended by what had happened. Probably other people had felt the same earlier, since some years after Dr. MacPhail's departure from Yugoslavia, and also subsequently, attempts had been made to set things right, and to give due recognition for all that this courageous and noble Scotswoman had done for our people. However, it seemed to me that all this was not enough, in view of her great achievements on the one hand, and the great injustice and ingratitude she had suffered on the other. As I reflected on this over many years, I came to the conclusion that the only suitable way of commemorating the name and the work of Dr. Katherine MacPhail was to write a book about her life, because a book is the most lasting and indestructible memorial; this is indeed clear from the twentieth century, when there have been so many attempts to destroy unacceptable books and consign them to the flames. So I set myself this task, since I regarded it as the only way to proceed, and indeed felt it was my personal duty towards both Katherine MacPhail and her family.

However, the preparation and writing of such a book, which required much preliminary research and collection of material, was no easy task, especially since it was undertaken as a spare-time occupation when engaged in a full-time profession; it was indeed a lengthy and laborious undertaking, which required the assistance of many individuals and institutions. Fortunately for me, all those from whom I have sought help have been most understanding and obliging, and it now gives me great pleasure, at the end of this task, which I hope has not been undertaken in vain, to express my warmest thanks to them.

The greatest help has certainly been that of my dear friend Mrs. Elspeth Biggs of St Andrews, a niece of the late Dr. Katherine MacPhail, who over many years has collected documents, photographs, and other material about the life of her aunt, and for whom I am sure that this book will be the greatest reward and expression of gratitude for all that she has done. Through her I have also obtained, apart from many other letters and documents, a copy of a manuscript by Shena Watson about a missionary hospital in India, dated 1948, and a letter from Basil Gardner-McTaggart to Dr. Katherine MacPhail, dated January 13th, 1935, now preserved in the family archives.

Katherine MacPhail did not herself keep a personal diary - as she said once about it: "I kept no diary of our days or doings – we were too busy or too depressed to go over again the events of each day,"- nor did she write her autobiography; but she did leave a large number of letters, written mainly to her mother, and some manuscript copies of public lectures, given for the purpose of raising funds for her humanitarian work, several published official reports of the work of her hospitals, and also a number of articles published mainly in *The World's Children*, in which she described her travels and her work; these have been a very important source of information. She also related her memories to Jean Bray, who included this material in a book, unfortunately unpublished, which has also been a very valuable source. Most of these letters and manuscripts are preserved in the archives of the Imperial War Museum in London, whose employees kindly showed them to me when I was pursuing my research in that museum in October, 1989. They also granted me the permission to use five photographs from their archives (HU56807, HU56808, HU56809, HY56810 and Q32072) in this publication; I owe my warm thanks to them.

I am also most grateful to the Save the Children Fund whose employees, in particular Mrs. Jane Button, Head of Central Information, kindly helped me to collect relevant material (in their possession), especially a number of articles, reports and notes relating to Dr. Katherine MacPhail and published in their journal *The World's Children*. For additional primary material related to the studies of Dr. Katherine MacPhail, her father and sister Isabel I should like to thank the staff of the Glasgow University Archives, especially Miss Moira MacKay, Assistant Archivist, for their help and patience. I received much help and support from the Vojvodina Archives in Novi Sad where I obtained many documents related to the building and upkeep of the Children's Sanatorium at Sremska Kamenica. I also met with much understanding in the museum of the Serbian Medical Association in Belgrade; I owe a special debt of gratitude to Dr. Žarko Vuković, who provided me with copies of a letter written by Dr. Katherine

MacPhail to this association on December 28th, 1973, and of the letter of Prof. Dr. Vladimir Stanojević to Dr. Katherine MacPhail, dated September 25th, 1974, and also a photograph of the slides which Dr. Katherine MacPhail presented to the Serbian Medical Association, from which many of the photographs appearing in this book were made.

I would like to thank the family of the late Dr. Branko Manojlović from Sremska Kamenica who allowed me access to his archives, where I found exceptionally useful reports which he submitted to the Main Regional Hospital in Novi Sad about the work of the Department of Osteo-Articular Tuberculosis (OAT) in Sremska Kamenica during the years 1955-61, and also other useful information. I would also like to thank Mr. Ilija Vidaković, a well-known lawyer in Novi Sad, who gave me valuable assistance in collecting material from the Local Public Records of the Land Registry relating to Sremska Kamenica in 1933 and later. I owe a special debt of gratitude to Mr. Ronald Keymer from St Andrews, who gave me much help in collecting material relating to that city, and to Dr. Jean Scott from Pitlochry who sent me important photographs and documents during the years 1986-1989.

Many other individuals, of whom several were Dr. Katherine MacPhail's contemporaries, gave me valuable help by means of letters, photographs and personal recollections, to whom I wish to express my thanks: Mr. Petar Ivić from Belgrade, who sent me a copy of his certificate of attendance of the fourth class of the elementary school in the hospital at Sremska Kamenica, dated June 5th, 1949; Prof. Milenko Došen of Novi Sad, with whom I discussed this subject during the period 1978-1979; Mr. Branko Bugarski from Novi Sad (letters and conversations, March-September, 1985); Mrs. Milica Ćirić from Novi Sad (letters, photographs, and conversations, March-September, 1985): Mr. Milan Ćirić from Belgrade (conversations and photographs, 1985); Mr. Ivan Koska from Sremska Kamenica (conversations, 1985); Mr. Svetislav Novaković from Sremska Kamenica (conversations and photographs, 1985), Mr. Ratko S. Stanković from England (letters, October 23rd, 1986, December 1st, 1986 and September 9th, 1987); Mr. Rade Kosanović from Sremska Kamenica (conversations, 1987); Mrs. Julka Skrjaga from Sremska Kamenica (conversations, 1988) Mr. Ivan Belina of Sremska Kamenica (conversations and photographs, 1988); Mr. Milovan Gašović from Belgrade (letter, 1991); Mrs. Olga Miladinović from Novi Sad (conversation, April 1996) and Major Ivan Zeljković from the Institute of Military Medical Information and Documentation, the Archives of the Military Medical Corps of the Military Medical Academy in Belgrade (letters and conversations, 1996-1997). To all these people, of whom many, sadly, are no longer alive, I owe a great debt of gratitude, because without their help this book could not have been written.

Finally I wish to extend my warmest thanks to Dr. Muriel Heppell, Emeritus Reader in the University of London and long-standing English Lector in the universities of Novi Sad and Belgrade, who kindly accepted the demanding task of translating this book into English, and thus enabled the story of the life and work of Dr. Katherine MacPhail to reach a much wider circle of readers.

Želimir Mikić
Novi Sad, March, 2007

Translator's Preface

I first heard about the "English Hospital" in Sremska Kamenica many years ago, in the late 1950s, when I was working as the English "lektor" in a newly-established English department, which later became part of the University of Novi Sad. I soon became a member of a local rambling club, and our walks through Fruška Gora often started in Sremska Kamenica. It was on one of these excursions that the "English Hospital" was pointed out to me, and I was told that the reason for this name was that an English lady (actually a Scotswoman) used to work there; but nobody seemed to know anything more than that. It was not until I read Professor Mikić's biography of Dr. Katherine MacPhail, some decades later, that I learnt the full story of this children's hospital and its dynamic founder. I was deeply moved by what I read, and by all that this Scotswoman had done in a place, which had become my "second homeland", as it had earlier been hers. I was particularly impressed by the closing words of this book: "It was always a hospital, but it always was and has remained a unique memorial of friendship and co-operation between people from different countries, of different nationality, beliefs and customs, but above all a lasting and inspiring reminder of human courage and nobility". This is indeed a valuable part of our heritage, and I hope that this English translation of Prof. Mikić's book will help to keep this tradition active and vibrant.

Muriel Heppell
March, 2007

Chapter 1

The MacPhail Family

The name of "MacPhail" is derived from the Gaelic language, and means "Son of Paul". The Scottish MacPhail family, with whom we are concerned here, originated on the island of Mull off the west coast of Scotland, north-west of Glasgow. The "Sons of Paul" who were the ancestors of Dr. Katherine MacPhail lived and farmed in the lovely green valley of Glenforsa for some 800 years. At the end of the third decade of the nineteenth century, Katherine's grandfather, Dugald Stewart MacPhail (1818-1887) left the island of Mull and went out into the world in search of a new and better life. He was the first of the family to show the courage and determination, and the inclination to seek out what was new and unknown which can be seen later in his descendants, and especially in his granddaughter Katherine. After leaving the island of Mull Dugald MacPhail went to Newcastle-on-Tyne, in the north of England, where he trained as an architect. Later he lived and worked for some time as an architect and clerk of works to the Duke of Westminster in Shaftesbury in Dorset, where a number of his children were born. Dugald MacPhail left this work for very high-principled reasons: in the building of a house for which he was responsible, against his will poor quality material was used; he therefore resigned his post and left Shaftesbury. After this, in 1868, the family moved to Edinburgh where they lived for several years and then, on his death, finally settled in Glasgow.

Dugald MacPhail was clearly a very enterprising, industrious and practical man, since he was able to earn enough to support a large family and to educate eight children. However, at heart he was a poet, continually troubled by nostalgia for his native country, his island of Mull. As he had an excellent knowledge of classic Gaelic, he began to write poems in that language, mainly dedicated to his island, and because of this he came to be known as "The Bard of Mull". His songs are still sung in Scotland, and his most famous poem, *The Isle of Mull* has become a kind of national anthem for the island, and is recorded on a gramophone record sung by the Glasgow Orpheus Choir. As a mark of gratitude the Gaelic Folklore Society from the island of Mull built a memorial to him in the valley of Glenmore (Fig. 1). The sturdy monument, made from the stones taken from his old cottage nearby, was erected to his memory in the early 1920s. On all four sides of the monument the open pages of a book with 4 verses of *The Isle of Mull* all written in Gaelic are carved in hard stone.

Dugald MacPhail was undoubtedly very devoted to his family and his children, and exceptionally liberal and progressive for his times, since he provided higher education for all his children, sons and daughters. Four of his sons, Donald, James, Alexander and John studied medicine at Glasgow University; the fifth son, William, devoted himself to religion and became a minister of the Presbyterian Church. Dugald's eldest daughter Kate became a nurse, Sarah a teacher of modern languages and Jessie a teacher of music. It is interesting that five of his children chose some form of medical profession; this characteristic of humanitarian activity and inclination towards medicine was inherited later by several of his descendants, including Katherine.

Dr. James M. MacPhail (1863-1929) was the second son of Dugald MacPhail, and was Katherine's oldest uncle. Although a "Scot of Scots", as his granddaughter Shena Watson put it, he was born in Shaftesbury, in England, and studied both medicine and theology at Glasgow University. From 1889 onwards he worked as a missionary in north-east India where he founded a missionary hospital in Bamdah (Santalia) in which he and his wife, Dr. Janet MacPhail, worked for the rest of their lives. His work was continued by his eldest son, Dr. Ronald MacPhail, also a doctor, who ran the hospital until his retirement, and then retired to the island of Mull, where he worked as a minister of the Presbyterian church; some years later he moved to Edinburgh, where he died.

James's younger son Russell became a teacher of English and the head of the Christian College of Madras in the Church of South India. He became a well-known publicist and author of a number of books; he died in Edinburgh. His daughter Jean became a nurse and worked in the Bamdah hospital and elsewhere in India, where she married Thomas Warren, a teacher in India; they moved later to Aberdeen where they had three children: Janet, Shena, and Andrew; they all were living in Great Britain where their mother Jean died in 1981. Shena, later Shena Watson, was the one who described later the work of her grandfather in India. [1]

James's third son, Dr. Dugald MacPhail (Fig. 1) also studied medicine but in St Andrews, thus breaking the long tradition in the MacPhail family of studying in Glasgow. During the Second World War Dugald was an officer in the Royal Navy, and was dropped by parachute into the liberated territory of Yugoslavia, where he organised an improvised hospital in a cave in the mountains. When orders arrived that all the British doctors and other officers were to leave Yugoslavia, Dugald refused to abandon his patients; he was then imprisoned, and after several months repatriated. After that he was sent to Burma, where he was parachuted into the jungle, behind the Japanese lines, where he treated the sick and wounded. Later he was decorated for his work both in Yugoslavia and in Burma. After the war he worked as a consultant psychologist in London, and later moved to Devon, after his wife's death. He died in Dorset in 1995.

James's youngest son Ian emigrated to New Zealand where he became a very successful sheep farmer. He called his ranch "Glen Forsa", after his grandfather's district in the island of Mull. During the Second World War he was badly wounded in Crete and imprisoned there, and later repatriated. After the war he continued to run his farm in New Zealand, where he died in 1994.

Dugald's fourth son, Dr. John MacPhail studied medicine in Glasgow and later worked as a doctor in Yorkshire where he married and had two daughters and a son.

Alexander MacPhail (1872-1938) was the youngest son of Dugald MacPhail, the "Bard of Mull", and Katherine's youngest uncle. He also studied medicine in Glasgow. He was a very active student and editor of the Glasgow University Magazine. There is an interesting incident about him recorded from this time of his life. When Lord Lister (1827-1912), a famous surgeon and inventor of antiseptic surgery, visited Glasgow University Hospital in which he had worked earlier, the students unharnessed the horses from his carriage, and themselves pulled the carriage to his house. Alexander MacPhail directed the whole incident from the coachman's seat. Later he became professor of Anatomy and the Dean in the Glasgow University, professor of Anatomy in London University, then a high official of the Ministry of Health and a professor of Anatomy in the Royal Academy of Arts, where he was particularly successful, as he had an excellent understanding of art. Elspeth Biggs said of him: "We remember him with great pleasure – he was very amusing, very well-informed about art, played on all keyboard instruments, sang wonderfully, spoke Gaelic, and, like his older brother Donald, left many fine pictures of Benderloch which hang on our walls".

Dugald's eldest son, Donald MacPhail (1854-1931) was one of the best students of his generation at Glasgow University, even though he had to help himself by working for a pharmacist in the evenings, because of his limited financial resources. After completing his studies on April 30th, 1877 he began to work as a resident at the Glasgow Western Infirmary, when he met and fell in love with Jessie Mitchell (1850-1925), daughter of a master-builder from Fife in eastern Scotland, who was working as a probationer nurse in the same hospital. The relationship soon led to marriage, concluded in 1881. Shortly after the marriage the young Dr. Donald MacPhail accepted an invitation to work in the County of Lanarkshire, and settled in the small village of Whifflet on the outskirts of Coatbridge, some 12 miles east of central Glasgow. This was an industrial area in the immediate vicinity of Glasgow, where there were mines and ironworks employing many workers, who lived modestly in typical estates with endless rows of houses consisting of a single room and a kitchen, often occupied by families of eight to ten members. Dr. Donald MacPhail gladly accepted the difficult task of working as a doctor in these surroundings, and later carried out this work with considerable energy and satisfaction, right up to his retirement. Among the inhabitants of this area, where Scots and Irish predominated, there was a considerable Polish colony, with whom Dr. MacPhail became very popular because he learnt Polish well enough to communicate with them in their own language. In addition Dr. MacPhail became well known as one of the first doctors in Scotland to set up permanent first aid and ambulance services. Because of his devotion to his work he became greatly liked and highly valued, and soon acquired a large number of patients, both among the poverty-stricken workers and farmers and among the wealthy inhabitants who soon joined him as private patients. For visiting his patients he used, summer and winter, a light, two-seater trap by which he was well-known throughout the district. When he went to visit distant patients in the surrounding villages, word soon got round that the doctor's carriage was coming (Fig. 2). This was certainly very difficult and responsible work, which demanded a strong will, self-sacrifice and love of his patients, and the MacPhails were clearly gifted with these noble qualities. Recalling these days, Katherine later related that during one severe winter, for five months her father daily visited a seriously ill patient after his regular surgery, and rarely returned home before nine or ten o'clock at night. In his rare leisure moments, and especially during his summer holiday, Dr. MacPhail enjoyed painting, and left behind him a large number of water colours.

In Coatbridge the MacPhail family lived in a fine house in Calder Avenue, with a courtyard and an orchard (Figs. 3 and 4) where Katherine and her sisters were born and spent their childhood. The first child in the family of Jessie and Donald MacPhail was Janet, born in 1884, then Annie, born in 1886. Katherine, the third daughter, was born on October 30th, 1887 [2], and the youngest, Isabel, in 1889 (see Appendix 4-6).

They were a very happy and close-knit family. Although the father, Dr. Donald, was kept very busy with his work as a doctor, he still managed to devote sufficient attention to his daughters, and what he could not do was supplied by their mother, Jessie, who took on the main responsibility for the house and children. Both parents were very devoted to each other and to their daughters, so that Katherine and her three sisters spent a very happy and care-free childhood in their spacious and comfortable family home (Fig. 5). There was no end to their toys, and interesting memories still exist from those times.[3] Their immediate neighbour was the local mayor, who also had two daughters, the same age as Katherine and Isabel. The little girls became friends and played together, and as they wanted to be in continual contact, they fixed a "telephone" between their rooms; it consisted of empty tins and string, which they stretched across both courtyards, which adjoined each other. How long this "telephone" functioned has not been recorded. Since Dr. Donald constantly used his horse and trap to visit his patients, he had a spacious stable in the courtyard, which the children often used to perform plays, and where they produced pantomimes, usually around Christmas. Later, when they were a bit older, they all took part in a group, which performed pantomimes in the church hall. The stables, it seems, were one of the favourite places for the children to play, and an amusing story about this has survived in the family memories. When she was still a little girl, Katherine decided to lay some eggs, so one day she placed some hen's eggs on straw in her father's stable, and sat on top of them in a suitable position until the chickens emerged; to pass the time she carved her name with a knife on a wooden partition. How long she sat there has not been recorded, but the eggs remained whole, there were no chickens and all that has survived is her name on the manger.[4]

The girls' education began at home, when they had private teachers; this lasted until they were old enough to go every day to the primary school in Coatbridge, some distance away. Later they attended high school at Hillhead Academy in Glasgow. During the week they stayed with their grandmother and aunts, and came home at week-ends. Staying with their grandmother was a special experience for the girls, which made a strong impression on them. Her house was full of books, pictures and music; and the company of their well-educated aunts, and especially of their uncle Alex and his learned friends, who often came on a visit, undoubtedly made a deep impression on all four girls and had a lasting effect on them. They started to attend school in Glasgow in pairs, according to their age. The first to go were the older sisters, Janet and Annie, who liked school, then Katherine and Isabel, who were not so enthusiastic and who wanted to run away from school and walk in the surrounding fields and woods. However all four girls were very bright and gifted, and after finishing school went on to study at Glasgow University (Figs. 6 - 10).

Katherine was the only one of Dr. Donald MacPhail's daughters who showed any interest in her father's work as a doctor, which she did early in her childhood. Ever as a small child she would go into her father's surgery and watch him examining patients or bandaging wounds. She also liked to accompany him when he visited patients in distant farms, which he usually did on Sundays, when she would sit proudly beside the coachman. In addition to this, her decision to study medicine and devote herself to a medical career was probably influenced by her two uncles who were successful doctors: James, who then directed a missionary hospital in India, and Alex, who was a professor of anatomy in the University of Glasgow (Fig. 11).

At that time it was unusual in Great Britain for women to study at all, and especially to study medicine. All that was expected of well brought up girls from good homes in that era was that they should keep house well and paint water colours – as a contemporary sarcastically remarked. Probably this was why Dr. Donald MacPhail was against Katherine studying medicine. When one of his colleagues once asked him: "And what would you say if one of your daughters wanted to study medicine?" he replied: "I'd sooner see her a policeman". However, Katherine had already shown a marked and persistent determination, and nothing would make her change her mind. Fortunately her parents, notwithstanding certain prejudices, were very liberal and progressive for those times. Like Katherine's grandfather Dugald MacPhail, her parents understood very well the importance of education, and their mother Jessie would say to her daughters: "We will not be able to leave you wealth or possessions, but we can at least give you all a good education to set you out in life".

So Katherine was one of the few girls who on 26th April 1906 enrolled as a student of Glasgow University to study medicine. In doing this she continued the family tradition, since already for many years at least one member of the family had studied medicine at this university, so the name of MacPhail was well-known there. However, Katherine was too proud to make use of this fact. On one occasion, during the students' practical work, an older doctor asked what relation she was to Doctor MacPhail. In a serious tone Katherine proudly replied: "It doesn't matter to whom I'm related. I am a MacPhail on my own and I stand firmly on my own feet". In fact "Kath" [5] was a very affable and friendly person, and made many friends among the students. She remained on friendly terms with some of her fellow-students all her life, and later they helped her a great deal by raising money and sending her medicines and medical equipment, and coming themselves to work with her in her hospitals.

Katherine was clearly a good, hard-working student, because records in the university archives show that she won some prizes as a student. She obtained a first-class diploma in practical zoology, and second-class in physiology, anatomy and surgery.

During her last years as a student Katherine began to help her father in his medical work. Ignoring the prejudice against women doctors, Dr. Donald MacPhail allowed Katherine to help him in his evening surgery, which, in view of his heavy work load, was a considerable help. This was the beginning of lasting professional collaboration, since in his later years, Katherine helped her father on several occasions, or took his place in his practice when he was ill. At that time, during the last years of her studies, Katherine began to be interested in children's diseases; and on one occasion she asked the chief of wards in the Sick Children's Hospital in Glasgow, who happened to be a close friend of her father, whether there was any chance of a woman doctor being appointed to a permanent post in the hospital. The short and discouraging answer was: "None at all, as long as I am in charge of the wards".[6] The lack of confidence in women doctors was then still considerable and deeply rooted, but this obviously did not trouble Katherine too much; she completed her medical studies successfully on October 12th, 1911 and began her medical practice as a newly qualified doctor.

As a young doctor Dr. Katherine MacPhail stayed in Glasgow, where she served as a   pre-registration house officer in the Glasgow Royal Infirmary, and after that she went to work with her father in Coatbridge. In the Medical Directory for Scotland for 1914, apart from her father Dr. Donald MacPhail, Katherine MacPhail was also included and described as an out–door assistant physician at Calder Avenue in Coatbridge (telephone number 176), that is, at the same address as her father.

The beginning of the twentieth century marked the beginning of a new era in Great Britain. In 1901 Queen Victoria died, after a reign of 64 years, and with her death there passed beyond return the so-called Victorian age of colonial rule, full of pomp and brilliance, but also of social restrictions and conservatism.

At that time the British Empire stretched over 11 million square miles around the world, "embracing seven seas", and was by far the strongest world power.[7] "The Victorian Age had made its mark. It had created or nurtured many British institutions – public schools, the professional civil service, military regiments, political parties, universities – and it had given the British a sense of stability and supremacy. British constitutional government was a model for the world. But the world was changing". On the other hand, over twelve million people in the country were living on the verge of constant hunger and 'in the grip of perpetual poverty'. The death rate in industrial Birmingham was 95.6 per thousand. Human beings were still cheap in England. It was the Golden Age, though, for the rapidly-growing moneyed middle class, and it was no longer easy to answer the question: who rules Britain? It was certainly not the 150 great families. Tory gentility could no longer hand down an undiminished tradition, and along with their power went much of the British pomp and plush. Gone, too, were the carriage flunkeys whose overcoats swept to their feet, and the boyish grooms with cockaded hats and white breeches. And going rapidly were more and more of the magnificent mansions. It was a time of growing contempt for old ideas, of willingness to challenge tradition and taboos, of a rather upstart arrogance. It was a time when people thought anything could happen, that convention was a cage that you broke out of in order to live your own life in your own way. It was a time of new ideas, magazines were filled with articles on everything new: The New Realism, The New Voluptuousness, The New Spirit, The New Woman".[7]

However, notwithstanding this increasing freedom, it was still a man's world. The Women's Suffrage Bill, despite 257,796 supporting signatures, was rejected by Parliament. In general men still regarded women as inferior creatures, and certainly there were few women who ventured to engage in any serious activity outside the home and family. However, the spirit of a new age, and the manifold changes that were taking place created a feeling of deep unrest among British women. Freed from the restraints of the Victorian era, women were fighting for all forms of emancipation, from details of fashion to high-level employment in public services and the right to vote. Corsets were abandoned, skirts shortened, and, thanks to the new trends in fashion, women could for the first time publicly show their legs. Public authorities began to employ women, and a significant advance in that direction was made in 1892, when seven government departments employed a number of "typing girls". The first woman doctor in Scotland was Dr. Marion Gilchrist who graduated at the University of Glasgow in 1894, and stayed on to work in Glasgow, where she later specialized in eye diseases.[8] The fact that Dr. Gilchrist stayed on to work in Scotland was also most unusual for those times, since among the students the idea prevailed that missionary work abroad was the right field of work, and actually the only field, for women doctors. At that time the suffragette movement was also very strong in Great Britain; the suffragettes fought, often in a very militant manner, for women's rights in general, and especially for the right to vote; in general public opinion was very hostile to them.[9]

Such was the social climate in Great Britain when Katherine was developing as a personality, and this undoubtedly had a considerable influence in determining her future.

One of the places specially loved by all members of the MacPhail family was the popular seaside holiday resort at Benderloch, a small village on the mainland opposite the island of Mull, where the family spent a month-long summer holiday, usually in August. Benderloch, which means "a hill between two lakes", lies at the foot of the mountain Beinn Lora, between Loch Creran to the north and Loch Etive to the south. The steep slopes of Beinn Lora descend almost to the shore, to the village of Ledaig where the MacPhail family usually stayed. The surrounding woods and sandy beaches, with wonderful views and romantic sunsets above the island of Mull provided a wonderful experience, which gave pleasure for years to all members of the family. They prepared for their holiday well in advance, rented a house and reserved a boat and a piano. During the holiday Dr. Donald MacPhail spent most of his time painting (Fig. 12), while the girls went for walks in the surrounding hills, rode their bicycles, and went rowing or bathing in the sea. Sometimes unusual things happened. During one of these unforgettable holidays, Katherine and Isabel went out on their bikes to the nearby mountain Cruachan where they wanted to climb the mountain and were suddenly lost in a thick fog. As they could not return home they spent the whole night in a huntsman's cottage; they were not greatly upset, and returned home the following day. Naturally, the whole family was extremely upset and afraid when their bicycles were found, but there was no sign of them all night. However the two of them were quite calm and contented, regarding the whole experience as an exciting event. Sometimes Katherine's uncles and their families spent their summer holidays there too, and it would happen that the MacPhails occupied nearly every house in the small village of Ledaig, where almost the entire family gathered together (Fig. 11).

For Katherine, Benderloch was a special place, an oasis of peace and bliss about which she always spoke with enthusiasm, to which she often returned, and about which she later yearned and dreamed during her long periods of absence.

And it was at Benderloch, one sunny afternoon in August 1914, that Dr. Katherine MacPhail heard the news of the outbreak of the Great War.

Fig. 1 Monument to the "Bard of Mull", Dugald Stewart MacPhail, in the valley of Glenmore on the island of Mull; the bard's grandson, Dr. Dugald MacPhail, is standing beside the monument (c. 1932). (Courtesy of Mrs. Elspeth Biggs)

Fig. 2 Dr. Donald MacPhail in his carriage in front of the family house in Coatbridge (c. 1900). (Courtesy of Mrs. E. Biggs)

9

Fig. 3 The house of the MacPhail family in Calder Avenue in Coatbridge, where Dr. Katherine MacPhail and her three sisters were born. (Courtesy of Mrs. E. Biggs)

Fig. 4 Katherine's mother, Jessie MacPhail, in the orchard of the house in Calder Avenue (c. 1900). (Courtesy of Mrs. E. Biggs)

Fig. 5 The four daughters of Jessie and Donald MacPhail (c. 1891); Left to right: Janet, Katherine, Isabel and Annie.
(Courtesy of Mrs. E. Biggs)

Fig. 6 The MacPhail family (c. 1910); the father and mother, Dr. Donald and Jessie, and Katherine, Janet and Annie are seated; Isabel is standing. (Courtesy of Mrs. E. Biggs)

Fig. 7 Katherine's eldest sister Janet after her graduation (c. 1902). (Courtesy of Mrs. E. Biggs)

Fig. 8 Katherine's older sister Annie after her graduation (c. 1904). (Courtesy of Mrs. E. Biggs)

Fig. 9 Katherine's younger sister Isabel after her graduation (c. 1907). (Courtesy of Mrs. E. Biggs)

Fig. 10 Katherine S. MacPhail after her graduation (1905).
(Courtesy of Mrs. E. Biggs)

Fig. 11 The MacPhail brothers in Benderloch (c. 1910); left to right: Alexander, William, Donald (Katherine's father) and James. (Courtesy of Mrs. E. Biggs)

Fig. 12 Katherine (in the centre), with her mother Jessie and her father Donald, who is painting, on holiday at Benderloch. (Courtesy of Mrs. E. Biggs)

Chapter 2

Serbia, 1915

The assassination of Archduke Ferdinand, heir to the Habsburg throne, and his wife, on June 28th, 1914 in Sarajevo by the secret Serbian organisation "Young Bosnia" resounded throughout the world; however, it did not give rise to any great excitement in Great Britain. "The murder of an Archduke meant no more to me than some tale of an imaginary kingdom in Zenda", said Mrs. Mabel Dearmer, as she recollected these days later; but she herself soon arrived in war-torn Serbia to work as a volunteer nurse. However, the situation soon changed. The wheel of history began to whirl with increasing speed, and many nations, one after the other, entered the war, in which finally 33 countries took part, with 1.5 milliard inhabitants, and 70 million mobilised soldiers. When Great Britain declared war on Germany on August 4th, 1914, war fever suddenly seized the country. "Recruitment centres were set up overnight, and men, some of them still beardless boys, waited enthusiastically in queues to volunteer; voluntary organisations and auxiliary units sprang up everywhere.... Throughout the country women trembled between excitement and indecision, uncertain at first what to do, although they were sure that the hour had struck for them to serve their country in some way, and not just 'to keep the home fires burning'.[10] Once she knew about the war situation, Dr. Katherine MacPhail firmly decided, without much reflection, to volunteer for active service in the British Army, and wrote immediately to the Ministry of War. A reply came quickly, expressed with military brevity, and, of course, negative. "Dear madam" it ran, "I have been instructed to inform you that the employment of women doctors in the armed forces is not under consideration at present." After this refusal she approached the Red Cross but received a similar answer. They too were not accepting women doctors. Then Katherine turned to Dr. Elsie Inglis, whom she had heard was trying to collect as many women doctors as possible, together with other medical personnel, in order to form women's voluntary medical units.

Even before the outbreak of the war, Dr. Elsie Inglis (see Appendix 2), worried by the constant rumours of approaching conflict, had set up a women's voluntary medical unit, whose members had studied intensively and engaged in practical work during the summer of 1914. Immediately after the outbreak of war, Dr. Elsie Inglis had sought means by which her unit, and other women who had received appropriate training, should be included in the nation's war effort; so she approached the Scottish Federation of Women's Suffrage Societies, with the idea of organising aid in order to equip a field hospital, staffed exclusively by women, which would be offered to the British Army for service in any field of war. In the minutes of the committee meeting of this women's organisation, held on August 12th, 1914, the following proposal of Dr. Elsie Inglis is recorded: "....that a hospital should be equipped ....staffed entirely by women, to be sent abroad, provided it is not needed at home." The proposal was accepted, and so the famous Scottish Women's Hospitals came into existence (abbreviated to SWH). The enterprise began modestly, with the aim of equipping a single hospital, but before the end of the war so many voluntary contributions had been received that 13 field hospitals were equipped, which operated in France, Belgium, Serbia, Romania, Russia and Greece.[10]

At the outset Dr. Elsie Inglis had offered this hospital to the British Ministry of War, but the offer had been firmly refused. An overtired official, unable to grasp the magnitude of this offer, had replied briefly: "My good lady, go home and sit still." However, Dr. Elsie Inglis did not allow herself to be discouraged, but immediately wrote to the French, Belgian, Russian and Serbian embassies, which at once gratefully accepted this offer. From then on the Scottish Women's Hospitals for Foreign Service, as they were officially called, began their active work, under the patronage of the Scottish Federation of Women's Suffrage Societies, and their headquarters were in Edinburgh, in the premises of this federation. The term "Scottish" was retained in the title of the hospitals because, as Dr. Inglis explained, "the idea originated in Scotland." However, the hospitals accepted not only Scotswomen, but also women from other parts of Great Britain, and even from other countries. The first, completely equipped, 200-bed auxiliary hospital, was sent to France in November 1914, and was located at the 13th century Abbaye de Royaumont, Val d'Oise; many others followed later. [11]

In October 1914 Dr. Elsie Inglis replied to Katherine: "The Ministry of War will not send women doctors to the front. They have definitely told us this. The Scottish Federation of Women's Suffrage Societies is organising hospitals, which will be sent out under the protection of the French or Belgian Red Cross, or even sent to Serbia where medical aid is desperately needed. Please let me know how old you are, whether you are physically strong, and what your special field is. Also, would you let me know whether you have had experience of surgery, or would you prefer internist cases? And when did you graduate?"

As the units intended for France and Belgium were already full, Katherine was in a dilemma as to whether she should go to Serbia, about which very little was then known in Great Britain. For most people it was a wild, unknown land, about which they did not know exactly where it was. "Well, I really hardly knew where Serbia was, but from what I have read I knew they were having a hard time in the war, and so I said to Dr. Elsie Inglis that I'd be very willing to go", said Katherine later. And so, without much reflection, and carried away by the spirit of the times and the desire for action, Katherine accepted the offer and joined a group of 30 women who comprised the staff of the first unit of the Scottish Women's Hospitals in Serbia.

The hospital was equipped as a surgical unit with 100 beds, completely supplied with all the necessary equipment, medical supplies, and basic foodstuffs. The staff consisted of five doctors, of whom Katherine was the youngest, trained nurses, hospital assistants and an ambulance driver. The director was Dr. Eleanor Soltau, and Annie Christitch, a young journalist of Serbian origin [12], was engaged as a translator; she left her job on the *Daily Express* to join this mission, where her task was also to teach the Serbian language.

In the course of making preparations, "a good deal of time was spent in getting a proper kind of serviceable uniform, grey, long, not very good fitting, with tartan round our hats and long cloaks nearly down to our ankles" (Fig. 13). "We looked very serious and stern in uniforms which were convenient and practical, but not at all attractive," Katherine recollected later (Fig. 14). "When we were being seen off at the railway station in London, a friend of one of the members of the unit, on seeing us, could not refrain from observing: 'Well, that crowd are very safe anyway.' He was quite right."

In the middle of December 1914, Katherine's unit embarked in Southampton on an Admiralty Transport ship which was carrying troops to the east, and which was sailing towards Malta, where the hospital disembarked. The journey to Malta was pleasant, and the members of the unit passed their time learning Serbian and getting to know each other better. Katherine, who had so far scarcely known the other members of the unit, was afraid that there might be many militant suffragettes. "During the leisure of our voyage, we had time to discover each other, after the first few days when sea sickness made most of us undiscoverable. We knew we were being sent out under the auspices of the "Suffrage Societies," wrote Katherine later, "and each was afraid that every other was a strong supporter, but were much relieved to find that almost none of us was what might be called 'strong', and that Serbia was the common bond, not suffrage. As few of us had known any member of the party previously, we looked at each other for a time very critically, as we were naturally curious to discover what we had been let in for in the way of co-workers." Katherine was obviously pleased to discover that the majority were not militant feminists, and that their common aim was to help those who were suffering or oppressed. "We were extremely proud to have the opportunity to show what women could do in the most difficult circumstances, but our real aim was the urgent need to help the Serbs", Katherine wrote later. "By the time we got to our journey's end, we had become friends, and we little guessed then what a mixture of happiness and troubles we were to experience in our short time as a complete unit together."

Most of members of this Unit knew very little of the country and people they were going to. "Most of us had the vaguest idea of what Serbia was like, we had read that it was a wild country with wilder people. Therein lay half of its attraction for the more adventurous of us" wrote Katherine in September 1916. "I remember on board ship, a letter being handed round all the members of the unit to read, warning us of the dangers we would meet in Serbia, how it was full of dark intrigues and unknown subtleties, how it was dangerous even to be alone, and impossible to be out after dark, how when we were travelling in trains, we were to talk with the utmost discretion, as information might fly rapidly the length and breadth of the country from our incautious lips – and how different it was when we arrived there – but the letter served to increase our ardour if not our discretion."

For Katherine, who had never been abroad before, everything was new and exciting. She wrote home from Malta: "Malta is more attractive than I could ever have imagined. The weather is like midsummer, warm and sunny, everywhere brilliantly light. Valetta is a town with long, steep, and winding streets, with unusual houses on both sides. The people are too easy-going to tire themselves by climbing up the steep streets, but ride in light, open carriages, drawn by Arab horses. As soon as you appear in the street, the drivers come and offer to take you wherever you want for a trifling sum. The shops are all practically on the street, and when you pass them the shopkeepers call you insistently to come in and look at their wares."

While they were waiting for further transport, the members of the unit visited places of interest, and spent Christmas there. It was first time Katherine had spent Christmas away from home, and she felt strange because of this, although the festival was full of events. They attended Christmas mass in St. John's Cathedral; in the afternoon a Scottish tea was prepared for them on the roof of their hotel; in the evening they attended a performance of "Aida" in the opera house.

Immediately after Christmas the unit again embarked on the boat "Nile" (Fig. 15), in which they sailed towards Piraeus, where they stopped for one day and took advantage of the opportunity to go round Athens. "What I remember most clearly about Athens," wrote Katherine, "was the wonderful air, and the scent of the many bunches of violets on sale at every street corner, and this at the time of New Year."

New Year's Eve found them on the Aegean Sea. "It was a full moon, and the dark, shadowed coast and the brilliant glittering sea all seemed a dream to us. I stayed on deck all night, and it was so beautiful," Katherine wrote later, "and I remember as it approached midnight, I went back and exchanged good wishes with a strange nondescript group of Britishers who were trying to bring in the New Year in the orthodox way. They were said to be the secret service, to be secret traders etc., but they turned out to be British Marines destined for Belgrade for work on the Danube." It was Katherine's first encounter with people with whom she worked a great deal later in her life.

At dawn on the first day of 1915, the "Nile" sailed past Mount Olympus, the peaks of which were covered with snow; and the same evening they arrived at Salonica. As it was already nightfall, it was decided that the passengers should stay on the boat until the morning. During the evening a cargo boat full of refugees from Palestine anchored beside them. Most of them were priests and monks whom the Turks had expelled from Palestine. Suddenly, when no one was expecting it, there was a sound of singing from the refugee boat, which echoed over the moonlit water. They were singing Christmas hymns and patriotic songs. They did not have to wait long for a reply; the Scotswomen answered their singing with psalms and their own national songs. It was indeed a lovely and unusual end to a pleasant and idyllic journey, a kind of farewell to their life before they were all faced with the horrors of war.

The staff and equipment of the Scottish Women's Hospital were unloaded in Salonica and transferred to the train in which they travelled northwards to Serbia. When they reached Skopje they learnt that they would not stop there, as they had expected to do, but would continue their journey further north, and that their destination was Kragujevac, where the main headquarters of the Serbian army and the army medical service were stationed. At Skopje railway station they were met and seen off by Lady Paget [13] who was there with the first hospital of the Serbian Relief Fund [14], which had arrived in Skopje in the middle of November 1914. She informed them briefly about the extremely difficult situation and enormous problems which awaited them; but they had seen enough of all this for themselves on their journey, about which Katherine later wrote in a letter: "As we passed through Skopje and Nish, we saw scenes which terrified us. We realised that, in this war-ravaged country, the situation of both soldiers and civilians was worse than we could ever have imagined." As they passed through Nish they were very warmly welcomed by highly placed government officials and representatives of the Red Cross; then early in January 1915 they finally reached their destination, Kragujevac, where representatives of the government also received them with great kindness. It was the first of many missions to Kragujevac. "We were cordially welcomed by the Serbian medical services. Their staff were exhausted because of their work with inadequate numbers of people in all the hospitals, which were in a desperate state," Katherine recollected later. "When we arrived at Kragujevac, which in peace time was a pleasant little town, there were scarcely any civilian inhabitants, because of the proximity of the Austrian troops; three weeks earlier they had all been evacuated. But the town was crammed with sick and wounded soldiers. Every available building was being used to accommodate them, from the military hospital, barracks, schools, down to the smallest wayside cafés .... It was an unforgettable picture of wartime destitution."

In Kragujevac they found an infectious diseases hospital with about 200 patients, working under frightfully difficult conditions, which shocked them by its appearance and general state. This was the First Reserve Military Hospital, headed by Major Dr. Dimitrije Antić, who had just recently been transferred there, when he himself had barely recovered from typhus; later he described his experiences in this hospital: "In its horror, the picture of the condition of the hospital when I took it over will always remain graven in my memory: in filthy rooms, corridors and staircases seriously ill soldiers, still wearing their uniforms,

19

dirty, infested with lice, lay on the bare floor crowded together against each other, so much so that it was impossible to get near them. Groans, cries for help, sighs, and the sound of the final death rattle reached our ears from far away! So, I had to take over a hospital with some hundreds of seriously ill patients, but without beds, without bedding or bed-linen, without disinfectants, medicines, medical instruments, and without syringes to give camphor and other injections, without enough doctors and nurses, and without the means of cooking and serving food! And in addition to all this, transports arrived every day bringing new patients." The unwashed and neglected patients lay two in a bed, or on the floor, in rooms and corridors, often without any bedclothes. Emaciated and in pain, they looked like living corpses. There was little fuel, the water supply constantly broke down, and there was not enough food. In addition the number of staff was nowhere near adequate; about this Dr. Dimitrije Antić [15] wrote: "With the sudden influx of typhus patients, and sudden deaths from this, and without enough of the necessary means of disinfection, soon all those working in the hospital began to succumb to typhus. First of all, naturally, the doctors .... All the doctors, medical assistants, nurses and sisters who worked in my hospital, until we got rid of lice, were infected either by typhus or a recurrence, first one, then the other......On one occasion, at the height of the epidemic, all the doctors collapsed without apparent reason, and I was left alone with over a thousand seriously ill patients!" In such a situation, often the only help available was that of overtired nurses working there, who could scarcely manage to give the patients an aspirin tablet, even if they could manage to get near them, since they were lying in extremely cramped conditions. In this hospital the Scotswomen met their compatriot, Dr. Elizabeth Ross [16] who was working there, and with whom they immediately made friends. Dr. Dimitrije Antić wrote about her as follows: "It is my duty, and this is the place, to mention with special gratitude the name of a colleague from Scotland, Miss Elizabeth Ross, who, as a volunteer, and at a most difficult time, quickly came to the help of my hospital. Day and night, without any fear for her own life, she worked tirelessly to treat soldiers with typhus."

The staff of the Scottish Women's Hospital were given a reasonably comfortable house to live in, which was, nevertheless, too cramped for their needs. They had to bring water from a distant well, and also to cut and chop wood for fuel. The kitchen was outside the house, in a small building in the courtyard; they had 6 to 8 Austrian prisoners of war to help them, whom they selected from a group which had been working on repairing roads. These people were extremely grateful to them, since otherwise they spent practically all their time out of doors, with no shelter and insufficient food and clothing.

From the various hospitals offered them, the Scotswomen decided to accept one situated in a small school building, about ten minutes' walk from the house where they lived. This improvised hospital had formerly accepted some

20

400 wounded men; however, they managed to limit the number of beds to 150, although they had equipment for only 100 patients. Dr. Eleanor Soltau, the director of the hospital, and her staff immediately set to work. In two weeks the rooms were emptied, walls and floors cleaned and disinfected, equipment and medicines unpacked and arranged, patients washed, given clean clothes, bandaged, and placed in clean new beds. Naturally the patients were satisfied, and extremely grateful, and at the same time very surprised and astonished. "The way we worked during that first fortnight was a matter of great astonishment to the Serbs, who said they had never seen women like us working so hard and so heartily before," wrote Katherine later.[17]

Very soon the hospital began to work at full capacity and even beyond this. Wounded men arrived from all sides, often travelling day and night from the battle field - dirty, mud-stained, with infected, stinking wounds, so that the hospital soon had three times as many patients as its normal capacity. In order to care for all the newly arrived patients, they took over and organised some surrounding buildings, and solved the problem of staff shortage by taking on more Austrian prisoners-of-war, who also performed other more difficult tasks (Fig. 16).[18] The hospital was also allotted four cafés in the town, which were full of convalescent patients, not yet well enough to return to their units; consequently they always had to look after some 400-500 patients. As regards surgical facilities, the hospital had a well-equipped operating theatre (Fig. 17), dressing room, and some isolation rooms (Fig. 18). Work continued throughout the day. Katherine, as the youngest doctor, usually worked in the dressing room, where there was a great deal of work, since most of the patients were rather neglected, with festering wounds which had to be dressed every day. "We were kept working in the dressing room from morning till night," wrote Katherine later, "as most of the men had terribly septic wounds". In addition Dr. MacPhail and her friend and colleague Dr. Adeline Campbell, a St. Andrews graduate, the two youngest doctors in the unit, were responsible for one of the "cafés" in the town, full of less seriously ill patients and convalescents. On one occasion Katherine diagnosed that in one of the wounded patients, a particularly tall and well-built young man, a bullet had remained lodged somewhere in his thigh. She immediately told him that the bullet must be removed, which he at first refused, but after a short, quite sharp conversation, conducted through another patient who knew some German, he agreed to this intervention. Dr. MacPhail's authority prevailed. Although she was young, and short in stature, about five feet tall, she was very determined and authoritative, which inspired the respect of her patients. This particular patient was taken to the hospital, wearing his pyjamas and bedroom slippers, and covered with a blanket; and Katherine removed the bullet there in the operating theatre; the patient was then taken back to his "café" with the bullet in his pocket. It was the first bullet Katherine extracted during her work as a doctor.

In fact the Serbian soldiers accepted women surgeons very gladly, although this was something quite unusual for them, since at that time women doctors were rare in Serbia, to say nothing of surgeons. Dr. Frances "Daisy" Wakefield [19], one of the surgeons in the Scottish Women's Hospitals in Kragujevac, explained this very well: "These simple young peasants respected women, especially as a symbol of the mother, which, of course, we were, considering the exceptional circumstances. Because of this they liked us better than the army doctors; they asserted that women surgeons were more considerate, that they were never rough, and in general more patient and tender. On the whole, that is true of most women."

Another problem with which the Scotswomen had to wrestle was mutual understanding. They had all studied Serbian intensively as soon as they set out on their journey, but their knowledge of that language remained minimal. Furthermore, there were also Austrian prisoners-of-war who spoke Czech and Hungarian as well as German, so communication in such a polyglot situation was quite difficult. In any case, knowledge of German was extremely useful. "For conversation," wrote Dr. Eleanor Soltau, who knew German, "four people were necessary. The head sister spoke English, the laundress spoke Serbian, I helped with German, and the kitchen-maid spoke German and Serbian."

However, in spite of all the difficulties, the work in the hospital soon became normalised. "A surgical ward, after the men were restored to comparative health was a cheery place to work in, and the men had such quaint ideas that always interested us. They always objected to the windows being open, and used to lie with their heads covered up under the blankets, but liked to have their feet uncovered so that when we went into the wards, instead of seeing a row of faces all we saw was a row of huge feet", wrote Katherine. "Sometimes, after the ward visits at night, we used to gather in one of the wards, and the patients and prisoners would sing together. They are very musical and have beautiful voices, and they used to sing long songs to us about the war and their homes and were always very proud of their children."

Because of the outbreak of typhus and other infectious diseases, the hospital staff were forbidden to visit Serbian families, civilian or military. They were also told on no account to shake hands with anybody, and not to visit public places or cafés, but to have meetings only with members of the army medical service. They kept company with one another, and rested when they could in the house in which they were living. They had their own cook, who was a member of the team and cooked for the staff, according to their taste, but they had considerable difficulties in obtaining food. "We lived for three months without butter, and often had no tea or sugar," wrote Katherine. "I remember our cook ordered calves' feet to make jelly for some of our nurses who were ill, and when they arrived, the feet were all right, but they were all shod with heavy iron shoes, as the cattle are all shod there. We never found out what the butcher thought we were going to do with the shoes."

The one form of recreation, which the Scotswomen could permit themselves, were short excursions to surrounding villages situated along the roads, which looked sad enough in those wartime years. On one such occasion, Katherine noticed a Serbian boy wearily floundering behind an ox-cart. He was in ragged clothes and peasant shoes, and looked wretched, and his sad, patient face reflected the misery and poverty of all the children who were the innocent victims of war. Deeply touched, Katherine took a photograph of the boy (Fig. 19), and later this photograph went round the world; that is, Katherine had it enlarged to the size of a postcard, and these postcards were sold at various humanitarian functions, and in this way contributions were collected to help the children of Serbia. This was Katherine MacPhail's first contact with the children of Serbia, which perhaps determined her future destiny.

At the end of January 1915, the spotted typhus which until then had been endemic in Serbia exploded into an epidemic of considerable extent, which violently attacked the entire country, including the foreign missions which had come there. The number of those afflicted rose sharply in February, and reached its highest point in the middle of March 1915, after which it suddenly began to fall.

Dr. Dimitrije Antić wrote as follows about this period in his hospital: "The greatest number of cases admitted in a single day was 120; an average number varied from 10-15 daily. The number of dead men was in harmony with that of the patients admitted: 19 dead was the highest number in a single day; otherwise numbers varied between 5-10-15 daily...At the height of the epidemic there was a frightful sight to be seen every day: piles of dead bodies, one on the top of another, uncovered, were carried through the town in open carts from the place where they died to the cemetery". [15]

Katherine wrote on the same subject: "The most trying time we had to experience was during the typhus fever epidemic, which was on us before we knew. The epidemic spread rapidly and thousands of people died within a few weeks. I don't suppose anyone knows accurately the figures, but it has been stated in reports that 100,000 soldiers died of it, and about 30,000 Austrian prisoners. What happened to the women and children, no one knows. The type of disease was very fatal at the beginning, and the mortality was as high as 80 %. Surgical wards were often dreadful enough, but nothing was so dreadful as the wards packed full of fever patients lying exhausted and helpless, with no one even to give them a drink of water except a few Austrian prisoners, who were so weary and weather-worn that they were nearly all doomed to take the disease themselves, and die sooner or later. The Austrian prisoners were in a worse plight than the Serbs, and I have seen them lying in stables and long cattle sheds, unattended except by those of them who were less sick than the rest.....The Serbs were absolutely over-whelmed by the epidemic, and they had lost a great number of their own doctors….They also lost a great number of medical students who were working in the hospitals."

Colonel Dr. Vladimir Stanojević also wrote about the terrible situation in Serbia during the typhus epidemic, when he was the director of a military hospital in Nish: "The situation in the hospital is not merely unsatisfactory, it is frightful…..The number of patients far exceeds the number of beds, so the patients, even those most seriously ill and delirious, and out of their minds are mixed up in beds piled together, under the bed, on the floor, even in the corridors. There is no service, since the nurses have either already died or lie themselves among those who are sick. The work of the nurses has been assigned to prisoners, who do not know the language of the patients, who look like ghosts, or to patients who have just got out of bed, and who can scarcely stand on their feet themselves. There are no doctors, since they are the most likely to fall ill and a large percentage of them die. From the total number of doctors in Serbia, 534 altogether, 132 have died and nearly all of the others have fallen ill. Confusion reigns everywhere in the hospital and affects all aspects of the work…..However, in the reception area more and more seriously ill people arrive, some already dead or dying. They are brought under primitive conditions, on wheel-barrows, or in oxcarts, crowded together like sardines, without straw, without any covering. All day they are dragged in carts to the hospital, over frightful cobbled pavements".[20]

Very soon after arriving in Kragujevac, Katherine became acquainted with Dr. Elizabeth Ross, who was working in the infectious diseases hospital. She wrote as follows: "Dr. Ross had been working in the Serbian fever hospital. I often visited her there, and the hospital was indescribable. But she worked on with a fearlessness and devotion to duty, which was an example to all. I visited the wards with her one night, and the wards and corridors alike were crowded with patients lying often two in one bed or three in two. The patients were in a filthy condition, but were too miserable to care. I also saw two Serbian girls, who had been working in the hospital and had taken fever. They were in a little stuffy room together, and one of them was delirious, and they were being attended by Austrian prisoners. Dr. Ross told me that she had discovered a woman in a little room that day, who had got in somehow or another, although it was a military hospital. She had typhus fever and had brought her little girl, five or six years old with her, probably because she had nowhere to leave her. Another woman with fever had also found her way into the hospital, and that little girl was living in the room with them and doing what she could for them". Soon Dr. Elizabeth Ross herself fell ill with a serious form of typhus, and as there were no medical sisters in her hospital the staff of the Scottish Women's Hospital came to her aid. Dr. Frances Wakefield acted as her doctor, and Louise Jordan or "little Sister Jordan", as they usually called her, and Margaret "Madge" Neill-Fraser provided nursing care; Madge Neill-Fraser was a health worker from Glasgow, and drove one of the unit's cars. In spite of devoted concern and care, Dr. Ross died, to the sorrow of all who knew her, and was buried one Sunday in February 1915. The next week "little Sister Jordan" died, and was buried with full military honours in the cemetery in Kragujevac (Fig. 20). The following week Madge Neill-Fraser fell ill and died and then Sister Agnes Minishull. "Those were the darkest days for us all, and the Unit was never the same again," wrote Katherine. "I remember Dr. Campbell, who was the other junior doctor with me, working in the theatre doing dressings, and she said to me: 'I wonder who we will bury next Sunday?' It was four consecutive Sundays we had buried four people."

In view of the extremely difficult situation, the Scottish Women's Hospital was obliged to take over the infectious diseases hospital in Kragujevac, with 200 beds; they immediately sought help from Great Britain, urgently requesting more staff to treat typhus. [21] Help came quickly, and since news of the terrible typhus epidemic had become widely known in the outside world, many other missions began to arrive in Serbia, and were of enormous help in crushing this terrible scourge. The greatest role in halting the epidemic was played by a group of specialists from the British Royal Army Medical Corps (RAMC), headed by Colonel William Hunter and Lieutenant-Colonel Stammers; [22] in accordance with their advice strict anti-epidemic measures were temporarily introduced. "Roads had been closed because of the fever, to all except to military people," wrote Katherine. "Rail transport was also temporarily stopped, so that all the inhabitants of Kragujevac were for a time in a sort of quarantine."

At the end of April 1915 a large field hospital provided by the Serbian Relief Fund arrived in Kragujevac; at the head of this unit was Mabel St Clair Stobart, one of the heroines of the First Balkan War and subsequently of the First World War (see Appendix 8). The hospital was set up outside the town in a large open space which had previously served as a venue for horse races; and very soon a little town sprang up there, consisting of over 60 tents with 300 beds, fully equipped for independent activity.

One of the exciting events of those days was a visit by Sir Thomas Lipton [23] one of the "tea kings" of Great Britain; he had conveyed a unit of the British Red Cross to Salonica in his yacht "Erin". Since he was already famous for his good works, a grand reception in his honour was organised in Kragujevac, which Katherine attended. "The reception was very amusing," she recollected later. "It was organised in the dining-room of an old hunting lodge belonging to Miloš Obrenović, head of the Serbian principality in the 19th century, then occupied by a military staff unit, and the orchestra of the Royal Guard played for us. When Sir Thomas entered the room, the orchestra greeted him with a loud cheer. He was very interested in us, and our work, and he was pleased to meet someone from Glasgow. We had a good chat, and as the night got on he got very cheery and he began to crack jokes. I must say I was very pleased the Serbs could not make out some of his jokes."

In the spring of 1915 military activity came to an almost complete standstill, and the surgical hospitals no longer had as much work as they had had earlier. The typhus epidemic also gradually decreased, and the situation became to some extent normal. Thanks to this change, Dr. Katherine MacPhail and Dr. Adeline Campbell were given a few days' leave; so they travelled to Skopje where they visited the infectious diseases hospital of the British Red Cross, which was still crammed with patients; the specialist staff was nowhere near sufficient, especially for night duty, so that during the night the patients were looked after only by student nurses. In addition Katherine unexpectedly had an opportunity to visit yet another place in Serbia. The Scottish Women's Hospital in Kragujevac had received an invitation from Sir Ralph Paget, the coordinator of all the British missions in Serbia, to send some medical sisters to a hospital in Smederevska Palanka, in order to look after a British doctor suffering from typhus. Since the hospital only had one sister, actually Sister Mackenzie, Dr. Eleanor Soltau, the director of the hospital, could not allow her to travel alone, so she told Dr. Katherine MacPhail to accompany her, and to report on the condition of the sick doctor on her return. When they arrived at Palanka, the Scotswomen found the hospital situated in a deserted barracks in an empty, muddy field, and in a pretty wretched state. The sick doctor was Dr. V.E. Haig, who had been only three weeks in Serbia. He was alone, since his colleague, a Swiss doctor, had died a short time previously. His condition was serious, he was being looked after by an Austrian prisoner with whom he could not converse because he did not know German, so he was delighted at the arrival of a British doctor and Sister Mackenzie. Katherine was very seriously worried by the state of the hospital, and her anxiety increased considerably after lunching with its staff. The fact was that everyone at the table was given a small bottle of alcohol, which he poured over the plate and then lit, after which he disinfected his plates and eating utensils. This was an understandable precaution, because stomach typhus and other intestinal infectious diseases were very prevalent; but still this considerably troubled and worried Katherine; however, after a brief hesitation she decided to stay for some time and look after her sick colleague. Another medical sister soon arrived, and by their joint efforts they managed to pull Dr. Haig through the crisis; then Katherine was able to return to Kragujevac, travelling by a night train. "I waited for daybreak the last two days sitting in a railway junction where we waited for hours and hours," Katherine wrote in a letter home. "Serbia is wide awake at night, and it was interesting to watch the people in the trains and at the stations. Travelling by night I came into more contact with people willing to help me in any emergency." And this was indeed her experience. As she was walking towards the station from the hospital, one of her legs sank deep into the mud, almost to her knee. As she was struggling to pull her foot out, an officer came along on horseback; and seeing her in trouble, he came up to her, and sitting on his saddle, he held out his hand, took hold of her and pulled her out of the mud; then he simply saluted and continued on his way. He must have thought: "Another of those English women," Katherine recollected later.

At that time, the end of April and the beginning of May 1915, while there were more than enough hospitals and doctors and other staff in Kragujevac, in other places there was a shortage of both staff and equipment, as Katherine had seen for herself on her journeys to Skopje and Palanka. Feeling that she was of little use in Kragujevac, and knowing that she could help in other places, Dr. Katherine MacPhail, with her friend Dr. Adeline Campbell decided, by mutual agreement, to leave the Scottish Women's Hospital and go somewhere where they could be more useful. With this in mind they approached the director, Dr. Eleanor Soltau, who was undecided, since she considered that they should not leave the unit, although she understood their reason for wanting to be more useful somewhere else. Like other members of the hospital, they had agreed to work for six months, without any salary; and as the period of their agreement had almost expired, they thought it was better to return home if they could not be sent somewhere where doctors were needed. As the two young doctors were very determined, Dr. Soltau suggested that they should all visit Colonel Lazar Genčić, the head of the Serbian Army Medical Corps; their suggestion met with his approval, and he immediately suggested that they should go to Belgrade and take over the infectious diseases section of the military hospital there; they accepted this suggestion, with the approval of Dr. Soltau. None of them could then imagine that this decision, in fact an honourable and unselfish act, would cause so much dissatisfaction and disapproval at their headquarters in Edinburgh.

The two young doctors immediately packed their bags and set off for Belgrade. But in these days travelling was not so simple. "We did all our travelling during the night," wrote Katherine. "We left Kragujevac at midnight, and were due to arrive in Belgrade at 8.30 in the morning, but we did not arrive till late in the evening, and had earlier in the day eaten everything we had with us. The distance was only about 70 miles, but we had to spend three or four hours at a junction waiting for a connection. It was perishing cold and we had to sit outside on the railway line, on top of our own boxes, huddled up in our coats or go into a stuffy reeking restaurant and drink beer, as it was the only safe thing to take. I will never forget that railway junction in my life. There we saw motley, miserable crowds of refugees on the way back to the remnants of their homes – women with families of cold, shivering children usually accompanied by the old grandfather, who carried all their household belongings in a pack on his back. They were hustled into horse wagons and travelled the whole dreary journey packed as closely together as possible. There were also hundreds of convalescent weakened soldiers, either being sent back to their regiments or to their homes. Then the regular troops going hither and thither, who usually travelled in large open trucks which were always brim full of men. Indeed, while travelling, we saw Serbia in a way we could have never seen it at other times." As soon as they arrived in Belgrade the young doctors had to return to Kragujevac because some of the doctors there had fallen ill; however, since they could, nevertheless, manage in Kragujevac without them, they immediately returned to Belgrade, so that during that week they travelled there and back, and four times waited for the day to break at the same station.

"Belgrade was a most interesting town to live in; it is beautifully situated at the meeting of the Danube and Sava" wrote Katherine later; "however, at that time Belgrade was an empty, deserted city. Grass was growing in the streets, and on the tramlines; the trams weren't working because the electric power station had been destroyed, and many buildings were in ruins." At the same time, the booming of cannon across the river Sava was a constant reminder that the enemy was very near. "We soon got used to the sound of the guns," wrote Katherine, "and twice during our stay the town was bombarded. When the guns started they sent a shiver through all the buildings, and we could watch from the hospital windows, the clouds of earth sent up by the shells, or the flames of the buildings afire."

In Belgrade Dr. Katherine MacPhail and Dr. Adeline Campbell took over the infectious diseases section of the military hospital, which was in a separate spacious building near the military hospital, occupied by 150 typhus patients. There they replaced an old and sick Serbian doctor, Dr. Hrnjiček, who went round the wards with them, handed over the patients, and left; they never saw him again. The equipment was poor and inadequate, and there were no staff. "The things were in a worse state than at Kragujevac," wrote Katherine, "as the town had never recovered from the invasion, and the hospitals were short of beds, clothing, and indeed everything, and the patients had often to be in their own uniforms on the floor.....We had the added difficulty of being without nurses, and had no equipment except some blankets, and a few sheets we had managed to gather together. We had to work with Austrian orderlies only, and the head of the household arrangements was a priest whose home was in Austria.....One day I found our priest looking out of the window through field glasses – he explained to me that he was looking to see if the spire of his church in Zemun was still standing. His heart was in Zemun, although it was really an Austrian town – this was the case with many of the people in Belgrade".[24]

The young doctors set to work with enthusiasm; they managed to get some bedding from Sir Ralph Paget, and Dr. Eleanor Soltau in Kragujevac also sent them some equipment; the building was cleaned and brought into some kind of order. The less seriously ill patients helped, and looked after those in a more serious condition, and for a short time they were helped by a sister from the Red Cross. Among the patients in the ward there were some in a very serious condition, as Katherine recalled later: "On one occasion a patient who was sitting on his bed, extremely rigid, beckoned to me to come to him; then he moved away the bed-cover and revealed his leg, which was blackened to the knee from gangrene, caused by typhus. The next day he was operated on, but unfortunately did not survive."

In spite of everything Katherine liked Belgrade, and later happily looked back on the time she worked there. "From our hospital we had a magnificent view across the Danube, away to the plains of Hungary, and many a beautiful sunset we saw from its windows....There were also beautiful acacia trees with their exquisite perfume and the streets in Belgrade abounded in pink and white chestnuts trees.....In the summer evenings at dusk, the patients in the hospital used to gather in a huge eager circle round one of the windows, where a gramophone was kept going to amuse them. They used to join in with the singing and the stronger ones would sometimes dance. Some of them would not have missed that hour in the evening for anything, and they looked more pathetic and appealing then, than at any other time. Down in another corner of the grounds under the trees, the Austrian orderlies would gather together and sing some of the most beautiful part-songs I have ever heard, to while away the time till bed. I will never forget those evenings, with the afterglow of the sunset over the river, and the patients and men moving about under the trees, burdened with the sadness of their country or their captivity."

Katherine MacPhail and Adeline Campbell were the first British doctors to come to Belgrade, and they did not have much opportunity for social life. Fortunately, there was a military hospital nearby in which then worked an American Red Cross mission, headed by Dr. Edward Ryan [25], with which they were able to communicate and find some company. In addition, there was a unit of the British Navy stationed in Belgrade, with whom Katherine had become acquainted on the ship "Nile" on which they had travelled to Salonica. The head of this unit was Admiral Troubridge, [26] "a very handsome and kindly old gentleman," as Katherine described him, with whom they became very friendly. His headquarters was near the private house where Katherine and Adeline lived, so he often used to visit them and bring them useful presents, such as a jar of marmalade, or some important news, which in that situation was likewise important for them.

At the end of May Dr. Elsie Inglis arrived in Kragujevac to take over the task of chief superintendent of all the Scottish Women's Hospitals in Serbia, and both the young doctors, separately, were invited to talk to her on account of their trip to Belgrade. Dr. Inglis showed considerable understanding for the reasons which Katherine put forward, but she still wanted them to join a new unit of a Scottish Women's Hospital which was due to arrive in Valjevo. However, she agreed that in the meantime they should continue their work in Belgrade, where she visited them on one occasion, thus conferring recognition of their strenuous work under extremely difficult conditions. Dr. Elsie Inglis reported all this in a letter to the president of the Scottish Women's Hospitals in Edinburgh: "On the train to Nish, 1 June, 1915. Drs. Campbell & MacPhail are at Belgrade running a little typhus annexe of their own. Dr. Soltau gave them leave to go, & I am sorry to say gave them some of our equipment. They have both been down to see me. I told them that what I *wanted* them to do was to join Dr. Hutchinson's Unit, Dr. Campbell as surgeon & Dr. MacPhail as Laboratory Chief, but their time is nearly up, & I did not *order* it, because – at this time – the unit was so out of hand that it was impossible to get an order carried out! The Committee need not trouble any more on that score, however! I saw Dr. Campbell first, & later Dr. MacPhail came down. By that time I had heard of this other scheme & I told Dr. MacPhail that I could not help either with sisters or equipment if they stayed on – as Mladenovatz would take all my resources. I have told them, however, that they must immediately send me a report of their work to send on to you – as they are wearing your uniform, using your equipment, & I will expect you to pay their expenses home. I am quite sure that what they are doing is quite good work. I have been amazed at what can be accomplished simply by British supervision in Hospitals here."

By this time the typhus epidemic was largely under control, and the number of new patients significantly less. However, it was just then, in June 1915, while she was devotedly treating her patients, that Dr. MacPhail herself fell seriously ill. She had contracted a severe form of typhus, and one mild June evening some Austrian orderlies carried her on a stretcher to the military hospital, where they took her in and she was looked after with great devotion by Dr. Edward Ryan and the doctors and sisters of the American Red Cross (Fig. 21). "I was in the Military Hospital," wrote Katherine, "and was looked after by the Americans who had me in their hands for ten weeks. I shall never forget their kindness, and owe my recovery in great part to the care and attention of Dr. Ryan and his nurses. I formed a high opinion of the work of the American nurses, and the skill of the American doctors."

Her illness was very serious; for some days she was delirious, and almost lost a leg from thrombosis, which appeared during her illness. In addition this severe form of typhus, with a prolonged high temperature, damaged her hearing, so that she remained permanently hard of hearing, which later caused her great difficulty, since her deafness gradually increased with the passing years. After her illness passed she lost all her hair, and for a long time she had to cover her head with a hat or scarf (Fig. 23). Later her hair grew again, thick and curly; then she kept it cut short, which was unusual at that time, because women wore their hair long. "She had to be different," was the comment of her niece, Elspeth Biggs.

Katherine's faithful friend and colleague, Dr. Adeline Campbell, continued to work in their department, and visited Katherine every day, right up to her recovery. After this, in view of the fact that her agreement had expired, she decided to return to Scotland, where she gave Katherine's family a detailed account of her illness and recovery.

Adeline Campbell and Katherine, after all the trials they had experienced together, became very close friends, as Katherine wrote later: "The other junior doctor, Dr. Adeline Campbell, was to become my closest friend, and after we left our unit to work independently in a Serbian hospital, we were never separate. She is always associated in my mind with Serbia, as we lived through so much and did so much together. Although vastly different in many ways, we were of one mind entirely about our work, and worked always in the greatest harmony. When our work led us to be cut off from all our friends, and we had the added difficulties of no nurses and no equipment, we felt that the fact we were so united, lessened the difficulties and loneliness, and increased appreciation of everything we saw and did. It is with the greatest of pleasure that we both look back on these days, and they were the very happiest, though in a way the most difficult days of our time in Serbia."

Another faithful visitor, who also visited Katherine nearly every day, was Admiral Troubridge, who invited her to become associated with the British Hospital for Infectious Diseases which had arrived in Belgrade that summer, but Dr. Ryan did not agree with this. As Katherine was exhausted after her serious illness, he insisted that she should go home to Scotland for a long period of convalescence, and Katherine finally agreed to this, with great regret; in her personal notes she wrote: "I was very sorry to leave Belgrade, and often wonder what has happened to all the people I knew there." For her devoted work, up to that time, she was awarded the Serbian Order of St Sava, fifth class.

While waiting for transport to go home, Katherine spent two weeks in a large, new field hospital of the SWH unit at Mladenovac. That summer there were four Scottish Women's Hospitals in Serbia – in Kragujevac, Valjevo, Lazarevac and Mladenovac, and three large units of the Serbian Relief Fund – one in Kragujevac, and two in Skopje, then the hospitals of the British Red Cross in Vrnjačka Banja and Skopje, the British Hospital for Infectious Diseases in Belgrade, and some other smaller units. Over 600 British doctors, medical sisters, nursing assistants and voluntary carers worked in them. In addition there were also other missions from Russia, France and America. At one time there were 50 British doctors working in the country. At the end of the summer of 1915 the inhabitants of Mladenovac, taking seriously the warning of Dr. Elsie Inglis about the need to secure safe drinking water, set up a fine memorial fountain, with the following inscription in English and Serbian: "In memory of the Scottish Women's Hospitals in Serbia and their founder, Dr. Elsie Inglis." This fountain was renovated and reopened on June 22nd, 1985.

After arriving at Mladenovac Dr. Katherine MacPhail was accommodated in a tent with Dr. Elsie Inglis for two weeks, and during this time the two women got to know each other better. The tireless Dr. Inglis made great plans for extending the activity of the Scottish Women's Hospitals in Serbia, about which she talked to Katherine, and promised her the direction of one of the smaller units when she returned from her convalescence, since she planned to establish several smaller units in villages where there was no medical service at all for the civilian population. Katherine was delighted to hear about Dr. Elsie Inglis's plans, and rejoiced at the prospect of her return, since she was firmly resolved to return to Serbia as soon as her health permitted.

Katherine returned to Scotland, to her native Coatbridge, in September 1915, and her father, Dr. Donald MacPhail, took over responsibility for her health and convalescence, while her family, who awaited her as a hero and a war veteran, were anxious to see her and hear her stories. However, her welcome at the headquarters of the Scottish Women's Hospitals was not so cordial. Her request to be enrolled once more in the list of members of this organisation was refused. She and Dr. Adeline Campbell had clearly broken the excessively rigid rules of this feminine organisation as soon as they acted independently, that is, they had sought work elsewhere and gone to some other place. Dr. Katherine MacPhail, offended by this decision, wrote a letter on November 19th, 1915, to Miss Mariss, the organising secretary, in which she said: "I had your note this morning informing me that the Committee have decided that they cannot put my name on their application list. I refuse to accept their decision until they can give me proof for the grounds of their refusal. These grounds you explained to me when I was in Edinburgh on Wednesday. Dr. Soltau could have dismissed us at the time we went to Belgrade, and later on Dr. Elsie Inglis could have dismissed us when she came out to Serbia. With their first hand knowledge of the circumstances neither of them did so. I feel there is something underlying all this disagreeableness since I came home, and apart altogether from the question of my ever going out to Serbia again, I must ask the committee for an explanation, for my own satisfaction. After the hardships I came through in Serbia I at least expected some appreciation of the work I did." Katherine requested a meeting with the main committee of the SWH in Edinburgh, and attended their meeting on December 3rd, 1915, about which she later wrote: "As I sat at this meeting of the committee, in front of this group of capable women who inspired my respect, I felt extremely small, isolated and exhausted after the recent unpleasantness, and wondered why they could be so severe with me. Nothing I had said to them was able to convince them of the sincerity of our actions, which had the approval of our superior, Dr. Soltau, of the head of the Serbian Army Medical Corps, and of Dr. Inglis." The members of the committee were indeed inflexible, and their final decision was that Dr. Katherine MacPhail could not continue to work in the Scottish Women's Hospitals. This was recorded in the minutes of the meeting: 3rd Dec 1915. "The question of Dr. MacPhail's application for re-appointment with the S.W.H. was referred back to the Committee by the Federation Executive Committee for further consideration. The Committee therefore considered the matter again very thoroughly, in the light of letters received from Dr. Inglis & Dr. Soltau, & also had an interview with Dr. MacPhail who attended for the purpose. After very careful deliberation the Committee felt that nothing had transpired to cause them to alter their previous decision not to reappoint Dr. MacPhail. The Chairman, on intimating this to Dr. MacPhail made it clear that the decision of the Committee was not arrived at on account of any dissatisfaction with her medical work, or her personal conduct, but solely on account of the attitude of criticism which she had adopted to her Chief Medical Officer, & her independent action in seeking to make arrangements to work elsewhere. It was further pointed out to her that the refusal of the Committee to reappoint her was in no way tantamount to dismissal." [27]

Dr. Adeline Campbell, who was also refused further work with the SWH, joined the Royal Army Medical Corps, which was beginning to accept women in its service.

Katherine, and also her family, were indignant at the decision of the SWH committee; on the other hand, it strengthened her determination to continue her humanitarian work. However, taught by her previous unpleasant experience, she decided in future not to attach herself firmly to any large organisation, but to act independently, as a separate individual, though she knew that this would be much harder. "So I was back at the beginning, but this time alone and independent, as an independent Scotswoman armed with faith and determination, though I did not know when or where I would start or finish", Katherine explained and concluded: "I hope to return to Serbia whenever it is possible to get into the country, to help with relief work." [17]

Although Katherine was very much determined to return to Serbia as soon as possible, she obviously could not do it at that time. But anyway, her family was rather disturbed about her intentions, and her father bitterly remarked once: "It's only queer people who want to go to the Balkans". Katherine commented that she had never met so many queer British people as she had in the Balkans. "Well, perhaps I was queer too", she said later, "but it was more an obsession that took hold of me." And, as she was unable to go back to Serbia she did everything she could to help Serbian people.

During the autumn of 1915, as soon as she had recovered sufficiently from her illness, Katherine got in touch with the Serbian Relief Fund in London, and set in motion a campaign for collecting contributions and other assistance for this organisation. She travelled throughout Scotland, attended fund raising meetings, giving talks on her experiences in Serbia, appealing for help for that suffering country, which at that very time was under the control of a much more powerful enemy. At that time the photograph of the poor, lost, ragged little Serbian boy, which Katherine had taken in the neighbourhood of Kragujevac, (Fig.19) was enlarged and sold as a postcard in schools and other institutions throughout Scotland; Katherine engaged all her family and friends in collecting help. In this way a considerable sum of money was collected, and handed over to the Serbian Relief Fund in London.

At the beginning of 1915, yet another member of the MacPhail family became involved in the war effort. Katherine's younger sister Isabel also joined the Scottish Women's Hospitals association, and completed a short course of training as a VAD nurse (Fig. 22), and travelled with her unit to France, where they were stationed in the region of Troyes, on the River Seine, east of Paris. Isabel stayed there until the summer of 1916.

During the time she spent in Scotland in the autumn of 1915, Katherine followed the progress of the war on all fronts very closely, and was deeply distressed by the news from Serbia, which was passing through a time of great hardship. It was with sadness that she followed the news of the overrunning of Serbia by the enemy and the retreat of the Serbian Army and people across the mountains of Albania to the Adriatic coast.[28] She also followed, as far as she could, the fate of her colleagues and fellow-workers who had remained in Serbia, a story later beautifully told by Monica Krippner in her book *Women at War*. Naturally, in such a tense situation, Katherine could not remain for long inactive; she could not long remain in peaceful Scotland when war was raging on all sides, and her help was so necessary in many fields of war.

Fig. 13 The staff of the first Unit of the Scottish Women's Hospitals for Serbia at the railway station in London in December, 1914, before their departure to Serbia (Dr. K. MacPhail is the second on the right, the only one with her cloak open. (Photograph courtesy of the Imperial War Museum, London)

Fig. 14 Dr. K. MacPhail in the uniform of the Scottish Women's Hospitals, before her departure to Serbia in December, 1914. (Courtesy of Mrs. E. Biggs)

Fig. 15 The staff of the SWH on the ship "Nile", on their way to Salonica at the end of December, 1914. Dr. K. MacPhail is standing, the second on the left wearing a white blouse and a dark skirt. (Courtesy of Dr. Jean Scott)

Fig. 16 The Scottish Women's Hospital in Kragujevac in the early spring of 1915: the wounded, staff and orderlies (Austrian prisoners-of-war); Miss Shepherd (smaller woman) and Miss McLeod in the top row; Miss Reid, sitting on a stretcher. (Courtesy of Dr. J. Scott)

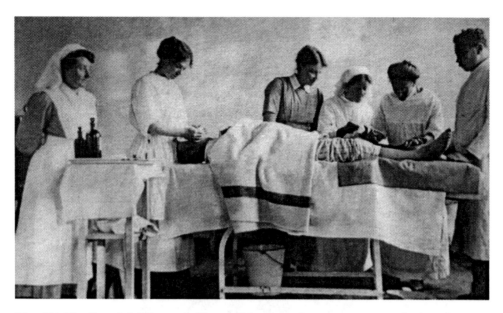

Fig. 17 The Scottish Women's Hospital in Kragujevac (1915): surgical work in the operating theatre. (Courtesy of Dr. J. Scott)

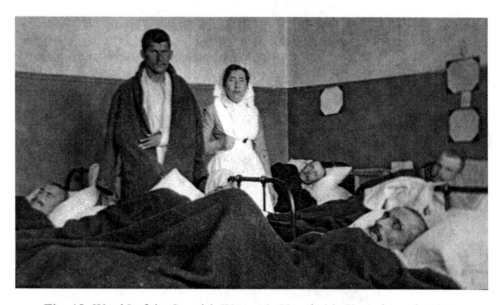

Fig. 18 Ward I of the Scottish Women's Hospital in Kragujevac in 1915. (Courtesy of Dr. J. Scott)

Fig. 19 "A Serbian boy in rags in the neighbourhood of Kragujevac in the winter of 1915". So wrote Dr. K. MacPhail who took this photograph herself; on the back of the picture it reads: "The cards are sold on behalf of the Children's Fund of the Serbian Relief Committee" (Courtesy of Mrs. E. Biggs)

Fig. 20 The grave of Sister Louise Jordan in the cemetery in Kragujevac; Sister Jordan died of typhus in 1915. (Courtesy of Dr. J. Scott)

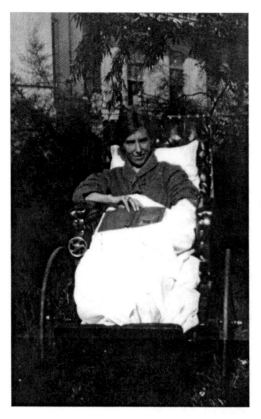

Fig. 21 Dr. Katherine MacPhail in a wheel-
chair during her convalescence from typhus in
the Military Hospital in Belgrade, in July 1915.
(Photograph courtesy of the
Imperial War Museum, London)

Fig. 22 Isabel MacPhail, Katherine's younger
sister, in the uniform of the SWH, immediately
before her departure to France in 1915.
(Courtesy of Mrs. E. Biggs)

Fig. 23 Dr. K. MacPhail, in a photo taken in the autumn of 1915 or early 1916 (at that time she always wore a hat, after the loss of her hair as a result of typhus).
(Courtesy of Mrs. E. Biggs)

Chapter 3

France, 1916

Since she could not return to Serbia, which was then occupied, in January 1916 Katherine approached the "Society of Friends", a Quaker organisation, which was then active in France.[29] Katherine began working at the *Mission Anglaise* at Châlons-sur-Marne, in the Champagne region, north-east of Paris, in a maternity hospital which was used during the war for the needs of both civilians and the army. The head of the *Mission* was then Miss Edith Pye, a devoted and tireless worker who worked in France throughout the war, and in recognition of her services she received the Legion of Honour. One of Katherine's duties was to go to the neighbouring town of Rheims, collect the homeless children and orphans, a dozen at a time, and take them back to Châlons, where they were in temporary accommodation until the French authorities sent them into the interior of the country. The town was not far from the front line, and was sometimes exposed to the bombardment of long-distance German guns. In such a situation, it was the task of all members of the mission to grab a child, or two babies, and hurry with them to the cellar where they took shelter until the bombardment stopped. In February and March 1916, Katherine spent some time in the nearby areas of Bar-le-Duc and Brabant-le-Roi, where she went round the nearby villages with a nurse and treated the civilian population. There she had an unusual experience. One day, while they were sitting in their village billet, drinking tea, they noticed a German Zeppelin falling down, hit by the fire of French soldiers. As they heard later it was the first Zeppelin shot down over France. "It was making a terrible noise, and we could see the crew, about ten to twenty men, rushing about helplessly in the undercarriage. Then it burst into flames and came down in a field quite near us. That same evening a general arrived from Paris to congratulate the men who had shot the Zepp. down. He decorated them then and there on the field with much congratulatory kissing on both cheeks, and cries of 'Vive la France', but I couldn't help thinking of the trapped crew, who were all killed, of course, and found it rather sickening", Katherine recalled later. Of course, Katherine who was by nature a true humanist, found such brutal scenes hard to bear, whoever was involved. But such is the nature of war.

At the end of March 1916 Katherine was moved to Sermaize-les-Bains in the same war-devastated region as the headquarters of the *Friends* for the district of Marne and Meuse. The administrative head of the *Mission Anglaise*, consisting mainly of builders, drivers, and men and women for the distribution of food and clothing over this wide area, was Marjorie Fry, and the head of the medical section was Dr. Hilda Clark. The unit was accommodated in the building of an old casino called *La source*, since before the war this place had been a medical spa. The offices, store-rooms, dining-room, a room for rest and recreation and a small dispensary were housed in the building itself, while the staff were distributed among surrounding wooden huts. Katherine was given the task of running a small hospital situated in a wooden barracks which the *Friends* had built as a hospital with 30 beds for the children of that district. The hospital was conveniently located, across a meadow from *La source*, on the edge of a wood, which stretched for several kilometers round about. Katherine was pleased to be working with children, and, of course, she grew fond of this hospital, and spent her free time playing with the children or strolling in the beautiful forest. However, she had little spare time, as, in addition to the hospital work, she took care of the staff of the mission, and also went round the neighbouring villages treating the civilian population, mainly the older people and children who had remained there. Most of the villages in the neighbourhood had been destroyed by enemy action; so the civilians, mainly peasants, lived in the less damaged houses, which had been sufficiently repaired for people to remain there; they were greatly helped by the *Friends*, who, among other things, had a building team. They were nice people, whom Katherine grew fond of, as she did of their district, which in normal circumstances was very beautiful, but at that time devastated and melancholy. In one of her letters home, dated March 6th, 1916, Katherine noted: "The countryside is very sad just now as most people have husbands or sons at Verdun. I never cease to marvel at the spirit of the women and they go on cheerfully from day to day". It was the time of the famous, long-drawn-out battle of Verdun, and the nearness of the front line could be felt on all sides.[30] On one occasion, as Katherine was returning from a visit to a sick child in a children's home in the neighbourhood, the car in which she was travelling simply could not cross the main road, along which was passing an endless column of heavy lorries full of soldiers hurrying to the front. The railway station in the vicinity, at a place called Revigny, where a train was waiting to take troops to Verdun, had been bombarded, so an entire division had to be transported in lorries, which had been passing that way all that day and night long.

Although she was extremely busy with the daily tasks, Katherine nevertheless found time to follow the events taking place in the world, and also medical literature. Her letters home show that she regularly received the weekly *Times* and also the *British Medical Journal*, and she often sought in her letters the advice of her father, Dr. Donald MacPhail, and discussed medical problems with him. Katherine also got on very well with other members of the unit, who were all Quakers, except for her, and she began to be interested in their convictions. She herself was very popular and well-liked, and many people marvelled at her work, and all that she had experienced in distant Serbia, to them an unknown and far away country. And in her appearance she was unique, since she had short, curly hair, which was very unusual at that time. In fact, Katherine had lost her hair when she had typhus fever, and for a time was almost bald, but the hair grew again, and was then short and curly, and because of this she looked like a boy, and was often teased about this. In the evenings, after work, the members of the mission gathered together in the main building of *La source*, where they spent their time talking, reading and singing. Thus it happened, on these social occasions, that a member of the team fell in love with Katherine and asked her to marry him, which she, naturally refused, since she simply did not have time for anything of this sort, which was unthinkable in her plans. This man was John Nickolls, who, in spite of being refused, remained on friendly terms with Katherine and many years later visited her in St. Andrews.[31]

A rare but great pleasure for the Quakers working in the devastated villages of France was a visit to their French headquarters, situated in the *Hôtel Britanique* (20 Avenue Victoria) in Paris, where Katherine stayed on a number of occasions and enjoyed visiting the sights of Paris.

In her letters to her mother written at this time, Katherine revealed that she had received an offer to go and work in Corsica. Lady Grogan from the *Serbian Relief Fund* in London, whose duty at the headquarters was to select and place staff in the institutions of this organisation, invited her to work in a hospital for Serbian refugees, mainly tubercular patients and convalescents. Katherine described this offer in a letter dated April 24th, 1916: "I had a letter from Lady Grogan yesterday asking me to go to a hospital for Serbian refugees in Bastia, Corsica. It's a hospital of 44 beds with an outpatient department as well. They ask me to stay 3 months and offer me a salary of £ 200 a year. Dr. Clark says she can spare me about the middle of May". In a letter dated May 10th, 1926 from Sermaize Katherine told her mother she was travelling to Paris, then to Marseilles and from there to Corsica. "Lady Grogan wanted me to go off to Bastia at once", she says, "but I cannot leave till the 15th". In a letter from Paris dated May 15th, 1916 Katherine wrote with pleasure that she had met there Dr. Ryan, who had treated her in Belgrade when she was ill with typhus, and for whom she had a very high regard. "It was a great pleasure to see him again and hear all his news. I hope I shall have the pleasure of seeing him again somewhere", wrote Katherine on this occasion. This was followed by a postcard from Nice, dated May 19th, then a letter from Corsica dated May 21st, 1916, in which she says: "I left Nice at 4 o'clock on Friday evening, and arrived at Calvi, a little port on the Corsican coast, at 4 a.m. the next morning".

On arriving in Bastia Dr. Katherine MacPhail was accommodated in the *Hotel Cyrnos*, and immediately started work in the hospital, which was located in the *Villa Kermakia* right on the sea-shore in a real Mediterranean setting. There was not a great deal of work, since the patients were for the most part taken care of and she had working with her a French doctor, a matron and three nurses, while the head of the mission was Miss Kathleen Courtney "an able administrator and a delightful friend", as Katherine put it. In a letter to her mother dated June 1st, 1916, Katherine writes: "At present there are no seriously ill patients. The Serbs have a very high opinion of this hospital. Today we had our photos taken, patients and staff" (Figs. 24 and 25).

One Sunday, a few days after her arrival, Katherine and Miss Courtney travelled to Ajaccio, where there was a unit of the Scottish Women's Hospitals, and where also stayed Sir Edward Boyle, head of the British missions in Corsica, with whom Katherine wished to become officially acquainted. They travelled by car, so Katherine had an opportunity to see the natural beauty of the island, which she noted in her letters: "The country we went through is the wildest and most magnificent I have seen yet. Wild jagged mountain ranges with snow capped tops, and all through the valleys, the strangest little villages perched up on the slopes of the hills like birds' nests." On the way they spent the night in a village, about 19 miles from Ajaccio, where there were some Serbian refugee families, and also some British humanitarian workers, so that Katherine had an opportunity to become acquainted at first hand with the condition and lifestyle of these refugees. Then she realised that the refugees in the villages were happier and more contented than those in the towns. In one of her letters dated May 25th, 1916 Katherine mentioned that the refugees with whom she had been in contact in Bastia, and who were accommodated in warehouses, were anxious to get out of Bastia and to move to the villages to "...start some sort of family life again. The Serbs are very sad and I wish we could do more for them".

In Ajaccio Kathleen Courtney introduced Katherine to the head of the mission, Sir Edward Boyle, with whom she then visited the Prefect of Corsica, and after this official business the girls left to make a tour of the town where, among other things, they saw the house where Napoleon was born, and also the church in which he was christened. In the afternoon they visited and went round a SWH Unit in Corsica, where Katherine met a number of her former colleagues with whom she had worked in Serbia, and in her letter of June 1st, 1916 she described that meeting: "Their hospital is very nice, and they seem well established. Dr. Inglis was in Corsica a few weeks ago....We had a great talk about all the people of our unit, and where they all are....How thankful I am that I am not in one of the SWH now", concluded Katherine, who was still feeling bitter and hurt because of her misunderstandings with the management of this organisation. Later, in a letter of June 20th, 1916, she also criticises the staffing arrangements of the Scottish Women's Hospital: "...What they do with all their people I can't think. They have a staff of 36 people! And we have 6, and they have only some 80 patients".

One of the problems which Katherine very quickly noticed was the condition of young Serbian refugees, of which there were many in Corsica; on this subject she wrote: "I examined about 50 of them the other day, boys of 13 - 14, and they are pathetically anxious to have something done for them .....Miss Courtney and I are very anxious to get the boys away from Corsica, and I suggested that I would try to get the ones who are still weak and miserable, and who are here without parents, into Dr. Hilda Clark's home in Haut Savoie, which she has just opened for refugee boys. I have written to her and also to Lady Grogan about it, and I hope I shall manage it." Unfortunately this attempt did not succeed, as will be seen later – however, help did come for some of these children. Those very days Miss Courtney travelled to London, accompanying a group of about a hundred Serbian orphan boys who were being sent to England.

Work in the hospital proceeded peacefully, in its usual way, as Katherine wrote: "The hospital is fairly full just now, but none of the patients give us much anxiety." However, some unusual things also had been happening: "We had a christening up at the hospital the other Sunday. The baby had been born in the hospital. A little boy of 14 acted as sponsor, as the baby's father is in Corfu. He was christened 'Slobodan', which is Serbian for 'liberty'. It was quite an interesting ceremony, strange and difficult to understand. We have a church service now every Sunday morning in the Club for the Serbs, and they all turn out to it very well."

The weather was already very hot, and Katherine avoided walking in the hot sunshine. But this enabled her to bathe in the warm sea. "I had my first bathe yesterday. We bathe from the hospital, which is just at the water's edge," wrote Katherine to her mother, "The nurses also bathe every day, as do the patients and orderlies." In addition, Katherine sometimes managed to go out riding in the evening and to visit some of the neighbouring mountain villages. "The other night, we all set off from the hotel with our knapsacks full of eatables, and climbed high up into the hills behind Bastia," wrote Katherine, in a description of those days. "We stopped at a little church, called Santa Lucia, and built a fire and fried eggs and bacon, and had supper in the moonlight. It was full moon, and the hills and sea were exquisite. After supper, we wrapped ourselves up in cloaks and slept out under the stars. We saw the moon set about 2 a.m. over the hills, and then the sun came up over Elba. We lit a fire again about 4 a.m., made coffee and had some breakfast, and then came down again about 6 a.m. to begin our day's work. We all enjoyed the coolness of the hilltops very much."

Katherine shortened her stay in Corsica considerably, and on July 3rd, 1916 she left the island for the mainland; the official reason for her earlier departure was to try and organise accommodation for Serbian orphans in the Friends' home in Haute Savoie. However, it seems that despite the leisurely stay in Corsica, Katherine was not happy there. She wrote that, owing to the "lack of medical work" in Bastia, she was glad to be getting away. The leisurely life on a Mediterranean island obviously did not suit her temperament and spirit, at a time when the whole of Europe was experiencing the chaos of war.

In a letter from Paris to her mother, dated July 18th, 1916, Katherine wrote: "Here I am in Paris after a long journey on my way back to Sermaize." After her return to the Society of Friends in Sermaize, Katherine tried to arrange the transfer of the Serbian orphans from Corsica to their house in Haute Savoie, but, unfortunately, this attempt was unsuccessful. Katherine attributed this failure largely to the Corsican government. She explained in a letter that her experiences in Corsica had been disheartening "as our hands were tied on account of the authorities…..The Prefect was a most impossible man and frustrated our plans in every possible way." In the same letter, describing the need for a hostel in the Alps, she writes: "We felt that something must be done for all the delicate refugee boys who were scattered all over France, working on the railways or in munitions."

At the beginning of August 1916 Katherine met her younger sister Isabel in Paris; Isabel described this in a postcard from Paris dated August 2nd, 1916: "Kath is motoring up from Sermaize to see me today – it is fine to think of." This was indeed a happy and pleasant meeting for the two sisters, prior to a lengthy separation, since Isabel, with her unit of a Scottish Women's Hospital, which was attached to the French Eastern Army (*Hôpital Aux. 301 Armée D'Orient*), was being transferred to North Africa, from which it would later go to the Salonica front, where the sisters would meet once more.

In the second half of 1916, a large part of northern France was occupied by German forces, who began to expel the remaining civilian population, mainly elderly people, women and children, invalids, that is, everyone who was of no use to them because they could not dig trenches or work in the fields. With the agreement of the International Red Cross, the occupying power sent these exiles from the occupied areas of northern France through Switzerland, back into the unoccupied parts of France at Annemasse, near Geneva, which was the frontier station where the transport ended, and where they were taken over by the French authorities and then settled in the interior of the country.

The Society of Friends made an offer to the French government to organise a welcome for these unhappy people, and to accept the most vulnerable women and children until definite accommodation was secured for them somewhere in the interior of the country. The offer was accepted, of course, and under the leadership of Dr. Hilda Clark the *Friends* quickly took over a hotel in the small village of Samoëns in Haute Savoie, in a beautiful alpine valley about 12 miles from the Swiss frontier and turned it into a home for refugees (*Maison Hospitalière*).

Katherine, who was in Sermaize at that time after her return from Corsica, liked this kind of work, and, on the other hand, she wished to escape for a time from the terrible scenes of the devastation and chaos of war; and she was, at her own wish, sent to take over the duty of doctor to this home, and arrived there at the end of September, 1916. In a letter to her mother from Samoëns dated September 26th, 1916 she wrote: "Here I am at my destination. This is my second day here."

The Home was situated in the Hotel "Bellevue", which could take about 80 women and children of all ages, who were looked after by a British team of about ten people of different professions. The director of the home was Miss Olwen Rhys, a Welsh woman, much admired by Katherine, and daughter of an Oxford professor. Among other things, she and Katherine had the task of travelling in a small mountain train, with some workmen, from Samoëns to Annemasse, on the Swiss frontier, where groups of refugees were waiting, sometimes consisting of about 500 people; they would then choose the most vulnerable women and children who were not fit to travel any further, and who urgently needed rest, medical treatment and convalescence.

The work in the Home was not too strenuous, as Katherine wrote in her letter home dated October 9th, 1916: "The work is fairly easy and I am beginning to feel rested. I have not had very much district work yet but the people are beginning to know that there is a doctor here and are coming from long distances." In her letters at that time Katherine mentions the possibility that she might join Dr. Kuss, a well-known tuberculosis specialist from Paris, with whom she would be carrying out research into tuberculosis. In a letter to her mother written on November 11th, 1916, she said she was "en route to Paris" where she talked to Dr. Kuss, but after this she nevertheless decided not to accept this offer. This kind of work was obviously too easy and inappropriate for her at that time when a violent war raged across Europe.

At that time one of the members of the mission was Francesca Wilson, a writer and well-known humanitarian worker in both world wars; in her recollections of work in Samoëns she described Katherine, with whom she became friendly: "Of my colleagues the most romantic was Dr. Katherine MacPhail. She was unassuming – small, with a mass of wavy short hair and a touch of melancholy in her Scotch voice, but she was romantic because of what she had done. In 1914 she had gone with the Scottish Women's Hospital Unit to Serbia. …..Dr. MacPhail had caught typhus herself – that explains her short hair, still uncommon in those days, also why she had taken a peaceful job such as ours was at Samoëns, for she was still convalescent. But she wanted to go back to her Serbs: they were not wild savages as people had imagined – they were wonderful, brave and uncomplaining and grateful for help." [32]

As soon as Katherine's presence became known, she began to do medical work in the neighbouring villages as well as in the Home; this was mainly with the local peasants, and the work was not difficult while the weather remained fine, as it was that autumn. "The autumn of 1916 was exceptionally brilliant, and my memory of Samoëns is of valleys and mountain-sides burnished with gold. In my recollection I am walking up a valley, brushing through gold with my feet, the sunshine filtering down through gold leaves on to me, and the torrent dancing beside me in a web of golden light" wrote Francesca Wilson about that period; "One night Dr. MacPhail, Maggie Adeney (one of our nursery helpers) and I took our supper out. We made a fire just before the moon rose, scrambled eggs and made tea. It was beside a stream by the roots of a pine tree, and the firelight showed white toadstools and glowed in the plaits of Maggie Adeney's red hair. Dr. MacPhail, with her shock of gipsy curls, looked to our romantic eyes like Medea as she stirred our saucepan with a stick. Then as the fire died, we saw the moon hanging among the trees, like some new miraculous, golden fleece. We climbed higher and lay down on the verandah of a chalet, abandoned for the winter months, and saw Lyra and Pleiades. When we walked back, we lost our way in a wood on the slope of Angolon and found how deceptive the moonlight was. We were always seeing a path shining white somewhere near us and finding it was only the moon on the aspen leaves or on the wet plantains. In the end we stumbled on the track again and got back in time for two or three hours' sleep." But: "The winter when it came was exceedingly cold. We lived in a world of ice and snow. The children tobogganed down the mountain paths with shouts of joy. The peasant women – there were few men left in the valley by this time – brought the hay down from the high meadows on sledges. Sometimes a summons came from a sick woman in some distant chalet, and I would go to her with Dr. MacPhail, envying the power her medical knowledge gave her" wrote Francesca Wilson.[32]

Katherine was very pleased with her stay in Samoëns. It was a beautiful, peaceful mountain district, with a real alpine beauty; the work was interesting, and not too difficult; she got on well with the members of the mission, all of whom liked and respected her and wanted her to stay with them, but her fate was clearly different. When the time for her departure came, the members of the mission organised a fine and unusual farewell party. Miss Olwen Rhys, the head of the mission, who had a very high opinion of Katherine, and also a poetic soul, arranged with the others that they should each compose a sonnet in Katherine's honour, which they then recited during an unforgettable farewell supper arranged on the eve of her departure, when they all wished her every happiness in her future life and work, which she certainly needed, since she was going away to meet new difficult trials, on the Salonica front.

Fig. 24 The "Villa Kermakia", used as a hospital for Serbian refugees in Bastia (Corsica), June 1916. (Dr. K. MacPhail, wearing a white coat, is standing in the front of the car). (Photograph courtesy of the Imperial War Museum, London)

Fig. 25 The staff of the hospital for Serbian refugees in Bastia (Corsica), in June, 1916. (Dr. K. MacPhail is sitting on the wall, second from the right) (Photograph courtesy of the Imperial War Museum, London)

Chapter 4

The Salonica Front, 1917 - 1918

In the early spring of 1917 Dr. Katherine MacPhail arrived at the Salonica Front. While she was still in France, Dr. Roman Sondermajer, head of the Medical Corps of the Serbian Army in Salonica, invited her to come to Salonica and offered her a place in one of the hospitals under his command, with a salary of 400 dinars a month. As can be imagined, Katherine, who had so much wished and planned to return to Serbia, did not reflect for long but immediately accepted this offer and soon afterwards arrived in Salonica. "It was my first paid job", she said later, commenting sadly on her situation at that time. This was indeed true, since right up to that time, both in Serbia and in France, Katherine had worked as a volunteer, without any financial reward apart from a short period in Corsica where, as a salaried doctor, she worked for just six weeks.

In Salonica Katherine found her younger sister Isabel (Fig. 26) who had arrived there much earlier with a Scottish Women's Hospital, which was attached to the French Eastern Army, with which it was sent from France first to North Africa and then to the Salonica Front. This hospital under canvas was situated on the outskirts of the town; the head of the unit was Dr. Louise McIlroy, whom Katherine had known from the Glasgow Royal Infirmary, where as a young doctor she had worked for some time under her direction. At Dr. McIlroy's invitation Katherine stayed for a few days in the hospital until she started her work. Dr. Sondermajer, to whom Katherine introduced herself immediately after her arrival, asked both her and Isabel to work in a large, newly-established hospital which France had given to the Serbian Army, and which was called Crown Prince Alexander's Serbian Hospital. Isabel did not hesitate and, delighted at the prospect of at once working with her older sister, decided to leave the SWH and join Katherine. However, since the hospital was still being established and did not yet have enough staff to begin work, the MacPhail sisters obtained some kind of leave, and had enough free time to go round the town and visit the numerous acquaintances they found there, including Dr. Edward Ryan and Admiral Troubridge, Katherine's old friends from Belgrade.

Salonica at that time was a very lively town, crowded with Allied soldiers in uniforms of many colours. There were Greeks, Serbs, Yugoslav volunteers, Britons, French, and dark-skinned Senegalese among the French colonial troops, Italians, and many others, all in new uniforms of different colours and design. In the town and the surrounding district there were many military headquarters, camps, hospitals and storehouses, and everything else that accompanies an army. Preparations were in progress for a big offensive, about which everybody was talking with excitement.

However, the leave, which Katherine and Isabel were enjoying, did not last long. Just a few days later the head of the Serbian Relief Fund in Salonica summoned them and asked them to go to their hospital in Sorović (today the Greek town of Amindeon, near the Greek-Macedonian frontier) to help to care for the civilian casualties from the bombardment of Monastir (today Bitola in Macedonia) and its neighbourhood; and of course they immediately agreed. Katherine replaced a doctor who had been transferred to nearby villages, and Isabel replaced a nurse in the women's ward.

The SRF hospital in Sorović was under canvas in a mountainous district where it was still very cold, and Isabel soon regretted leaving Salonica, where it was already spring. "The mountains are covered with snow. We have storms of wind and rain and it is bitterly cold, and in Salonica the tamarisk and wisteria are out", wrote Isabel. But this hospital had some advantages to which Isabel had not been accustomed in her SWH unit, namely there were hospital orderlies always available for all the coarse tasks, something not to be dreamed of in the SWH, where they had to do all the jobs themselves. Moreover there were some interesting people in this hospital, with whom the MacPhail sisters soon became friendly. The hospital secretary was Ann McGlade, known as Nan, [33] a very capable, hard-working and popular person, whom Katherine knew from her time in Kragujevac, and with whom she later shared a flat in Belgrade. Then there were two nurses, Hilda Willis and Rose Stone, who were later to work for some time with Katherine in Macedonia and Belgrade, and Dorothy (Dot) Newhall, [34] a sanitary officer, whom Katherine had known in Kragujevac and with whom she would later work in Belgrade. In addition, in the nearby town of Ostrovo (today the Greek town of Arnissa), on the northern shore of Lake Ostrovo (today Lake Vegorritis in Greece), there was a large and well-equipped Scottish Women's Hospital, known under the name of "The America Unit", because the money for its establishment and upkeep was collected mainly in America. The head of the hospital was Dr. Agnes Bennett.[35] Naturally, when Katherine and Isabel had some free time, they used to visit this hospital, and Dr. Bennett, like Dr. McIlroy in Salonica, invited Katherine to come and work in her hospital. Working here abroad, they obviously did not know about the decision of the Edinburgh committee of the SWH. Of course, Katherine politely refused this offer, and instead moved away to work in villages immediately behind the front line.

In fact there were no doctors at all among the civilian population of that area, because they had all been called up for military service; in addition there was a great danger of epidemics breaking out. The authorities, wishing to help the civilian population and to prevent the outbreak of an epidemic, which would be a serious problem, especially at a time of preparations for a big offensive, sought help from the SRF hospital in Sorović, which then organised teams sent to the war zones in the north as outpost clinics to provide medical help for civilians, particularly the vaccination of the inhabitants. One such team, which included Sister Hilda Willis, Sister Rose Stone, Isabel temporarily, and Dorothy Picton as a cook, under the leadership of Dr. Katherine MacPhail, was sent to the village of Brod, situated on the south-eastern side of the Monastir (Bitola) plain, a few miles from the noise of the war. The village with some 400 inhabitants, had been almost completely destroyed by constant battles, and the villagers were living in shelters made from half-ruined houses. The mobile dispensary was set up in one of the few houses which had an undamaged roof. The unit members were accommodated in tents, which they set up at the edge of a cemetery, which surrounded the ruined village church; because of this they used to remark jokingly that they were "feeling very much like the living among the dead." They were exposed to the boom of cannon almost every day and night, and they could see the enemy shells as they fell on Monastir (Bitola). However, they could enjoy a beautiful view across the plain to Florina, Bitola and the Albanian mountains. In the surrounding villages there were military camps containing Serbian, Italian and French troops, and the camp of a British motor transport unit, while the main body of British forces was some distance away, further east.

The small team was warmly welcomed in the villages and everyone tried to help them as much as they could. "Everyone, as always, is as good to us as can be, and thanks to many gifts we have our tents comfortable and dainty," wrote Isabel. The orderlies who had been assigned to them by the Serbian army were also very useful for a variety of tasks. Nearby, at the edge of the village, there was an Italian warehouse, and their officers, gallant by nature, were happy to be able to help the British unit, and supplied them with some specialties such as tins of tuna fish, macaroni, and sometimes even food from frogs' drumsticks. The Italians also made them a mess, using empty milk boxes filled with sand, so that the members of the unit "felt as though they were in a real house." There was also an Italian transport unit stationed nearby, and their colonel would lend his vehicles for the British to use whenever they needed. The Italians were certainly kind, nice people, but as Katherine later recounted, not especially famous as soldiers. They liked music, singing and a fine voice more than war or military skill. It so happened that, at that time, an amusing anecdote about the temperament of the Italian soldiers circulated among the members of the British missions. During the night, while there was a battle going on, the commanding officer's voice was heard ordering his soldiers to advance: "*Avanti soldati!*" Complete silence reigned, and no one moved. Then the same command was heard again, but again, nobody moved. Then the same command was heard again, but again, no one moved. The commanding officer, already very upset, cried out a third time, in a loud, deep voice: "*Avanti soldati!*" In a silence, which reigned once more, suddenly a cry of amazement was heard from his soldiers: "*Che bella voce!*" True or not, the Italian soldiers were very helpful to them, and Katherine got on very well with them.

The work in their small dispensary developed smoothly, the people had confidence in the new doctor, and the peasant women from the surrounding area, "in all their homespun embroidered garments and yards and yards of horse or goat hair cord wound round them", gladly came to seek her advice. Immediately after their arrival in the village, in the course of a single day, Katherine's unit vaccinated all the inhabitants of the village, and then began to go round the neighbouring hamlets, right up to the front line. On the occasion of these visits, which had an official character, the village headman greeted them, an old man with much authority, who took them round the village and showed them the houses where there were sick people. In fact, these were huts with earthen floors and open fire-places, and very little furniture, and Katherine was often astonished at the primitive conditions under which these people lived. On the other hand, she was fascinated by their unusual, multi-coloured national costumes. On one occasion she asked a sick woman to remove her girdle so that she could examine her, and calculated that it was wrapped round her body 23 times.

During May it began to be unbearably hot, and Katherine complained in a letter home: "....the heat is terrible, the only cool time being very early in the morning or late evening. Our tents are almost no shelter in the scorching sun." At that time, in June 1917, Isabel left Brod and returned to Salonica, to her post in the Crown Prince Alexander's Serbian Hospital, which had at last begun to work. The hospital was in a fine, spacious building, in beautiful grounds, and very well equipped, so that for Isabel it was real luxury, after two years of living under canvas. The doctors were Serbs who had studied in Vienna, Paris, or Prague; at that time it was not possible to qualify in Serbia, as there was no medical school in pre-war Serbia. The director was Dr. Ljubiša Vulović, a specialist in diseases of the nose, ear and throat, later professor in the Faculty of Medicine in Belgrade; "one of the most handsome and charming people I have ever met," was how Isabel described him. The nurses were Serbian, French and British, and in charge of the nursing staff was Mrs. Simka Jovanović, the wife of the Serbian minister for internal affairs, the only "female minister", who was working as a medical sister. She was very popular, and everybody called her "Auntie Simka". Although the staff were drawn from different countries, it seemed that there was no problem of communication among them, about which Isabel wrote: "We all had our meals together, and I don't think you would ever find a dinner table where conversation was carried on in four languages with such ease, and ranged over so many different topics."

Isabel was appointed to a surgical unit with 30 patients, but she had some very highly experienced orderlies, so that she had little to do in the unit, and actually was most concerned to see that everything was in order for the doctor's visits. She was satisfied both with her work and her accommodation; "The only thing I grudge is being separated from Kath," she wrote home.

During the summer Katherine continued her work in the villages in the Bitola valley, mainly inoculations. "I have been almost to the front line, where every day we can hear the booming of cannon from the other side, " she related, "we have been round the villages of the Bitola valley, where we have treated women and children. However, the most important part of our work has been vaccinations. We have vaccinated about 100 people every day." The work had also its amusing side. On one occasion, while working in a village with a mainly Turkish population, Katherine was amused to see how the men pushed their wives forward to see what would be the effect of the injection. The women there all wore the veil, and only their frightened eyes could be seen, and they were so shy that they scarcely revealed a small part of their upper arm to receive the injection, which otherwise they accepted without any fuss. Before they began vaccinations in a village, the unit would inform the inhabitants of surrounding hamlets, some of them quite distant; then the villagers in long processions, led by their headmen, would come in columns to the designated place. While the unit was working, the men, women and children would gather together in groups while they waited, exchanging news, so that for them this day became a kind of holiday gathering. One day, Katherine's unit, working from the morning until late in the evening, inoculated 1,200 people.

Because they were working in a quite remote and distant village, one of the problems facing Katherine and her unit was that of supplies, about which she wrote: "Food is a great difficulty and we are often short of supplies, as they are only delivered every four days, and then what we've ordered doesn't always come." She also missed books to read. "Tell father the British Medical Journals are coming through again all right and I am glad to have them," Katherine wrote to her mother; "We often feel starved of something decent to read. The rubbish some of the camps gather in the way of novels is not worth reading. I have been lucky to have a few good books lately, but it just makes me long for more. I often long for some new jokes too – the old ones get so threadbare, so if you know of any, send them on."

During the summer Katherine travelled to Salonica, where she wished to have a few days' rest. She stayed with Isabel in Crown Prince Alexander's Serbian Hospital, which, after the primitive mountain villages, seemed to her "sophisticated, cosmopolitan and safe." However, in spite of this she still did not want to take up her position in the hospital, but asked Dr. Sondermajer to allow her to return to work in the villages, where there was so much to be done; he gave his approval of this, but only until September.

On returning to her unit at Brod she found a serious situation. An unknown disease had appeared in the villages, causing deaths among the adults, and particularly among the children. In a single village some twenty-six children died in the course of one week. The illness began with diarrhoea, followed by swellings on the feet, which gradually spread to the arms, hands and face. Of the sick people sent to the hospital in Sorović, 40 % died, and the death rate was higher among those who could not be sent to the hospital. Dr. MacPhail was convinced that they were dealing with a disease caused by long-term malnutrition. The population who lived in these war-devastated regions, in great

55

poverty, were certainly short of food; there was no livestock, milk, or milk products, and very little fruit and green vegetables. The rice, flour and beans, which they received as humanitarian aid, was also insufficient, so their diet was not varied enough in form and quality, and consisted mainly of maize flour. Later it was established that they were dealing with a then little known disease, especially in that part of the world, called pellagra, which appeared as a result of a monotonous diet with insufficient vitamins. Simply by improving the diet, the disease was quickly eliminated.

During the summer of 1917 it was extremely hot in the Bitola valley; dry winds blew, and the earth became dried and cracked; all this had a bad effect on Katherine. "I never longed more for the sight and smell of trees as I did during those months on the parched plains," she wrote nostalgically, feeling lost and extremely lonely. One of the rare sources of refreshment which she could take advantage of at that time was to go away for a day or two high into the mountains, to the hamlet of Jelak, under the main mountain peak called Kajmakčalan, where there was a section of the SWH Motor Ambulance Column.[36] This settlement of wooden huts built for them by the Serbian Army was situated in wild mountain scenery, surrounded by pines and fir trees and deep ravines. One of the members of this unit, Elsie Corbett [37] described it as follows: "Our Jelak camp was a lovely place: the fir woods began just above us, but looking back you saw nothing but the wildest mountain country, with fantastic rock masses tumbled over it ......we looked across a valley so deep that you could see the backs of eagles wheeling far below, with Kajmakčalan rising in majesty beyond." Of course the way up to Jelak was extremely difficult, steep, winding, with very sharp bends, on the edge of deep chasms; but for the brave drivers who were members of this unit this was no obstacle to conveying many thousands of wounded men, for which they were highly valued and respected by the Serbian soldiers. Dr. Milorad Dragić, later a well-known Serbian medical historian, also recollected these brave women, about whom he wrote: "During the First World War, after arriving at the Salonica Front from Corfu, I found myself as a medical student on military duty at the Divisional First Aid and dressing station .... Our job was to receive sick and wounded men from the front, which was very near us, give what help was needed, and if necessary evacuate the sick and wounded further into the interior.... They were brought from the front to our dressing station on mules, with comfortable seats on both sides of the saddle, and their further evacuation from our first-aid post was carried out by cars driven by women from Scotland." The gratitude and esteem of the Serbian soldiers was shown in a number of ways. Elsie Corbett provides evidence of this; in her book [38] she describes an interesting incident with one of the older soldiers, who otherwise performed auxiliary duties; such a soldier was known as "čiča" ("uncle"); their task here was to keep watch and help the drivers at the sharp bends on the mountain roads: "One day one of the SWH ambulances was stopped on the way up a steep road by a warning board on the hairpin bend, and behind the ambulance a convoy of British M.T. wagons slowly slid to a stop. As they did so the old "čiča" vanished from his post for a moment behind a boulder, and reappeared with an old bully beef tin, in which was arranged a bunch of wild flowers. This with great delight, he presented to the 'Goddess in the Car'. It was not difficult to imagine the feelings of the M.T. men who had had to halt their convoy for this act of devotion, and their wagons restarted on the steep bend." The members of this unit were very friendly toward Katherine, and some of them, particularly Elsie Cameron Corbett, Marjorie Pope Ellis from South Africa and Florence Harvey from Canada (Fig. 27), often gave up their time off to drive Katherine on her visits to the remote villages, and were also to contribute a great deal to her later work in Belgrade.

Just before the end of the summer of 1917, the SRF Hospital at Sorović was transferred to Germijan, near Brod, and Katherine's dispensary in that village, the "shambles of a place" as she put it, was therefore closed. At the same time she was due to report at the Crown Prince Alexander's Serbian Hospital in Salonika in connection with her job there. However, Katherine was firmly convinced that her medical help was needed much more in the outlying villages, and with great difficulty she managed to convince Dr. Sondermajer of this; in the end he gave in and agreed that Katherine should continue to work in the villages in the rear, near the front line. In making this decision Dr. Sondermajer, who badly needed doctors to work in his military hospitals, was probably influenced by the ever-present fear of an outbreak of infectious diseases among the local people, which could be the beginning of a more widespread epidemic among the civilian population, and also among the widely dispersed military personnel. So, Katherine remained working in the Bitola valley; her headquarters was in the half-ruined village of Bač, just a few miles away from the SRF hospital in Germijan. At this time, her friend Dr. Edward Ryan, to whom she showed the surrounding villages, and the wretched conditions under which these people lived, especially the children, visited Katherine. These scenes, together with her determination to help these people, were so convincing that Dr. Ryan immediately moved into action, and through the American Red Cross he managed to obtain for her a kind of mobile dispensary, provided with drugs, dressing material, and foodstuffs, so that Katherine was able to extend her medical work by improving the nutrition of vulnerable children. The poverty of the children specially affected Katherine; she was extremely sensitive about this, and what she saw and experienced in the Bitola valley probably determined her future journey through life. "I saw there deprivation and disease among the children," she wrote, "and what a lot needed to be done in the future to care for them and improve their condition."

In Bač Katherine lived in a single-storey house, built in the Turkish style. The owner and her children lived on the ground floor, and Katherine was given a room on the first floor; she was extremely fortunate to be surrounded by four walls, since there were only a few houses left in the village; she was especially grateful that there was an iron heating stove in her room, because she knew that winter in those parts could be very cold. The Serbian Army assigned to her two helpers, a driver called Pero (short for Peter) (Fig. 27), and a pitiful handicapped soldier as an assistant, whom Katherine described in the following words: "He is a wounded soldier who has lost the sight of one of his eyes, and is now out of the army. He is doing very well for me, but as he and I are both pretty ignorant of cooking matters, we are living very much at the mercy of chance. Luckily for me, I have friends who will ask me out to dinner occasionally, and that way I will keep my weight up!" Pero was a simple Serbian peasant, always cheerful and smiling, extremely popular with everybody. He was faithful and attached to his doctor, and drove her around throughout her stay in that area, all over the district, and under the most difficult conditions; and on one occasion she promised she would take him to England after the war. He was certainly very clever and resourceful, which at that time was indeed important, since there was a great and permanent shortage of just about everything; it was especially difficult to obtain lamps and spare parts for the car, so Pero had to do the best he could about this. On one occasion he drove Katherine to the British camp at Jelak, where a concert was taking place and many guests had gathered. Their car had no headlights since they had been damaged. Pero did not attend the concert, and when Katherine found him afterwards, he proudly informed her that their car now had three headlights. At that time, the lamps were not fixed to the cars and could easily be removed, so it was not difficult to suggest how Pero had come by them. At first Katherine was very angry   at this, since it seemed to her a very inappropriate way of paying her debt to her British hosts for an enjoyable evening, and, naturally, she said so to Pero. However, he just smiled and said: "It's all right; I got them all off French cars!" Since all the cars had then gone their separate ways, it was too late to do anything more about this.

The winter of 1917-18 was bitterly cold in the mountains of Macedonia and the travelling to the distant villages was often a perilous experience, as Katherine recalled later. Once, in early January her car stuck more than axle deep in mud, two kilometers from the village she was going to visit, and all the efforts to pull out the car were futile. She and Pero walked the rest of the way; Katherine did her rounds in the village, looking for cases of typhus fever, which had occurred again, and after that they set off on borrowed horses to retrieve the car. By this time it was snowing hard and the car was still immoveable. Their only chance seemed to be to ride to the nearest Serbian Army camp for help. When they arrived Katherine was somewhat astounded and perplexed when the Colonel there insisted that they should stay the night. Noticing her confusion the Colonel explained laughingly that he could not send his officers out on such a night. She was given one of the officer's huts to sleep in and was rather alarmed as she settled down for the night, to hear a loud hammering outside. The Colonel had sent a soldier to put a lock on the door, "because I know how dangerous you think we men are!" The next morning it was still snowing hard and Katherine, accompanied by Pero and two officers, rode 7 miles, to the nearest military ambulance station, where she was revived by tea with rum, a favourite drink in such weather. "I don't remember ever having been so cold", she said. "It made me realise something of what the retreat over Albania must have been like at times, and also what the soldiers at the front have to suffer." It took six horses and 20 soldiers to get her car out and back on the downward road.

One of the best-preserved houses in Bač was the school building in which the heir to the throne stayed when he came to visit the front. That winter, on St. Andrew's day (on December 13th, according to the old, Julian calendar) Crown Prince Alexander came to celebrate his *slava* [39] among the soldiers, and Katherine was invited to this celebration; this was the first time she had seen and met the prince. This was also her first *slava*, and, not surprisingly after this serious feasting she needed two days to recover.

Katherine regularly visited the surrounding villages with her mobile dispensary and carried on with her work. Meanwhile, at her request, her family and friends in Scotland had gone into action and collected warm winter clothes and shoes; and when all these things reached Katherine she had great pleasure in giving them as presents to poverty-stricken women and children on the occasion of her visits.

However, there were more difficult and unpleasant tasks. One night, after midnight, the local civilian district chief, accompanied by some men carrying lamps, knocked violently on Katherine's door and woke her up. When she came out, completely astonished, they told her that an important official in a neighbouring village had shot himself, and that she, as the only doctor in the district, must come and see him. Katherine quickly got herself ready, summoned Pero and went with her escort to that village. There they found the official in a small upstairs room lying behind the stove with a wound in his head, and with a revolver beside him. Katherine examined him, and reported that he was dead. The district chief then demanded that she should perform an autopsy. Katherine, naturally, was very unpleasantly surprised by this request. Earlier she had helped and taken part in post-mortem examinations, in well-equipped hospitals; but here, in such conditions, and alone? It was unthinkable! She tried to get out of the situation by saying that she did not have the instrumentation for this task, however, to her amazement once more, they produced a box of instruments, and she had no way out. The corpse was taken on to the balcony, where there was more room, all those present were sent away, and Katherine set to work. Of course she had to open up the skull, which for her was the hardest task; and who else should then come to her aid than the faithful Pero, the only person who stayed with her. When Pero saw how she was struggling to saw the skull bones, he simply took the saw from her and did the job. When they had finished the post-mortem and other formalities they left the officials to write their report and quickly departed. "As we went home, I remember being seized with a fit of shivering from the intense cold and a feeling of nausea in the pit of my stomach" said Katherine. "Pero looked at me and although it was his only wrap, he took off his scarf and put it round my head without a word", said Katherine later, as she recalled this unpleasant event.

Pero continued to act as Katherine's driver right up to her departure to Scotland, and then he returned to his regiment. However, after the war he appeared in Belgrade, where he found Katherine, and again worked for her for a time; she then fulfilled her promise and enabled him to visit Great Britain.

It is quite understandable that life was not easy for Katherine at this time. Wartime conditions were difficult, and she was the only civilian doctor in a devastated and poverty-stricken district immediately behind the front line, all around her was poverty and distress; however she bravely and persistently continued the work she had begun, for which she was greatly loved and appreciated. Fortunately quite near, in the village of Germijan, there was a SRF hospital, where there were performances of music and dancing every Saturday; then she was always welcome at the British camp at Jelak, and the surrounding camps of the Serbian Army; her old friend, Admiral Troubridge with his staff was staying at one time in a nearby village; so Katherine had plenty of friends in the neighbourhood to be with her at difficult times. It was at that time that she became acquainted with Miloš Ćirić, who, while still a medical student, had fled at the beginning of the war from Novi Sad, which was in Austria-Hungary at that time, and enlisted in the Serbian Army as a volunteer; he had crossed Albania with them, and then been stationed on the Salonica Front, where he, as all other medical students in the Serbian army, fulfilled the duties of a medical auxiliary. In fact, although these students were officially just doctors' helpers, they very often fulfilled the duties of doctors who were in short supply, and because of that the soldiers regarded them as doctors, which they then in fact became. So it happened that, during the war, their firm friendship began, which lasted until the end of Katherine's stay in Yugoslavia, and was strongest while she was working in Sremska Kamenica, when Dr. Miloš Ćirić, already a well-known specialist for pulmonary diseases, lived and worked in Novi Sad. Miloš (Miša) Ćirić, like others, developed a great respect and gratitude to Katherine; this is clear from a letter he wrote, in quite formal English, to greet her at Christmas: "My dear friend, Today, I would like to comprehend in my wishes for you all the possible good that any vivid imagination ever made desirable. At first, I wish that my warm feelings may find the right way to your heart and a home in the recesses of your soul. May your spirit remain for ever gay and youthful; may your soul remain for ever noble and pure; may your heart beat for my nation as warmly as at present. And, if there is love in your heart, or a germ of it, may it grow into the ardent passion while never ceasing to be the noblest and tenderest self-expression of individuality. This is all I wish for you and Miss Isabel for the Christmas. With brotherly love, M. Ćirić."

While Katherine had celebrated Christmas on her own at Bač Isabel enjoyed, at the Crown Prince Alexander's Hospital, the traditional Serbian Christmas festivities.

Christmas in Serbia is celebrated on January 7th, as the Serbian Orthodox Church uses the so-called Julian calendar, which is thirteen days behind the new Gregorian calendar, and the festive procedures traditionally start in the afternoon of the January 6th. Thrilled by the experience Isabel wrote: "On Christmas Eve, about four o'clock, just at sunset, we had the ceremony of *Badnjak,* or burning the yule-log. In a big open space there was a small fire burning and by it stood the Director as master of the house to receive the blessing of the visitors. Two soldiers then came up carrying huge branches of oak. After saluting the Director and being welcomed by him, they put these on the fire and he threw handfuls of sugar and wheat as a symbol of plenty. While the fire was blazing they danced the *kolo* [40] and served wine, tea and coffee at intervals to all of us who were sitting round the fire. As usual, of course, we were called away to an immediate operation – a case of strangulated hernia – but everything went well and we were in time for supper at 7.30 p.m." … "In the barracks the floor was strewn with straw and candles – a symbol of Christ's being born in a manger – and we had a meagre (!!) meal of five courses of fish, cakes, fruit etc. Then we danced, had music and played games till midnight. Early in the proceedings an orderly came in and announced that the pig had been killed and cleaned, weighed 12 kilos, and was now being roasted. It was for this feast that we waited until midnight, when we all sat down to table again and had roast pig, salad and cakes. I went off to bed thoroughly exhausted at 2.30 a.m., but the others went on until 6 a.m. We have luckily not got very much work just now and everyone can be free to frivol and visit their friends. But with all the gaiety, one is struck more than ever by the sad fate of all these men."

During the winter and spring of 1918, the situation on the Salonica Front was relatively quiet. Apart from occasional skirmishes and exchange of gunfire, there was no major activity; everything was quiet, in the expectation of a big offensive, about which everyone was talking and waiting for, and trying to guess when it would start. In such a quiet situation, there was both time and opportunity for various other activities, so the Serbian soldiers from the surrounding camps gladly sought the company of the girls from the British missions in the neigbourhood. Katherine later recalled an incident, which vividly expressed the atmosphere of that time. One day in the spring of 1918, the officers of a large military unit, stationed some distance away in the mountains, invited Katherine and eight other girls from the SRF hospital in Germijan to their unit's *slava.*[39] That morning the officers came for the girls with horses, and they all rode off happily up to the mountain, expecting to return at the usual time of 10 p.m. After a long ride in the fresh mountain air, they all enjoyed the *slava* lunch, accompanied by gipsy music, since one of the soldiers played the violin very well. Then they followed the *kolo* (Fig. 28) [40] and there seemed to be no end to the celebration. No one noticed that night had already fallen; and when the girls, accompanied by a few officers, finally set off to go back, a fog descended, which significantly slowed down their movement along the mountain paths, so that they arrived at the hospital in Germijan much later than the appointed time. The girls quietly withdrew into their tents, and the officers then accompanied Katherine to her village, which was quite near, and everything seemed to be all right. However, their late arrival had been noticed, and, because of this, on the complaints of the hospital administration, the Serbian officers were strictly forbidden to visit this hospital. One of these officers was Colonel Panta Draškić, who was a friend of Prince Alexander, the heir to the throne. Now, he was a big, strong man, and during the retreat through Albania, when the prince developed appendicitis, he carried him on his back for several kilometers to the nearest hospital, where the prince was operated on. Naturally, the prince could never forget such an act of devotion, and Panta Draškić, whom he from then on regarded as a personal friend, was rewarded by the gift of a ring with a beautiful sapphire, which the colonel wore with pride. The next time the prince came to visit the front, Colonel Draškić complained to him about the "out of bounds" order, which was a blow both to him and his colleagues, since they missed the company of the girls from the hospital, and the regular Saturday entertainments, which were held there. The Crown Prince immediately sent an urgent message to Vojvoda Živojin Mišić, Commander-in-chief of the Serbian Army (*vojvoda* - lit. duke - was also the highest military rank in the Serbian army), from whose headquarters this order had come, and asked for horses and an escort in order to visit the hospital. And very soon, accompanied by those same officers who had been under the "out of bounds" order, the prince visited the hospital, where they were all warmly welcomed and received with great pleasure; and after this the infamous order was forgotten to the great pleasure of everybody.

From time to time Katherine visited Salonica, in order to get supplies for her mobile dispensary; on these occasions she always stayed with Isabel. Katherine looked forward to these visits when she could return to civilisation for a short time, have a rest, and visit her friends. During one such visit in the summer of 1918 Isabel introduced her to Flora Sandes (see Appendix 7), who was then already one of the legendary figures of the war in Serbia; she was then in Crown Prince Alexander's Serbian Hospital for a minor operation, that is the removal of bits of shrapnel, which had remained after an earlier wound. A close friendship immediately developed between them, which was to last until the end of their lives. Katherine wrote home about this meeting: "I like her very much and our mutual enthusiasm for the Serbs gives us a lot in common. She is dressed in a Serbian sergeant's uniform, which suits her very well. Yesterday we went into the town together to lunch and I helped her to buy a pair of trousers and leggings. The Serbs all love her and look on her as a kind of mascot."

As everything was quiet on the Salonika Front in the summer of 1918, and there were no signs of the long-awaited great offensive, Katherine began to make preparations to go home to Scotland. Actually, the main reason for this decision was the need to help her father in his medical practice. In fact Dr. Donald MacPhail, who had a very extensive practice, remained alone since his two assistants had been called up into the army, and he could no longer do so much work himself. At that time, in Britain, as in the rest of the world, there was a widespread pandemic of the so-called "Spanish influenza", which greatly increased the number of his patients; and when Dr. Donald MacPhail himself succumbed to influenza, Katherine no longer hesitated. She and Isabel announced their departure, and the relevant authorities, though reluctant to lose two such devoted experts, accepted their reasons, and approved their departure, with gratitude for what they had done. Katherine was awarded the "Order of St. Sava", fourth class, for her work in Macedonia, and a medal of the Serbian Red Cross, while Isabel was awarded the Serbian "Cross of Charity"; she had already been awarded the "Médaille des Epidémies" for her work during epidemics in France.

And so in August 1918 the MacPhail sisters left Salonica and returned to their native Scotland; however, as soon became evident, their stay at home did not last long.

Fig. 26 Isabel MacPhail, Katherine's younger sister, in Salonica, 1917.
(Courtesy of Mrs. E.Biggs)

Fig. 27 On the Salonica Front, 1917; Dr. K. MacPhail is sitting in the car, beside her driver Pero. Florence Harvey is sitting in front of the car, and Marjorie Pope Ellis standing beside it, both ambulance drivers. (Courtesy of Mrs. E. Biggs)

Fig. 28 On the Salonica Front, 1917-1918; Dr. K. MacPhail is dancing the kolo, with an Allied officer on one side and a Serbian officer of the other.
(Photograph courtesy of the Imperial War Museum, London)

Chapter 5

Belgrade, 1919 – 1934

After her return to Scotland, Katherine had no time to rest. First of all, her father was ill, and she had to concern herself with his health, and then she had take over most of his patients, since the only help available was an older doctor unfit for military service. But this was a problem at first, because the patients had doubts about women doctors. It happened that one day, a woman patient who was waiting for the doctor was not a little surprised, and offended, when Katherine arrived. However, everything ended well, and later she jokingly said to Katherine's father: "You said you would send another doctor, and you just sent a bit lassie!" But during the great influenza epidemic, when there were so many sick people and so few doctors, there was no room for prejudice. On the other hand, Dr. Katherine MacPhail, with her inborn authority, decisive manner, medical knowledge and style of approach soon dispelled all doubts and suppressed all prejudices, and became very popular with her father's patients. Many of them later gave her all the help they could in the various humanitarian activities she and her family organised to help Serbia and Serbian children. Of course, the fame of her war service on various European fronts also contributed to all this. Her sacrificial work during several years of war could not pass unnoticed, and the citizens of her native town of Coatbridge were proud of her. Soon after her return home Dr. Katherine MacPhail was proclaimed an honorary citizen of Coatbridge, and on the occasion of a special celebration on August 15th, 1918 she was given the Freedom of Coatbridge and presented with a gold watch (Fig. 29). Also at this time Isabel received an Imperial Nursing Medal for her care of the wounded. So the two MacPhail sisters, and their father, were included in the book of meritorious citizens of Coatbridge who had particularly distinguished themselves in the Great War.[41]

Katherine and Isabel followed the events on all fronts with great interest, especially those on their own Salonica Front, where, in September 1918, the long-expected great offensive finally began, and they were delighted by the successes of the allied forces in breaking through this front; at the same time they regretted that they themselves were not present at these great events. Then they both decided, without much reflection, to return as soon as possible to Serbia.

Isabel was the first to go; she attached herself to the YWCA (Young Women's Christian Association), where she was accepted as a worker in a charitable kitchen. She and Eleanor Cave left London in October 1918 for Salonica, but by force of circumstances they arrived in Gallipoli, which was, to quote Isabel, "the last word in filth and decadence, with   Spanish flu raging." Since for some military and naval reasons they could not get transport to Salonica they were obliged to take a roundabout route by way of Corfu and

Albania, so they embarked on a naval vessel, which took them to Corfu. While they were waiting for further transport they accepted an invitation from a colonel who had taken over the house of a former German Consul "with beautiful furniture, a library of German and English books, fine table linen, china and crystal, and a cellar full of good wine, and he simply revels in using them all to full advantage". From Corfu they passed to Albania where they were the guests of Italian soldiers who transported them to Bitola in Macedonia, by way of a newly built road over the Albanian mountains, and as they came down from the heights to the plains round Bitola, "the decline, with all its windings, continues steadily for twelve and half miles, and we had to stop periodically to rest the brakes", recalled Isabel later. They found Bitola in a state of chaos. "Troops of all nationalities thronging the streets, refugees pouring in on their return journey in wagons, mule carts and lorries, camps moving their equipment, a French band playing in the square, pandemonium, crush and overpowering noise"….Isabel wrote. "As we sat waiting in the station for our train to the YWCA Headquarters at Salonica, a train load of women and children in trucks passed through, refugees going home. They had been 17 hours in the train already, and would have to turn out and sleep on the ground, perhaps travelling on next day without anything to eat. It makes me feel absolutely helpless and overwhelmed."

When they finally reached Salonica, Isabel and her travelling companion joined their canteen which was awaiting further orders, so they had a few days to recover from their long and strenuous journey, about which Isabel wrote with pleasure to her family: "We are enjoying the quiet and comfort after not having had our clothes off from Friday morning to Monday night." They stayed in a small hut for the staff, and nearby there was a Serbian unit whose commanding officer helped them to settle in, about whom Isabel wrote: "He is one of the nicest Serbs I've ever met, most sincere and interesting. Today is a howling day of rain, wind and thunder, and he has been most thoughtful for us, has had a small stove in our hut, and keeps us supplied with wood, which is at a premium. Also he has nailed up all the cracks in our windows." As well as these purely practical contacts and assistance, they obviously discussed more complicated questions which troubled and confused many Serbian soldiers who came into contact with foreign missions; about this Isabel wrote: "He cannot understand our mentality at all, or what makes the British want to come out to this kind of life, or our education, which makes us women work as no other women like us do. He got his first impression of British women with the Sir James Berry Unit at Vranje, where he was nursed through typhus just before the retreat. He has a great admiration for all things British and has just given his own son aged 13 to a Mr. Riddell [42] to be his adopted son for some years to come."

In November Isabel's unit was sent to the South-Serbian town of Vranje, to which they travelled in a convoy of ten vehicles. The roads, over which an advancing army had already passed, were in a frightful state, and between Skopje and Leskovac their carts became stuck in deep mud, so that they were obliged to spend one night on the road. "It was dark and wet with mud inches deep all round us and an icy blizzard blowing", was how Isabel described that night. "My chauffeur rigged up his coat and blanket as curtains round the front of the car, but they always blew down and at last I just lay a shivering bundle of wraps on the front seat while he went inside on top of the truck we had brought with us." At about five o'clock in the morning they were woken up by the cheerful voice of an Englishman from a heavy lorry, which had stopped alongside them; he offered them hot tea, which in those conditions was an unimaginable luxury. They exchanged a tin of sardines for a cup of hot tea, and heard the joyful news that five pairs of oxen and twenty Bulgarian prisoners of war were on their way to pull them out of the mud. Once free of the mud, they pushed on north, but again the roads were appalling and rather than risk another roadside night, they decided to stop in a village. A Serbian peasant and his wife agreed that Isabel and Eleanor Cave could sleep in their one room for the night, and that the men could eat an evening meal round their stove. They had had no food all day and the drivers set to and cooked huge platefuls of bacon and eggs, much to the interest of the family. Eggs at that time could not be bought for money, but were exchanged for tins of petrol – four eggs for one tin. The Serbian family who accepted them were terribly poor; the husband had just returned after being interned in Bulgaria, and they were without decent clothes, even without pots, pans and cups, everything was taken or destroyed during the war. Isabel was much touched by their hospitality in such circumstances.

When they finally reached their destination at Vranje they organised and set up a charitable kitchen, which gave free food and tea to all who asked for it. There were then many people who were hungry, and they just besieged the charitable kitchen, or canteen, as that institution was then called, so that armed soldiers had to be summoned to keep order.

As soon as the canteen began to function regularly, Isabel decided to return to Salonica to secure stores for the canteen, and to collect her heavy luggage including her much needed fur coat, which had been lost in Corfu and then finally found. This time she decided to travel by train, in the hope that this would be more reliable. In fact, the railway was in even a worse condition than the roads, and she found out that very soon. No one ever knew when the train went or how long it would take to get to its destination. "Like the Mull steamer it is never due, it just arrives", she remarked. Isabel finally got on a train with a crowd of British, Greek and Serbian soldiers, into an open goods train, which was travelling south. While it was day-light it was quite a novelty to sit at the open side of the truck and enjoy the scenery, but all too soon it was dark and the wind and rain blew in on them. Some time after midnight the train stopped suddenly in front of a bridge across the river Vardar; the bridge was damaged and the train could not cross it. The travellers had a choice: they could either stay in the train until morning and wait for lorries which would take them further, or they could cross the bridge on foot, and then walk along a damaged section of

69

the railway line, about two miles altogether, to the following train which would take them further. Although it was a moonless night, Isabel and some of the British soldiers nevertheless decided to set out on foot over the badly damaged bridge, with the swollen river roaring beneath it. When they reached the train on the other side they were delighted, though once again it was a case of open goods wagons, which were so dirty that they could not lie on the floor, but sat through the remainder of their journey wrapped in their cloaks, throughout a bitterly cold night.

When Isabel finally returned to Vranje, with five lorry loads of supplies and her luggage, she decided that at least for some time she would not travel anywhere; she wrote home: "Travelling is such business that now I am here I mean to stay here if I can. I wonder where Kath is by this time. I expect as soon as she comes out, she will have to find her way to Belgrade – a long round journey from here these days. We may have Christmas together with luck."

While Isabel suffered during her travels through the devastated Balkan region, Katherine had other problems. In London she was collecting the documents needed in order to travel to Serbia, which at that time was not easy. She had no large organisation behind her to secure all the necessary permits and documents; she was acting as an independent individual and had to arrange everything herself. First of all she requested permission in the Serbian Legation to return to Serbia, to do the same work as a civilian that she had done previously. The Legation accepted her application, but then she had to secure the permission of the British authorities, which was quite complicated. From London she wrote home: "I have had a most unfortunate day – waiting my turn in the British Permit Office. I was there from 10 a.m. to 4 p.m. waiting my turn and when it came, the officer told me I should have been to the Foreign Office first and until I had been there he could not put my passport through. I rushed down there on his advice to find that the place was closed, which he might have known, so that the whole thing begins again tomorrow."

At the end of November 1918, having collected all the necessary documents, Katherine set out on her journey. Her capital consisted of £ 25.00, which she carried with her. The clothing, footwear and other necessities, which she and her family, friends and patients had collected to help Serbia were separately packed and sent through the Serbian Red Cross in Great Britain. From London Katherine travelled to Paris, where the British king George V was then on a visit; she did not manage to see him, but enjoyed watching the parade on the Champs Elysées, where "the poor, weather-beaten troops got a great reception as they rode past the crowds on the Champs Elysées, and the people rushed out to give them roses, carnations, mimosa and every sort of flower." From Paris she travelled to Toulon where she waited for a passage by sea to Dubrovnik on the Dalmatian coast, from which she would have to travel by train through the newly acquired provinces of Bosnia and Hercegovina and Croatia to Belgrade. Toulon was then crowded with refugees from Serbia, civilian and military, who were eagerly waiting to return home. There, Katherine became acquainted with Miss Darinka Grujić, who was also travelling to Belgrade. Darinka Grujić, an enthusiastic and goodhearted young woman, who had been looking after Serbian orphans and refugees in France since the beginning of the war, and now planned to take them back to Serbia, asked Katherine, in the course of their conversation, whether she would be interested in working with her? This acquaintance, which was later to develop into a lasting friendship, turned out to be very important for Katherine's future work. After they had waited for several days in Toulon, the ships to take them to Dubrovnik finally arrived; then there followed an extremely difficult train journey, through Sarajevo and Slavonski Brod to Zemun, which lasted three days and three nights. The carriages had only bare wooden benches; there was no heating or lighting, and a bitter wind blew through the broken doors and windows. The train crawled along at a speed of about 4 – 6 miles per hour, and stopped at every station, sometimes for several hours. However finally, at three o'clock in the morning one December night, they arrived at Zemun, on the opposite bank of the Sava River to Belgrade, where they had to wait until morning for a ferry to take them across the river, as the railway bridge had, of course, been blown up.

At that time, as Katherine remembered it, Belgrade was terribly changed. Practically everything was demolished and destroyed and those houses still standing looked dilapidated. Crowds of people, most of them badly dressed and undernourished, wandered about the streets, and there were large numbers of foreigners. "The streets are so full of all nationalities that it doesn't seem to belong to the Serbs at all", wrote Katherine, describing these days. There was not a single hotel functioning, and Katherine was delighted when she found her old friends from the Salonica Front, Nan McGlade and Dorothy Pickton, who had arrived from Macedonia with their charitable kitchen immediately after the army, and were already settled in Belgrade. They helped her to find a room near them where she could stay until she found more permanent accommodation and could see how her plans would work out. She soon made contact with friends from the Transport Unit of the SWH with whom she had made friends in Jelak at the Salonica Front. This was the first ambulance transport unit, which had arrived in the town immediately after the army, for which they earned the personal decoration of the Medal for Bravery from Crown Prince Alexander. Two SWH units had also arrived in the town, to help with the reorganisation and arrangements of the existing hospitals in the city, which were in a wretched state. But, of course, Katherine had nothing to do with them whatever.

Immediately after her arrival Katherine reported to the Ministry of Internal Affairs and obtained permission to stay in the town and engage in humanitarian work; she hoped she would find Darinka Grujić, whom she had heard was staying in Dubrovnik to see to the transport of her luggage, from which she did not wish to be separated.

Soon it was Christmas, but there was little joy in the ruined and impoverished town. "It is quite impossible to buy anything here in the way of clothing, material and so on, although food is more reasonable here than in some parts", wrote Katherine to her family. "Tomorrow is Christmas Day, and I am going to the SWH Transport Unit for dinner, so we will probably have a merry time. I am afraid the Serbs will be very dull and sad on their Christmas. There is no feeling of the war being at an end here, and indeed in some ways it seems the worst part of it. I hear that Isabel is in Vranje, away beyond Nish, so I shall not have the chance of seeing her for a while anyway."

At that time, in devastated Serbia and Belgrade, there was indeed an enormous need for every kind of help from abroad, from medical service and assistance in looking after orphans and invalids, to help with food, clothing, footwear and everything else. The large number of foreign humanitarian missions in Belgrade at that time wanted in some way to be involved in these efforts, and to start their work, but regarding this there was at that time considerable chaos in Belgrade, as described by Francesca Wilson, a well-known humanitarian worker, who was then in Serbia: "Relief work for the Serbs during the war was well done on the whole, and was mainly in the hands of two bodies – the Serbian Relief Fund and the Scottish Women's Hospital Unit. In Serbia itself, until the Retreat in 1915, and after that on the Salonika Front, relief was mainly medical. The spheres of the various hospital units were well defined and did not overlap…But Serbia after the war was, for a while, complete chaos. There were dozens of different organisations struggling for a foothold. The newly constituted Government of the new kingdom of Serbs, Croats and Slovenians, later Yugoslavia, with a population that had leapt from four-and-a-half to nearly fourteen million, and a territory that had expanded enormously, had enough on its hands without having to be polite to all sorts of foreigners who importuned it for buildings, transport, personnel, priority and privilege. Ministers of Departments could not tell who was important, and did not like to be rude to earnest Anglo-Saxons, who had left their own countries, ostensibly at great sacrifice and with the most benevolent intentions, and who dangled before their eyes all sorts of benefits for widows and orphans, for the diseased and maimed and blind. As a rule, they promised the same buildings to half-a-dozen different people and gave it to none of them. Heads of missions were frantic over unimplemented promises and unanswered requests. There was no co-ordination amongst them or enough attempts to find out what the Serbs wanted themselves. In June, 1919, General Fortescue [43] established a child welfare society in an effort to co-ordinate foreign and national work on behalf of the child population, but it was only partially successful; it should have had wider powers and have existed from the start." [32]

In this somewhat confused situation immediately after the war, Dr. Katherine MacPhail was the first among many foreigners who got herself organised and set to work; and as early as the beginning of 1919 she opened the first children's hospital in Belgrade. The first report of this hospital contains the following statement: "Serbia at this period was in a terrible plight. Everything was disorganised and no facilities for hospital work were obtainable. This meant that children were dying daily for lack of proper medical attention….In December, 1918, the use of an abandoned Austrian Barrack, which had last been used as a stable, was obtained. Bugs were many and beds were few. With the kindly help of the various Allied Relief Missions equipment was obtained and a start was made. Two English Sisters who had been working with the Serbs on the Salonika front joined Dr. MacPhail to begin this new piece of work and with their help the hospital was soon set going." [44]

In the course of a few weeks after her arrival in Belgrade, Katherine managed to secure a shed in Studenička Street, found beds, bedding and staff, and secured food supplies for her small patients. "Perhaps because things were in a terrible muddle, I got help just by asking", Katherine explained later. Certainly her remarkable power and ability to infect others with her own enthusiasm, and to win them over to her own ideas and plans reached its full scope; this same power, a kind of magic, was often useful to her later in her life. Isabel described this ability of her sister quite simply: "Kath never has to ask people for things, they are just given to her."

The most important event, which enabled Katherine to begin her work successfully, was the arrival of Darinka Grujić in Belgrade; she arrived in an open wagon with her luggage and equipment. Later Katherine wrote about her: "Darinka Grujić was one of the greatest characters I have ever known. I knew very little of her background except that she had lived for some years in America, and had many new friends there, and that her family were a real Serbian family who lived in one of the small towns near Belgrade. We were attracted to each other in the first place because we had the same urge to get ahead with work to help the homeless and needy. I never knew anyone with a warmer heart, and almost nothing was too difficult for her to surmount, when it was a question of helping forlorn children and their families. I realised this as soon as I met her in Toulon, waiting to return to her own country. She told me that she had had a Home in the south of France for about 200 children, many of them orphans, whom she collected in Greece after her country was overrun by the Germans in 1916. Some children had made the retreat over Albania to the coast, and others had escaped over the frontier into Greece. Darinka Grujić found a home for them near Nice, and was now, at the end of 1918, going back into Serbia to find a home there for them, if they did not find their families. It was for her I waited when I reached Belgrade, and asked the Ministry of the Interior if I could wait for her arrival to see if we could do something for the many children who were being brought to Belgrade from the interior. So it was with delight that I found her, shortly after my arrival, just before Christmas. I never knew where she got all her funds from, but I knew that she was friendly with a wealthy

American family named Frothingham.[45] There were two sisters, I think, and a brother, Major Frothingham, who came to Serbia in connection with the American Red Cross. He had formerly given her generous support, and continued to do so for many years. She seemed to know everyone in Belgrade, including all the ministers and officials, and was immensely popular."

As soon as she arrived in Belgrade Darinka Grujić managed to get hold of five barracks in Studenička Street, very near the military hospital, and she let Katherine have one of these for a children's hospital. The sheds were in a terrible state – dirty and neglected, without water supply or electrical installation, which had been destroyed, and with broken windows – so that practically all the missions to which they had been offered had refused them. They had to be cleaned from top to bottom, repaired, and made ready for work, so Katherine immediately got down to this task. Her old friends, the British sailors of the Danube Flotilla under the command of Admiral Troubridge, who had also returned to Belgrade, came to her help. They quickly cleaned, repaired and re-painted the barrack, of course in Dreadnought Grey, the only paint they had. Katherine also asked for assistance from Colonel Kidd, head of a medical unit of the British Army, which happened to be then in Belgrade, and asked him to inspect the barrack, which, it turned out, had already been offered to him and which he had refused; she also asked him to help her to install a sterilizer in the barrack, which he did. From Miss Annie Dickinson [46] at the Red Cross she managed to get 25 military beds, bed-linen, blankets and various other things; in addition Annie Dickinson agreed that the Red Cross would pay the salary of two nurses if they could be found. Very fortunately there were at that time two nurses, Rose Stone and Hilda Willis, staying in Belgrade on their way home; they had earlier worked with Katherine in Macedonia, and when they heard about her new hospital they decided to stay and work with her again. Two British VADs also offered their services; they were Betty Jealous and Jean Martin. Betty Jealous stayed with Katherine for three years, and Jean Martin through the first, most difficult months. Most of the medicines and material for dressings were obtained from the American Red Cross.

In the immediate vicinity of the sheds the Serbian Relief Fund opened a charitable kitchen for a neighbouring school, and Katherine succeeded in arranging that this kitchen should also supply food for the children in the hospital; in this way the question of food was settled, at least for beginning, and the municipal authorities promised to supply wood for fuel. Two old friends of hers from the Transport Unit of the SWH in Jelak, the Canadian Florence Harvey and Marjorie Pope Ellis from South Africa (Fig. 27) were at that time transferred to a transport unit of the SRF, and when Florence Harvey learnt about the founding of a new hospital, she offered to be responsible for transport, free of charge in her own car, and stayed with Katherine for the whole year. All these intensive efforts and assistance bore fruit, and the hospital soon accepted its first patients. At the end of January 1919 Katherine wrote home: "With generous help from the various organisations, we went quickly to work and there is always a large crowd of mothers and miserable, sick, underfed children who have come from all over the country to seek help in the hospital. The general frustration and mental exhaustion made things difficult for us all, and we had to expend a tremendous amount of energy in getting our doors open and beginning to work." A few days later Katherine again wrote home: "Our little hospital is a great success and we have one ward of 20 patients open. I have also an out-patients, and the children come up in shoals from the different orphanages in a terrible state of health. We hope to have another 10 beds ready soon, but the lack of heating has hindered us, and also the fact that we cannot get straw to fill the mattresses…The other day one of the Scottish Women's Hospital commissioners out from England came to visit our place and was so impressed that she gave us a donation of £ 40. It is a great boon and just what I was needing most, as we are always wanting money for extras, such as eggs and any extra food and medicine we can buy. I have spent a little over £ 10 of my own money, and as you say you have £ 25 and can send it out, we can go on quite comfortably for a bit. The difficulty is that we don't constitute a unit of any relief organisation, which makes the responsibility greater."

During the first months every bed in the hospital was occupied, and many children passed through the out-patients clinic every day. The work in the clinic was the most tiring, because the British method of working was quite unfamiliar to the patients, and communication was made considerably more difficult by lack of linguistic knowledge on both sides. There were large numbers of dressings done in the clinic, and apart from that it also organised the distribution of food, clothes and medicines, and the children were always given a cup of cocoa, so it is quite understandable that the hospital soon became very popular (Fig. 30). Dr. Katherine MacPhail herself did all the medical work, since at that time there were very few doctors. In the whole of Serbia only about a hundred of them had survived the war, so it was very difficult to find a doctor who was free; in addition there was never enough money even for the most basic needs. Fortunately Katherine's old friends, Admiral Troubridge and his Marines, were still there, and they again came to her help. Their surgeon, Dr. Ibbotson, a "most enthusiastic operator" from the Middlesex Hospital in London, arranged an improvised operating theatre in the house where he was living, which was quite near the hospital, and where he could perform minor operations. Katherine helped him with his surgical cases and they formed an operating team, and soon, one night they performed their first mastoid operation with Katherine giving the anaesthetic. In return he attended to the surgical cases in Katherine's hospital, and if any of her children needed an operation, they were able to do it in his operating theatre, as there was no room for one in the barracks.

Moreover, Dr. Ibbotson was a gifted pianist, and played at a number of fund-raising concerts in Belgrade, which were organised for the benefit of the children's hospital. Katherine described the first such concert as follows: "Miss

Coleman, attached to some other mission, and two Serbian ladies, got up a concert for us and we had a most delightful evening in a hall in Belgrade, which was a cinema. The people turned out most enthusiastically and we made a clear profit of £ 130.00 willingly given by many who had little money for themselves...We had the hall draped with the naval signalling flags. Admiral Troubridge was there, General Fortescue, the British Minister, the British Consul and many other British and foreigners. Darinka Grujić made a speech in her strange mixture of Serbian and American English, but in the middle, she forgot my name. 'Oh, you all know who I mean', she said impatiently, and there was a great shout of 'MacPhail', while the hall rang with laughter."

At that time Dr. Katherine MacPhail certainly became extremely popular in Belgrade, so that she succeeded in maintaining her hospital from various kinds of donations and other help; it had no other source of income, and cost a great deal to maintain. But, as she herself wrote, the children themselves provided a great motive for help from everyone: "The children made the best appeal of all, and as they had to be cared for, we got help more readily than I would have believed possible." A considerable amount of material and medicines was obtained from the numerous foreign missions, which were gradually beginning to leave Serbia, and they all wanted to help the hospital. They also received an unusual present for these circumstances from the sailors under the command of Admiral Troubridge. The marines found on the Danube an abandoned Austrian barge full of children's toys, including a large wooden rocking horse. Of course they soon took all the toys to the hospital and gave them to the children, who were absolutely delighted, especially as until then many of them had never had the opportunity to see real toys. There were some rather strange gifts too, as Katherine recalled later. So, it was really no surprise when one day Major Howie of the Serbian Relief Fund offered her a couple of mules. Katherine, not wishing to refuse anything, which might be useful, accepted them. But the mules proved to be a problem. Katherine decided she had no use for them, and offered them to Father Mardari, a priest who had lived many years in America and now was living in a monastery near Belgrade. He duly bought them for 3,000 dinars and no more was heard of them for some time. Then Father Mardari turned up in a fury, and said: "You must take your mules back. They are doing so much damage in the orchards, I will give you 3,000 dinars to take them away." The mules were finally given to the mayor of Belgrade and were used for scavenging work in the town – two beautiful mules which were ultimately all that was left of the British Army in Serbia, coming originally from the Salonica Front, concluded Katherine jokingly.

Soon after the hospital opened Katherine obtained new living quarters, in the same requisitioned house as she had lived in 1915 when she fell ill from typhus. This house had previously belonged to an artist; during the occupation it had been damaged by the Austrians who had removed nearly all the furniture, so that all that remained were pictures and sculptures and a piano. In addition to

Katherine, Nan McGlade and some other friends from the charitable canteen moved into this quite comfortable four-room building, and they settled in very pleasantly with their camping equipment. However, the winter of 1919 was harsh and Katherine complained in her letters home: "We have deep drifting snow, high winds and freezing cold." In such grim weather heating problems occurred because of the serious fuel shortage in Belgrade, but once again Admiral Troubridge and his Marines came to the rescue, and supplied them with wood from the stores of their unit. Katherine kept herself on the salary of 400 dinars (about £ 20) a month, which she received from the Ministry of Internal Affairs, which was barely enough to live on. "We lived very frugally", she wrote later, "and what we hadn't we did without – and usually what we really needed turned up miraculously." For their consolation they had the piano, which Dr. Ibbotson often played for them and their friends and the staff of the hospital.

For Katherine the happiest event at this time was the arrival in Belgrade of her sister Isabel. In order to be nearer Katherine Isabel left the charitable canteen in Vranje run by the YWCA and offered herself as a voluntary worker in the Joint Supply Commission in Belgrade, headed by General Fortescue, [43] where she helped with the distribution of clothing and footwear to invalids and impoverished demobilised soldiers, many of whom had no shoes and went about in rags. Isabel, who had moved in with Katherine, was of course very impressed with all that Katherine had achieved during these few months, and delighted to be able to help her in any way she could.

In the early spring of 1919 the hospital was already too small to receive all who sought help there; this was especially the case regarding the large number of children suffering from tuberculosis, of whom there were many, as always happens after a war; and this was a direct result of poor nourishment, bad hygienic conditions and other misfortunes resulting from war. Dr. Katherine MacPhail soon noticed this and at once began to seek a solution. She heard that at that time at Topčider, the park and woods some five miles from Belgrade, there was an open pavilion, which had earlier been used for children, but which was now empty and abandoned. The pavilion was situated on a hill, right at the edge of a forest, surrounded by meadows, so it was ideal for treatment by means of fresh air and sunshine, which, in addition to good food and rest, was at that time the only form of treatment for tuberculosis. Katherine quickly made up her mind, obtained permission from the government, succeeded in securing the necessary repairs and obtaining equipment, and by Easter 1919 the pavilion with 40 beds was ready to receive the first patients. As soon as the weather allowed the pavilion was opened, and 40 small patients, mainly those with tuberculosis and convalescents, were admitted (Figs. 31 and 32). Two tents, left by one of the departing missions, were set up beside the pavilion for the staff, and Mary Baker took the charge of the premises. She had worked with Katherine earlier in Corsica, and as soon as she learnt about her hospital in Belgrade she wrote and offered to come and help her as a voluntary worker, which Katherine eagerly accepted. Mary Baker stayed a whole year in Belgrade, and when she returned home she took with her to England a young boy, a war orphan, whom she adopted, and who remained there living with her family.

The pavilion in Topčider soon proved to be a very successful enterprise. Under the devoted care of the staff, the children soon grew better in the fresh air, to the great joy of their parents who visited them regularly, and to the satisfaction of the many guests who came to see the hospital, which became a popular place for many native and foreign visitors. One day, unannounced and unofficially, the Crown Prince Alexander came on a visit; he wished to see the son of his adjutant and friend Colonel Draškić. This was the same officer from the Salonica Front who had been forbidden to visit the SRF Hospital in Germian. When Katherine opened her hospital Colonel Draškić begged her to help his son who, while living in France as a refugee, had developed a tubercular shoulder joint. Katherine accepted him for treatment, first at Topčider, then in Dubrovnik, after which the boy recovered and later became a famous violinist. Among the many friends and visitors who came to see her was her old friend from the Salonica Front Miloš Ćirić, who had been demobilised and decided to continue his medical studies, which he completed in 1920 in Prague. It was on this occasion that Katherine gave him her photograph with the greeting "Ever yours sincerely", which, as it turned out, had a much wider symbolic significance. This was on May 5th, 1919, as is written on the back of this beautiful photograph (Fig. 33).

As time passed and the work continued to expand, although Katherine was satisfied with the success so far achieved, she began to realise that the existing capacity would soon be inadequate for the increasing number of patients, especially in view of the fact that it would be impossible to use the Topčider pavilion during the cold winter days, so she began to consider extending the hospital. A good opportunity soon appeared: a quite large house in Miloš Veliki Street in Belgrade, near the Military Hospital, which had earlier been requisitioned for the accommodation of the Danube fleet under Admiral Troubridge, had remained empty after the British sailors left Belgrade, and Katherine immediately moved into action to secure this building for her hospital. She was helped in this by her friend and protector General Fortescue, who managed to arrange with the relevant authorities that this house should be assigned to Dr. Katherine MacPhail for the purpose of extending her hospital. It was a quite large private building, light, solidly built and well maintained, with sufficient space for 50 beds, especially when Katherine managed to exchange the large military beds which she had had in the barracks for proper wooden children's beds, of which many more could be accommodated. In addition a small operating theatre was established for minor surgical operations, while the more difficult cases, which required more extensive surgical intervention, were sent to the state hospital. Likewise a large out-patients department was established for mobile patients (Fig. 34).

The new hospital began work in November 1919, and then it was no longer some sort of improvised institution, but a real hospital. "This became a Hospital of fifty beds and as such was awarded recognition by the Serb-Croat-Slovene Government as the first Children's Hospital in Serbia," according to the first official, printed report of this institution. And it was indeed the first children's hospital in this area, officially recognised and known as the *Anglo-Serbian Children's Hospital*, abbreviated to *A.S.C.H.* [44] This official recognition was important not just as a matter of protocol; it brought with it definite advantages: the Ministry of Social Policy approved regular financial support for the hospital, whose expenses rose considerably as the scope of its work widened. There was then an increase in the number of staff, and Katherine employed four qualified British nurses, two British VADs, and some local girls who nursed children under the direction of trained medical sisters. For a few months she had help from two Scottish doctors who had been previously members of one of the Scottish Women's Hospitals before they went home. However, this was not enough for the greatly increased number of patients, and Katherine, who herself had so far done all the medical work, was obliged to seek help. The first two doctors, who came to work with her were Dr. Niko Miljanić, then a young doctor, later a professor of the Faculty of Medicine in Belgrade, and Dr. Garnier, a French woman doctor, who had been the head of a French Mission for the care of children, known as *Goutte de lait* ("A Drop of Milk"). Soon after the hospital was opened the Ministry of Health asked Katherine to accept sick newborn babies from a maternity hospital; this led to the establishment of a special section for newborn babies, under the charge of the most experienced medical sister.

That autumn it became clear that the pavilion in Topčider could only be used during the summer months; it functioned in this way for some years, until 1924, when it was closed. Meanwhile, the number of small patients, especially those with tuberculosis, continued to increase. Then Katherine had the idea of finding some place on the coast where children with tuberculosis, and other convalescents, could be accommodated; so she asked General Fortescue (who else?) to look for such a place during his travels round the country. Very soon, on his return from Dubrovnik, the general reported that he had found an ideal place at Lapad, a suburb of Dubrovnik with a beautiful beach, where the nobles had their attractive summer palaces. There was there a villa, which had been requisitioned from its Austrian proprietor, where the military authorities had planned to open a rest home for convalescent officers, but it was still empty. Without losing a moment Katherine personally approached Vojvoda Živojin Mišić, who was then chief of the general staff of the Serbian Army, and whom Katherine had known from the time she spent at the Salonica front. When Katherine explained to him that the villa in Dubrovnik ought to be used as a place to treat convalescent children, he immediately gave orders that the villa should be handed over to the Anglo-Serbian Children's Hospital for further use. Isabel, who had then come to work full-time in Katherine's hospital, travelled to Dubrovnik to see the building and to try and find equipment for it. While she was staying in Dubrovnik Isabel heard of an abandoned Austrian hospital near Zelenika, a small place in Boka Kotorska (the gulf of Kotor) some 31 miles from Dubrovnik, and at once went there to investigate. To her surprise, she found the hospital abandoned, but complete with beds, bedding and other material, and a pleasant young Serbian officer who was looking after everything with his soldiers. This was Vasa Srdić [47] who was later to play an important part in Katherine's life. When he heard Isabel's story, Vasa Srdić told her to take whatever she needed, and in addition he at once organised the loading and transport of the equipment to Dubrovnik. Isabel selected 60 beds, with bedding and other equipment, and returned in triumph to Lapad. Since the building itself was in good condition, not much time was needed before the "Villa Bravačić", as it was called, was opened in February 1920. So the children from the Anglo-Serbian Hospital in Belgrade came to Dubrovnik, then those from the children's home run by Darinka Grujić, and those from the carpentry school of Annie Dickinson in Vlasenica.[46] For the period of the two years, during which this hospital functioned, every six weeks sick and malnourished children arrived in special carriages provided by the Red Cross in Belgrade, and returned home restored to health, strong, and suntanned. For children who still remembered the horrors of war, the "Villa Bravačić" must have seemed like paradise on earth. And in fact it looked so to many: "Anyone who has seen the Dalmatian coast of Yugoslavia knows it as one of the most beautiful in the world – the translucent blue-green Adriatic caresses a rock strewn shore garlanded with vine and olive, figs and cypress, aloes and oleander, and the air is as wide as heaven," reminisced Katherine later.

At this time one of Katherine's colleagues from Glasgow, Dr. Agnes Salmon (Fig. 50), who had worked for some time in the Belgrade hospital, visited the "Villa Bravačić" with her husband James, who was an architect. He was so delighted with the hospital that after he returned to Scotland he tried to secure funds for Katherine to buy the villa, which he described in the following words: "It lies half a mile from the nearest house (a vine tender's lodge), approached by an avenue of tall cypresses which leads to wrought iron gates set in an arch in the great 30ft wall surrounding the two acres of garden. This gate leads onto a broad terrace, above and below which are innumerable other terraces. Some are broad, forming cloistered courts, some long, narrow cypress lined alleys, some reached by long stairs through archways and past mysterious vaults and chambers used in the preparation of olive oil, or for the storage and treatment of fruit. In November, geraniums were flowering on the terrace, and cyclamen were blooming, while varied butterflies and, later in the day, great blue bodied moths fluttered around. Nothing but joy seemed to exist there. The little war orphans, feeble and ailing, played and laughed all day. The staff, British and Slav nurses, the Russian cook and the soldiers who carried water, chopped wood and played with the children, all were gay. Life here was like a dream, like a fairy tale, like a story from the *Thousand and One Nights*. Every day a sister led a little band of children out through a postern door, down cobbled paths and steps, among semi-tropical trees and flowers, to the little bay, and there they bathed and basked naked in the sun." Unfortunately James Salmon was unable to collect enough money for Katherine to buy the "Villa Bravačić"; and when the villa was finally returned to its owner it was sold for a large sum of money; and two years later the hospital had to be closed.

During the two years when it was used the "Villa Bravačić" was run by Sybil Kenzior, an Englishwoman and a friend of Katherine's from Belgrade, and then by a Scotswoman, Elsie Chalmers from Edinburgh, who became so fond of Dubrovnik that she stayed on after the hospital was closed and married a Russian émigré and widower, whose two children convalesced at the Villa. They lived in Dubrovnik until 1941, when her husband was called up and when she returned to Scotland taking the two children with her; and, as Katherine remarked later: "She made a very happy home for the children." Naturally, Katherine herself often visited the "Villa Bravačić", and her sisters Isabel and Annie, or Nan, spent a lot of time there helping with the work; Isabel had actually organised the whole institution from the beginning, together with Sybil Kenzior, and Nan arrived there in the summer of 1920 (Figs. 35, 36, 37 and 38) and stayed there till 1922 when it was closed.

At that time Belgrade, which had been very badly damaged during the war, began to be repaired and restored. Those inhabitants who had fled returned; damaged houses were repaired and restored to their former state; shops, hotels, cafés and restaurants were opened. The theatres began to work again, new cinemas and cabarets were opened; life gradually returned to normal. The Anglo-Serbian hospital, in addition to its basic medical function, became a kind of meeting place where many British people, Americans and Yugoslavs gathered together. It was the first place, after the British Legation, almost always visited regularly by all guests from Great Britain. The hospital also arranged fund-raising concerts, which were always well attended; and the first ball organised by the hospital raised 7,000 dinars, which was enough to purchase some new children's beds, which were brought by boat down the Danube from Vienna to Belgrade. In order to provide her colleagues with some opportunity for relaxation and entertainment after their difficult work, every other Saturday Katherine organised evening performances in the hospital with music and dancing; these were held in the reception centre for out-patients, which was emptied for this purpose. These performances soon became very popular, and many guests, native and foreign, gathered together there; the hospital benefited from them considerably both financially and socially. There was no other place in Belgrade, apart from the Diplomatic Club, which in any case was accessible only to diplomats and their guests, which offered similar opportunities for entertainment and getting to know people. Very near to the hospital there was an empty space where the British and Americans obtained permission to make a tennis court; this provided yet another opportunity for the hospital staff to meet a number of interesting people. Katherine herself was not interested in tennis, but from childhood she had loved riding, and on a suitable occasion she bought a horse, which was looked after and fed by a cavalry officer, Captain Tešić, who had the right to keep two horses. In return he used Katherine's horse when necessary. This officer often accompanied her on her rides; she also often had the company of Katherine Brown, who had worked as a cook in one of the SRF hospitals with which she had come to Belgrade, where she stayed on to work as a secretary in the British Legation, since she had a good knowledge of Serbian. She stayed there until 1941, when she returned to Great Britain with the rest of the embassy staff; there she continued her work as a secretary in the Foreign office.

The staff of the hospital, which became a very well-known and important institution in Belgrade, were often invited to various celebrations and receptions. Hence they were all invited to the reception in honour of the birthday of the Prince Regent Alexander, which was held in the Officers' Club. There the prince talked at some length, and very cordially, to Katherine, although she was not a diplomat; he then explained to Lady Young, the wife of the British ambassador Sir Alban Young, who was standing beside him, that they were old friends from the Salonica Front. Katherine was also regularly invited to receptions at court, and they were all on a number of occasions invited to the British Embassy, where they were always welcome guests.

Katherine often visited nearby villages, where she would go and see children who had previously been treated in her hospital, and where she came into contact with local residents. Sometimes these visits were rather unusual; one day, as Katherine evoked later, she was driving round some of the villages near Belgrade and then she sighted a gaily-coloured blanket apparently lying out to dry on the veranda of a dilapidated house. As she was always on the look out for peasant embroideries, which could be sent home to Scotland and sold to raise funds, she stopped the car and went to investigate. There she found three boys crawling out. The smallest, who must have been about two years old, had swollen glands in his neck and the distended stomach of the half starved. Katherine asked for their mother, and the eldest murmured something about prison, but he was not very coherent, and Katherine looked up the nearest neighbour. He told her that the mother had been sent to prison for stealing the food to give to her children – the father had been killed in the war and the mother could not work to get money to feed them, and meanwhile the neighbours were doing their best to keep the children alive. Katherine immediately told him to bring the children next day to her hospital, and he seemed rather relieved at the prospect. Anyway he turned up with the children next morning, and the two elder children were placed in a SRF orphanage, while the youngest, Ljubo, was admitted to the hospital, where he stayed for many months, and became a great favourite. Their mother later claimed him and his brothers when she was released from prison.

Katherine and Isabel had a pleasant opportunity to become familiar with the hospitality and some of the local customs of the people of this area. About this Katherine wrote: "By degrees we got to know Serbian families and were welcomed into their homes. But we had our first experience of lavish Slav hospitality when we were asked by Darinka Grujić to celebrate her brother's engagement, a ceremony which was of considerable importance to the Serbs. By then she had been transferred for some months from the barracks in Belgrade to a lovely country house on the banks of the Danube north of Belgrade at Kamenica, which before the war had belonged to a Hungarian Count. It had beautiful large spacious rooms with a pillared terrace running the whole length of the front, and it stood in lovely grounds. Count Karacsonyi, the owner, had had an extensive vineyard and orchards, and had used prisoners from the large prison nearby at Petrovaradin to work in them. When some of these prisoners were set free, if they had been good workers he took them to work on his property. Many of them settled for life in Kamenica and brought up large families. Darinka Grujić was given this beautiful place for her 200 orphans, and settled down to many years of happiness for herself and the children. There was no orphanage atmosphere. It was a real home for the children and their elders. It became a favourite place for a day-off expedition for many of the foreigners working in Belgrade."

The "wonderful house on the banks of Danube", as Katherine described it, known as the "castle" in Sremska Kamenica, built in 1840, surrounded by a beautiful, large park, was a summer house of Count Eugen Karacsonyi from Budapest till the First World War. After the war it was confiscated and an orphanage was located there from 1919 till 1933. It was supported financially by Major John Frothingam, [45] and was known as the "Serbian-American Home". This home was headed through all that time by Darinka Grujić or "Mummy Grujić" as the children used to call her.

Isabel, writing of the same event, said: "It was to this beautiful place that Darinka Grujić asked about 70 of us to celebrate with her on the occasion of her brother's betrothal – and what a celebration! We travelled from Belgrade by car or by boat, and about 9 o'clock in the evening, sat down to a great spread, the long tables being beautifully decorated with rose leaves by the children. Wonderful Serbian dishes were served in abundance, and wine from the vineyards – a feast which lasted well into the night. There was a gypsy orchestra, which played all night, and singing and dancing, especially the *kolo*, the Serbian national dance, round a huge log fire outside, in which everyone joined. This was kept up all night. Some of the guests rested on the terrace in wraps till dawn came. Somehow there was accommodation, somewhere for the tired guests to snatch a few hours' sleep, to waken up to find a large breakfast going. After breakfast, a walk round the lovely park, more gypsy music, more *kolo* dancing till lunch, and then we set off home. Never had we had such a house party."

These were pleasant days, when many new friendships were made, and also real romantic attachments. On one occasion Katherine wrote as follows: "We inevitably made attachments, and, inevitably, detachments. Lots of good friendships were cut short, as people were on the move the whole time, especially in the early days after the war. So we took our happy times when we could, and they remain as memories, sometimes happy, sometimes sad." Katherine herself was too wrapped up in the hospital work to make any lasting attachments; indeed so much so that anybody who became attached to her inevitably had to become attached to her hospital, which was part of herself. This had become her life. What had begun as an adventure had long since become a mission.

In the summer of 1920 Katherine and Isabel had, for them, a rare and exceptionally happy visit. In August their parents and their elder sister Annie came to visit them from Scotland. Dr. Donald MacPhail managed to find a colleague who would take over his practice for three months, so he was able to take some leave and set out on a long journey, which he and his wife had prepared to take some time ago. They travelled by train to Venice, and then by boat to Dubrovnik where they stayed for some time. They stayed in a hotel in Lapad, from which it was not far to visit the "Villa Bravačić" and enjoy the beauties of the Dubrovnik coast. Katherine's father, who liked to paint water-colours, had brought his painting kit with him to Dubrovnik, and filled a whole sketch-book with drawings in bright Mediterranean colours, which are still preserved in the family archives (Fig. 38). As her parents wished to see the children's hospital in Belgrade too, Katherine took them from Dubrovnik by train; and for this purpose she managed to secure a special carriage, in which they travelled to Belgrade in reasonable comfort, for those days. In Belgrade they were given a warm welcome by Katherine's friends and the staff of the hospital; and after going round the hospital they were very impressed indeed, and proud of all that Katherine had accomplished. When the time came for them to return to Scotland, Isabel also decided to return home with them, as she had decided to begin there her career as a secretary. This was the end of Isabel's "Balkan interlude," as she herself called it; after this her life took quite a different course, and her secretarial work took her to quite different parts of the world (see Appendix 5).

However, Katherine did not remain alone, her elder sister Annie (Nan) MacPhail, stayed in Dubrovnik to help her with the children. She had learnt Serbian, and as she was a trained teacher she began to teach the older children, especially the boys who had come from a home and carpentry school in

Vlasenica, a small town in Bosnia, run by Annie Dickinson. Nan liked this work with boys, and later in 1922, when "Villa Bravačić" had been closed, she moved to this school to work as a teacher until she returned home to Scotland in 1923 (see Appendix 4).

One of the greatest difficulties in the work of the Anglo-Serbian Children's Hospital at that time, and also in that of other hospitals, was the lack of trained Serbian nurses. Instead of them work was done by untrained women or men who had worked as orderlies during the war; so Katherine had to rely mainly on British nurses, of whom there were fewer and fewer. Because of this she began to think about opening a training school for nurses, since at that time there was no such school in Serbia. When a mission from the American Methodist Church came to Belgrade during 1920, Katherine got in touch with them, and put before them her plan to open such a training school in Knez Miloš Street, where her hospital was situated. They agreed with this and promised full financial support, but on condition that her hospital should move to another site. Katherine then sent Sister Rose Stone, who was still one of the hospital's nurses, to Britain for the necessary training in sister tutoring, while she herself began to search for a suitable, reasonably large building to accommodate the staff of her hospital, which had already become a problem in Belgrade. Then she heard of a building that had been damaged during the war, and was at that very time being repaired and renovated; it was situated in Višegradska Street, in a very convenient location, very near the State Hospital. When she made enquiries about this hospital Katherine learnt that the owner was Kosta Jovanović, then mayor of Belgrade; so she at once went to see him to ask if it would be possible to rent part of the building for her hospital. However, to her great surprise, he offered her the opportunity to buy the whole building for the sum of 100,000 dinars, or £ 5,000 sterling, instead of renting it. She liked the building very much, both because of its size and its location, and found this offer very tempting indeed. She wanted this building, but she did not have such a large sum of money, nor any idea how she could obtain it. Fortunately, at that time Elsie Cameron Corbett, one of the Katherine's friends from the Transport Unit at Jelak, [37] who had always been very favourably disposed towards Katherine and had valued her work, left her the sum of £ 1,000 (about 20,000 dinars) for her hospital as a parting gift; so Katherine offered this sum to Kosta Jovanović immediately, and promised to pay the remaining 80,000 dinars in the course of six months; he agreed, and the contract was settled. "It was an act of faith", said Katherine later, "for I had no idea where the rest of the money was coming from." Anyway, the Anglo-Serbian Children's Hospital soon moved into its new permanent house in No 20 Višegradska Street, where it was officially opened in February 1921. The outstanding sum of money to pay for the new building was, fortunately, collected in time. The Child Welfare Committee, which distributed money from various foreign services sent to Serbia for child welfare, contributed

40,000 dinars. Of this money a large amount came from the Save the Children Fund from London, although Katherine did not come into direct contact with this humanitarian organisation till later. Then, Marjorie Pope Ellis, one of Katherine's friends from the Transport Unit of one of the Scottish Women's Hospitals (Fig. 27), who had returned home to South Africa, collected £ 1,000 (about 20,000 dinars) there; the remainder was collected from various fund-raising performances in Belgrade, and from other donors; a Serbian officer called with 1,500 dinars collected from a group of officers of the Serbian Army, and a lawyer from Sarajevo brought 650 dinars collected in one of the hotels there; the J.P. Coates Trust, Paisley, Scotland, gave £ 1,000. In that way Kosta Jovanović was paid at the end of the agreed six months, and Dr. Katherine MacPhail could continue her work in peace in the new hospital building.

At the same time, during the year 1921, the Training School for Serbian Nurses began its work in the old building in the Knez Miloš Street. There is information about this in the first report of the Anglo-Serbian Children's Hospital for 1921: "This training school is supported financially by the Board of Foreign Missions of the Methodist Episcopal Church. The school is the first of its kind in Serbia. It is regrettable but true that at present the nursing profession, in other countries one of the proudest assets of womanhood, occupies in Serbia a very inferior position. The training school is doing a lot to alter this state of things and its establishment in connection with the Children's Hospital is further evidence of the value of the work of the Hospital not only in its more obvious aspects but as a factor contributing to progress and enlightenment in the medical work of the country." [44] At the beginning ten young Serbian girls were admitted to this school; they also lived there, so that it was a kind of boarding school. Sister Rose Stone gave theoretical lectures through an interpreter, and the practical work was done in the wards of the new permanent children's hospital. This small school worked in this way until 1923, when a state school for training medical sisters was established. Katherine herself was a member of a state committee, which was formed to create that first State Nurses Training School. But even then the Children's Hospital remained the base for practical training, where future sisters spent six months learning to care for sick children (Fig.39). During the time the hospital was in Belgrade, some two hundred probationers passed through the hospital.

The Anglo-Serbian Children's Hospital in its new quarters in Višegradska Street (Figs. 40, 41 and 42) had 70 beds, which were divided between a surgical ward, a medical ward, and one for newborn infants (Figs. 43 - 46). In addition the hospital had an operating theatre with modern equipment provided by contributions from Scotland, and it was therefore called the *West of Scotland Operating Theatre*. These contributions were actually the money which James Salmon, the husband of Dr. Agnes Salmon, had raised to purchase the "Villa Bravačić", and as that money was not enough for the purchase of the "Villa Bravačić" it was decided that it should be used to equip the operating theatre in the Children's Hospital in Belgrade (Fig. 47). In addition the hospital had a spacious out patients' department, and a dispensary. The new building was clean and spacious, and all its rooms were large and light. The walls of the children's rooms were decorated by a Russian artist, a friend of Katherine's, with pictures from Russian fairy tales (Fig. 43). New proper metal beds, specially made for children, were imported from Vienna and brought into the hospital instead of the old wooden ones that had been found to harbour bugs. The other equipment was also renovated, so that, for those days, the hospital was exceptionally well equipped and run. During 1929 Dr. Leonard Findlay, at that time Professor of Pediatrics in Glasgow University, visited the hospital, and after the visit he described his impressions vividly: "So far as medicine in Serbia is concerned, the one desideratum is efficient nursing. The medical men are just as well educated and efficient as in any other country. Their work, however, in the care of the sick and in the study of diseases is handicapped through the want of efficient nursing such as obtains in this country. Many of those I spoke with admitted that this was so. Now the Anglo-Serbian Hospital just supplies the necessary stimulus in this direction. It stands in marked contrast to all the other hospitals in Belgrade. In it there is ample evidence of the hand of the professional nurse, and the various Serbian medical men who work in it cannot speak too highly of the facilities for work granted and of the efficiency of the care of the patients. Dr. MacPhail co-ordinates all the various activities, and one cannot visit the hospital without being impressed by the great amount of first-class work which is being done. It is the development of the modern nurse and the organisation of the modern hospital which I consider are the greatest benefits which will accrue from the example of the Anglo-Serbian Children's Hospital."[48]

At that time Katherine had to rely on four British sisters: Sister C. King, who worked as head sister (Figs. 43, 45 and 46), Sister G. Matthews (Fig. 48), who came from the King's College Hospital in London as a theatre sister and was in charge of instruments and of the operating theatre, where there was always a lot of work. Then there was Sister C. O'Rorke (Fig. 49), who was the head sister in the out patients' department; she later contracted tuberculosis and died in 1931, after a long period of illness in Switzerland. Betty Jealous (Fig. 48) was there for four years and then went home and married a naval officer who had once served with the Danube Flotilla in Belgrade. Nurse Katie Heilbut, who had just finished a course in infant nursing in Geneva, was there for four years. When Sister King left the hospital, Katherine appointed as matron Katherine Ogilvy, who had worked in Serbia during the war. In addition to them there were others who worked in the hospital at different times: Sisters R.A. Stone, H. Willis, B. Friend, B. Dickson, M. West, M. Jackson, Buckland and Miller, then the VAD nursing auxiliaries: Miss M. Baker, Miss. J. Martin, Miss Force, Miss Craigie, Miss Dickson, Miss Risely and Miss Collinson. In addition to these trained foreign sisters and nursing auxiliaries some Serbian partly trained girls also worked in the hospital; and in later years there were Yugoslav sisters who had been trained in the newly opened training school, and who gradually replaced the foreign nursing staff (Fig. 48). However the head sister or matron was always an experienced British sister. [48]

During the first years of the hospital work Katherine was helped for short periods by four of her colleagues from Scotland, who usually came for six months; the most faithful of these, it would seem, was Dr. Agnes Salmon (Fig. 50), who made several visits to Belgrade, and whose husband collected money in Scotland towards equipment for the operating theatre. As well as her, there was also Dr. Mary Ferguson, Dr. Margaret Leitch and Dr. Vida Perry (Fig. 48). Later, when the scope of the work in the hospital increased considerably, the Ministry of Health appointed some permanent Yugoslav doctors; many others worked there temporarily, mainly young doctors who gained practical experience there.

Among the physicians who worked permanently in the hospital for longer periods, or even stayed there until it closed, there were some very well-known Belgrade doctors. First of all, Dr. Dimitrije Jovčić, a well-known child surgeon, later a professor in the Faculty of Medicine in Belgrade, carried out pediatric surgery in this hospital for many years. In fact Dr. Dimitrije Jovčić, trained in France, was the founder of the Surgical Section in the Children's Department of the State General Hospital in Belgrade in 1921. In 1923 the Children's Surgical Section, the first of that kind in Serbia, became part of the Anglo-Serbian Children's Hospital, where it had much better accommodation facilities and superior working conditions; and it stayed there until its removal into a new building that was completed in 1931; in later years it developed into the Children's Surgical Clinic under the guidance of Prof. Dimitrije Jovčić. A little later, during 1929, Dr. Svetislav Stojanović was appointed to the staff of this hospital; he was then a young surgeon who had recently been studying in France; later he became a well-known orthopaedic surgeon, head of the Clinic for Orthopaedic Surgery and Traumatology in Belgrade and a professor of the Belgrade Faculty of Medicine; he continued to be Katherine's associate and devoted friend throughout the time she lived in Yugoslavia. The hospital owes a great debt to him for the high standard of its orthopaedic work. Dr. Miloje Vasić also worked with them as a surgeon in the hospital. Another colleague over many years was Dr. Vladimir Bogdanović, an internist (Fig. 49), and Dr. Uroš Ružičić, then a young pediatric specialist, who later became head of the Pediatric Clinic in Belgrade and professor of pediatrics in the Faculty of Medicine in Belgrade. When Dr. Ružičić, on the recommendation of Dr. Katherine MacPhail, spent six months of specialist study in the Glasgow Sick Children's Hospital, working with Professor Leonard Findlay, Dr. Milan Sokolović replaced him in the hospital. During the First World War, after the retreat through Albania, Milan Sokolović was evacuated to Scotland, where he completed his medical studies in Edinburgh. He worked in the hospital for two and a half years and there he fell in love with Katherine Ogilvy, the head sister, and soon married her. After their marriage he and his wife moved to Nish where he became a well-known pediatric specialist. Unfortunately he tragically lost his life during the Second World War when he was killed in an air raid. Other doctors who worked in the hospital for different periods of time were Dr. Desanka Prekajski, Dr. Jelica Petrović, Dr. Desanka Kutlić, Dr. Marija Roknić, Dr. Milorad Jovanović and Dr. Siniša Radojević, later professor of anatomy in the Belgrade Faculty of Medicine. With Katherine's help two Serbian doctors went to Scotland to work and specialise for some time in the Glasgow Sick Children's Hospital under professor Leonard Findlay, and when he subsequently visited Belgrade, he wrote: "With consummate wisdom, Dr. MacPhail has chosen for the completion of the staff of the hospital, Serbian doctors and nurses, so that side by side, British and Serbian men and women work in perfect harmony. To me there is nothing more certain than that a better understanding and a greater appreciation of these two nations by one another, will arise from this co-operation in such a work of humanity." [48]

When Katherine Ogilvy left the hospital to get married, Katherine appointed Agnes Hardie as matron; she came from the Shadwell Children's Hospital in London unlike most of the British nurses in Belgrade, who had worked in Serbia during the war. "Miss Hardie", as everyone called her, was a very gifted and popular sister, who succeeded in maintaining a very high level of service, and stayed with Katherine until the outbreak of war in Yugoslavia in 1941. Another long-standing and popular hospital figure was Miss Alice Murphy, who was the secretary and the housekeeper of the hospital (Fig. 50). "Murphy", as everyone called her, was born in Saint Petersburg, of a Russian mother and an Irish father; after the Russian revolution she fled to London, where she found work by selling handwork and embroidery in a shop belonging to one of Katherine's acquaintances; this was where Katherine got to know her during one of her visits to Great Britain. When Alice Murphy heard about the hospital in Belgrade, she immediately asked Katherine to take her there and employ her. As Katherine could not promise her a large salary, they agreed that "Murphy" should compensate for this by giving English lessons to Serbs and Russian refugees in Belgrade. Katherine never regretted that she had accepted Alice Murphy, who proved to be an exceptionally competent and irreplaceable secretary, as well as a good friend, who stayed with Katherine till the end. Although quite different in character, "Miss Hardie" and "Murphy" got on very well together, and complemented each other, and, to the satisfaction of everybody, managed the work of the hospital together over many years, first in Belgrade and later in Sremska Kamenica.

Dr. Katherine MacPhail, as the superintendent of the hospital, was always extremely busy with administrative and organisational tasks, but she did not neglect her medical work, especially in the out patients clinic, to which about 100 patients came every day. Katherine's friend and comrade Miss Flora Sandes, who happened to be present on one occasion, wrote: "It is early yet, only 8 a.m., but already work is in full swing in the Out-Patients' Department. The big waiting room is crowded to overflowing, but still every minute brings some new arrival. Many have travelled all night by train from some distant part of the country; more have been, since dawn, jolting over the rough roads in a bullock wagon; more still have come on foot from some outlying villages; but, one and all, they await their turn, unhurried and uncomplaining, with that patience characteristic of the Serbs. Their faith in the British is touching; their babies' lives are at stake, and they will go through much for the privilege of having them doctored here – the only hospital in the whole of Serbia exclusively devoted to children. Wherein, one wonders, lies the magic of the name, *Anglo*-Serbian Hospital?" This wonder was also explained by Flora Sandes: "You can hardly find a cottage in Serbia where some member of the family will not anxiously enquire if you can tell him the whereabouts of some British sister – name unknown, but whose appearance he describes minutely – who nursed him during the War. 'She was like a mother to me. If I had been a general she could not have given me more care,' he says admiringly. More has been done by these unofficial ambassadors of Britain to cement friendship in the hearts of another people, than by all the diplomats that have ever been born. The tradition is being nobly carried on by the Anglo-Serbian Children's Hospital." [49] The hospital was certainly very popular and well-known, and always very full; all the beds were occupied, so that large numbers of children could not be accepted in the hospital but were treated as outpatients. As can be seen from one of the first statistical reports of the hospital from the year 1921, in the course of one year 386 children were treated in the hospital, and 4,742 as out-patients.

At the end of 1921 a detailed report of the work of the hospital from 1918 to 1921 was published in English, which described both the history of the hospital and its various activities. [44] This report included a large number of letters that the hospital had received from prominent people in the country and abroad, on the occasion of its move into a new building, and its very successful work up to that time. The most important sign of recognition was a letter from Nikola Pašić, then head of the government; it goes: "I would like to express a sincere appreciation for the work which has been done for this country by the Anglo-Serbian Children's Hospital through the efforts of Dr. K.S. MacPhail. The work of Child Welfare is one of the most urgent and pressing needs of our country. This institution is one of the examples of what can be done in a practical reconstructive manner and one which is worthy of not only the thanks of our people but of all possible aid and support", (signed by Nik. P. Pashitch). The letters appreciating the work of the hospital from Dr. Ivan Ribar, Speaker of the Parliament, the Ministers of Public Health, Social Politics and Public Instruction, as well as the letter from the Mayor of Belgrade showed clearly the sympathy of representative public opinion. By this time the hospital had become a show place in Belgrade and had many foreign visitors who also highly appreciated its work like the Bishop of Gibraltar, Harold Buxton, who, after his visit to Belgrade, wrote in the *Gibraltar Diocesan Gazzette*: "The ten days at Belgrade which followed were very full of interest and opportunity. I found a full and excellent programme arranged for me. I could not possibly mention all of these, but almost the very first was a visit to Dr. MacPhail's Hospital for Children, a romance in real life of what the courage, devotion and skill of a solitary woman in a strange land can achieve. Beginning after the war, when her war service in a Scottish nursing unit in Serbia was done, Dr. MacPhail started by looking after a few derelict suffering children, with no idea that she was beginning a great and splendid work. But the knowledge that there was one whose love and skill were ready to care for sick children brought more and more to her. Soon she had more than she could do unaided, and sought for help, getting at first, food and garments, and a shed, then skilled helpers and money, and proper premises. It was a heroic effort, and is even now a hand-to-mouth enterprise, needing and deserving continual support. But a solidly built, well-equipped hospital, on high ground, and in a quiet spot now exists. Forty thousand little patients have been through her hands, and day by day they come in from every part of Serbia, north, south, east and west, brought by travel-weary anxious mothers who leave their little ones in Dr. MacPhail's keeping, with hope and confidence. What a debt of gratitude Serbia owes to women from Scotland; quiet, practical, highly trained, unemotional women, whose power of love is as tenacious and wise and clear-eyed as it is silent and deep and tender."

Meanwhile, from the financial point of view the hospital was passing through great difficulties. During 1920 and 1921 all the foreign missions left Serbia, so there was no further help from that source, as it was generally considered that this country had obtained the immediate post war help it needed. However Katherine knew that large sums of money had been collected in Britain and in many other countries, and felt that at least some of that money could be used for rehabilitation in a country as devastated as Serbia. In letters to the "Scotsman" and the "Glasgow Herald", she wrote: "It is quite erroneous to say that there is no further field open for medical and nursing work in this country. Indeed the need is just as great, and almost greater, than it was during the war, as the Serbians have been left with a heritage of children, youths and old people still suffering from disease, which is the direct outcome of all those years of privation and war, and who have seen health and hope offered to them by the many missions and hospitals which are now being withdrawn rapidly on all sides. The closing of these missions leaves them poorer than before, as they now know what was brought within their reach in the form of good nursing, and clean and bright hospitals and medical attention." The country was really impoverished, with soaring inflation and the government did not have enough money to finance the continually increasing needs in various aspects of life. Although the Anglo-Serbian Children's Hospital did receive some assistance, Katherine could not count on maintaining the hospital from this source. "I know with what difficulty they distribute fairly the little money they have at their disposal," wrote Katherine. "I know that they are having to close down sanatoria, which are the most urgent need, solely on account of lack of means. They have made considerable strides in these questions since the war, and have as high aims in children's work and public health generally as any other country, but they lack the means with which to carry them through." In order to secure the regular functioning of her hospital, Katherine had to make continual efforts to raise money, in the country, and to an increasing extent abroad, and especially in Great Britain. Fortunately, there were always donors whose contributions enabled the hospital to continue its work without interruption. One such benefactor was an American, Mr. Leo Casper, who was a representative of the Carnegie Trust, and came to Serbia to make arrangements for the building of a Carnegie Library in Belgrade University. He became very interested in Katherine's work, and on his return to America he collected many thousands of dollars for the hospital, and contributed to its improvements. After a visit to Glasgow, when Katherine gave a lecture in Queen Margaret College, some friends in Glasgow formed a committee to organise help for the hospital. The chairman of this committee was Dr. A. K. Chalmers, head of the Glasgow Public Health Department, with whom Katherine had worked for a time in 1914, before her departure to Serbia. Another colleague with whom Katherine had worked in Glasgow before her departure was Professor Teacher, professor of pathology in Glasgow Royal Infirmary, who had just at this time sold his yacht, and at once gave half of this money to the hospital fund. However, as Katherine herself was wont to say, her most important "committee" in Scotland was her family, who all, over many years, worked with enthusiasm to collect funds for her and her hospital.

At the beginning of the twenties Katherine's father, Dr. Donald MacPhail, retired, and the family moved from Coatbridge to Hamilton, where they found a new house, Cadzow Lodge, which was now home to the three unmarried daughters – Annie, Katherine and Isabel. Katherine's older sister Janet, who had married Dr. James McFarlane in 1913, also lived there with her three daughters, but a little later, they moved to the village of Chapelhall, some 3 miles east of Coatbridge, where they had a house outside the village with a huge garden. One of their daughters, Mrs. Elspeth Biggs, remembering that period, wrote later: "We had to walk a mile to catch a bus to Hamilton Academy, in all weathers, but we didn't mind that, and sometimes finished our homework in the bus! For the first year that we were in Chapelhall, we had to stay at Cadzow Lodge during the week, and only go home at weekends – this was because my younger sister, Ann, was too small to reach the step of the bus." Isabel then looked after her parents until 1923, when she went to work in China. That same year Annie returned home from Yugoslavia, and from then on she stayed with her parents, whom she looked after until they died. Jessie, her mother died in Hamilton in 1925. Her father Donald then went to live with his eldest daughter Janet in Chapelhall, where he died in August 1931. Jessie and Donald, the mother and father, were buried beside each other in the churchyard of Old Monklands Church in Coatbridge where they had spent most of their lives, and where their four daughters had been born.

Annie at that time was actively engaged in various local organisations, but most of all in organising help for Katherine, so she was the most active member of Katherine's "domestic committee". Of course during these years Katherine came home from time to time; her niece, Elspeth Biggs, then a little girl, living with her two sisters first in Hamilton, then in Chapelhall (Fig. 51) says: "Katherine's work continued to thrive, but she had to keep up her search for financial support, and came home to London now and then, to consult with the *Save the Children Fund* (SCF) and give lectures, as well as going to her home to see her family. She kept us three nieces supplied with lovely cosy Serbian slippers, and when we grew out of them, there were bigger ones sent. I don't know much of this period, in the middle twenties, except for the fun of her visits, and the pride of the whole family in her work."

In Belgrade also a hospital committee was formed which took care of the business aspects of the hospital, offered some sort of protection and exercised an advisory role. This committee included Major J. Hanau, who had previously been an assistant to General Fortescue on the Joint Supply Commission, and had stayed to work in Belgrade after that mission was completed; K.S. Patten, the American Consul, and James B. Clark, director of the British Trade Corporation in Belgrade, who was the honorary treasurer of the hospital. "They do not want to interfere in the running of the hospital at all, and are willing simply to back me up officially," was how Katherine explained their role. "They have proposed that the house and land should be registered as my personal property, lent by me for the purposes of the hospital, so that it can never be taken out of my hands, until I want to give it up. All sorts of things like that, they will decide, which will make it easier for me, and not too much personal responsibility."

During 1922 Dr. Katherine MacPhail came into personal contact with a large new charitable organisation, which was later to play a significant part in her life and work. This was the *Save the Children Fund* (SCF), a British organisation with its headquarters in London.[50] In August 1922 Katherine attended an international conference on the protection of children in Geneva, where, as always, she tried to get help for her hospital; and with this object in view she approached the *Union Internationale de Secours aux Enfants,* which directed her to the *Save the Children Fund* in London, or rather to Mr. L.B. Golden who at that time was its General Secretary. He was immediately interested in the work of her hospital. This Fund had already given some help to her hospital through a common programme acting with other organisations; however, from then on the Fund began to offer the hospital directly much more significant assistance, without which the hospital would surely have been closed in the difficult years which followed. In this way, thanks to help from the SCF, in 1925 the hospital acquired X-ray equipment and equipped modern premises for sterilising instruments for operations. During 1926, Miss Eglantyne Jebb, the founder and honorary secretary of the *Save the Children Fund*, visited the Anglo-Serbian Children's Hospital during a tour of the Balkans, and was full admiration for its work. "What impressed Eglantyne at the hospital was Dr. MacPhail's complete authority," her biographer Francesca Wilson wrote later. "Things seemed to be running with extraordinary efficiency and yet with a kind of miraculous ease. Everyone obeyed Dr. MacPhail, but she was always quiet and relaxed, and seemed to make no effort. It was natural that the nurses and the children and the anxious peasants who brought them should obey her, but what was strange was that the Serb doctors and officials obeyed her too, they who had never before taken orders from a woman." However, it never seemed that Katherine was giving orders to anyone, "she simply discussed the matter in hand, and caused everyone to agree with her." At that time Eglantyne Jebb was received by Queen Maria, who was very interested in work with children, which she explained in the words: "I am deeply in sympathy with all kinds of work for children. I am a mother myself." On this occasion, through Eglantyne Jebb, Queen Maria thanked all the members of this charitable organisation for their constant and unselfish help to the Anglo-Serbian Children's Hospital.[51]

At the beginning of twenties, by which time there was a Faculty of Medicine in Belgrade, [52] the university authorities considered the possibility of extending the Anglo-Serbian Children's Hospital and turning it into a university clinic, which was badly needed, both because of the increasing demand for the contemporary methods of treating sick children, and also for training students in the newly established medical faculty. The committee of the SWH in Edinburgh had at that time sent two delegates to Belgrade to discuss plans for building a memorial hospital in honour of Elsie Inglis; so the university authorities wished to suggest to this delegation that the relevant funds should be invested in extending the existing Anglo-Serbian Children's Hospital; Dr. Katherine MacPhail agreed with this, since she considered it necessary to accept any suggestion that would contribute to the welfare of children. After all, she had nothing against the SWH, and she had actually a high opinion of their work as could be seen from her own words: "No organisation among the many which came to Serbia made such an impression on the Serbs as did the Scottish Women's units. Throughout the length and breadth of the land, the British women are remembered in the peasant homes and talked about by the old soldiers. And its individual members, wherever they were, and whatever work they were doing, made a lasting impression on the Serbs of what women can do and be. I knew Dr. Elsie Inglis in 1915 in Serbia and I remember how enthusiastic she was about helping these people, and she was full of all sorts of schemes for increasing and extending the work. The Serbs were our staunch allies during the war and looked to Britain as the great power to help them when they were losing all they had. Those of us who have gone through the war with them can never forget this. And today it is still true if we put aside political differences and international unrest. Most of the missions have had to leave Serbia from lack of funds, but they leave behind them an open field of work almost untouched. The few remaining institutions supply a real need and are encouraged by the Serbs themselves to continue the work."

When the delegation of the Scottish Women's Hospitals arrived in Belgrade, the suggestion of the university authorities was put to them and the delegates went round the Anglo-Serbian Children's Hospital; however they were dissatisfied because there were male doctors working in the hospital. When they raised this question Katherine replied that they employed both men and women in the hospital, and British and Serbs and other nationalities, but that they always made every effort to choose the best qualified individuals, with the most experience; and that from this point of view feminist principles did not come into consideration. Naturally, this answer did not satisfy the delegation from the committee of the SWH, who on principle accepted only women into their ranks, so the proposed plan to extend the Anglo-Serbian Children's Hospital was rejected. The funds raised were later used to build the *Dr. Elsie Inglis Memorial Hospital for Children and Mothers* in Belgrade, which, unfortunately, soon ceased work because of financial difficulties. This hospital was then bought by the State Railways and turned into the so-called *Railway Hospital* that still exists; and there is preserved there a commemorative plaque in memory of Dr. Elsie Inglis in Latin: *In memoriam Elsie Inglis amicae Serborum certissime.*[53] The delegation from the Scottish Women's Hospitals then donated a considerable sum of money to build a laboratory in the Institute of Physiology of the newly-established Faculty of Medicine, which institute was situated immediately behind the Anglo-Serbian Children's Hospital. So the idea of extending this hospital fell through, and Katherine had to continue on her own and to seek other sources of financial support.

One of the most important events of the summer of 1922, which, as became obvious later, had considerable influence on the work of the Anglo-Serbian Children's Hospital, was the wedding of Princess Maria of Rumania and the young King Alexander on June 8th, 1922. There were great preparations for that day in Belgrade, in which the hospital took part too, and about which Katherine wrote as follows: "I have never seen things in such an upturn as they were in Belgrade. People were working day and night by the hundreds in the streets to get them paved before the day, and I think they took up every street in Belgrade. We did the same in hospital, had it all enclosed with proper palings, all the broken stonework repaired, and painted everything up so that we look better than we have ever done." On this occasion Belgrade had its first visit from a British prince, the young Duke of York, later King George VI, who was best man to the young bridal pair. Katherine hoped that the Duke of York would have time to visit her hospital while he was in Belgrade, which he did, to the general delight and excitement of all its members. The visit was very official, and the Duke of York came with a large suite, which included the King's cousin Prince Paul, and the British Ambassador Sir Alban Young. "They were all done up in full uniforms and looked overpowering," was how Katherine described this visit. "However, we struggled through, and I found that the Duke was shyer than I was. He was very nice and I introduced him to all the English and Serb staff. Prince Paul was particularly interested in the hospital, as he said he never knew that it existed. The Duke recognised Sister King, our head sister, whom he had seen in a nursing home in London a few years before, and had quite a friendly talk with her. That same afternoon all the British colony were asked to the Legation to a reception, so we were presented to him again."

Katherine was delighted with this visit, although it was "a terribly formal affair", since such connections and visits certainly provided a strong recommendation for her hospital and her work. On this occasion it was an exceptional recommendation for her to come into contact with the new queen, whom she wished to act as patron of the Anglo-Serbian Children's Hospital. In this respect Katherine counted on specific British connections, since Queen Maria was a great-granddaughter of Queen Victoria.[54]

In December 1922 Katherine wrote home: "I had an audience with the Queen and found her very nice and willing to be very interested in the hospital. She agreed to become Patron and to do anything she could to help me. The Queen of Rumania (Queen Maria's mother) was there too and she was just as interested as her daughter. They made me quite at ease at once, and we had a friendly talk. She seems a nice, simple girl, a bit burdened with her role as queen." So, to Katherine's great pleasure and relief, the Anglo-Serbian Children's Hospital gained a highly-placed patron and protector in the person of Queen Maria, who fulfilled this role over many years, first in Belgrade and then in Sremska Kamenica. This protection and help from such a highly placed person as Queen Maria proved to be exceptionally significant for the progress and subsequent activity and maintenance of the hospital.

In the summer of 1923 Katherine again met the Duke and Duchess of York. On her return from London where she had given some lectures at meetings arranged by the *Save the Children Fund*, and collected some financial help for her hospital, Katherine travelled on the Simplon Orient Express from Paris to Belgrade; and at breakfast on the first morning on the train she saw the Duke and Duchess of York, who were also having breakfast at the other end of the dining carriage. It later turned out that they were travelling to Belgrade for the wedding of Princess Olga and Prince Paul. After breakfast, when Katherine had returned to her own compartment, the conductor came up to her and said that a gentleman on the train was asking for her name. Katherine was taken by surprise and at first she hesitated, but when the conductor insisted she gave him a visiting card with her name and the name of the hospital. A little later a colonel came to her compartment and introduced himself as the Duke of York's equerry, and told her that the Duke had recognised her in the restaurant car and wanted to know her name. He also conveyed an invitation from the Duke that they should meet during the half-hour pause at Milan, when Katherine was introduced to the Duchess of York. [55] During a pleasant conversation the Duchess expressed a wish to visit the hospital, which she had heard was one of the most interesting places in Belgrade.

Although she only stayed in Belgrade for two days, the Duchess of York kept her word and came to visit the hospital, where she charmed everybody. "Everybody fell in love with her," wrote Katherine later. "She spoke so naturally and was so delighted with the children. She specially liked the little ones and, of course, was high in praise of the hospital altogether. One of the children presented her with a bouquet as she left, and said in his best English: 'A present from the children', which he had been repeating to himself all afternoon so as not to forget. It was all so unceremonious and natural that it was a great pleasure to show her round." The Duchess kept up her interest in the hospital and if any of the nurses were in England at International Nurses' Conferences at which she presided, she always asked for news of the hospital and its work.

Because of constant financial difficulties Katherine approached many people for help, and in May 1923 an appeal for help was printed in English, since most of the donors were from abroad, and most of all from Great Britain. The appeal contained the following words: "Of the children treated in the Hospital on an average one third are orphans. Many of the former soldiers bring their children to hospital from quite distant parts of the country, because they themselves were nursed in British Hospitals on the Salonica front, and now wish their children to have the care of a British Sister and the comfort of a British Hospital." As regards the expenses of the hospital, Katherine reported: "Three thousand pounds will keep the Hospital for one year, while £ 50 will keep a bed for the same period." In the same appeal Dr. Katherine MacPhail reported that 35-40 % of her patients were children with tuberculosis, most often tuberculosis of the bones and joints; this was a specific problem which she describes as follows: "Of these tubercular children, a large number had to remain in hospital *for months and in several cases for over a year*, as there was no means of having them cared for in their homes or in the institutions whence they came. They were mostly orthopaedic cases, having treatment in extension or in plaster. To attempt any cure at all in such cases necessitated a long period in hospital and in this way beds which might have been used for acute illnesses were taken up by these chronic cases and considerably lessened the turnover of patients. The question of these tubercular children is a very difficult one, for, if left at home, they are a source of infection to the whole family, and, on the other hand, there is no place where they can get proper treatment except in hospital." [56] That was in fact a major problem at that time, which would finally induce Katherine to plan and open a new hospital specially for such cases.

During the past years the hospital worked intensively without a break, with varying degrees of difficulties, and tens of thousands of sick children passed through it. At the same time it became a kind of special *memorial* of good will and mutual human understanding. At the end of 1925 Katherine described the situation as follows: "The Anglo-Serbian Children's Hospital in Belgrade grew out of nothing but a great necessity in a time of grave distress immediately following the Armistice. It stands as a living and sentient memorial to the good will of hundreds of friends in England and other lands for the people of Serbia, and for the comfort and health of over 40,000 children who have passed through our hands." [57]

The number of patients in the hospital grew from year to year, as can be seen from the official statistical information up to the end of July 1925. Until then 3,421 children had been treated as in-patients in the hospital, and 37,075 as out patients.[57]

Among the numerous small patients in the Anglo-Serbian Children's Hospital there were many children of Russian émigrés in Yugoslavia; on account of this in 1926 the Russian Red Cross awarded Dr. Katherine MacPhail a medal. The explanatory text accompanying this medal contained the following words: "During many years you have always met with constant care, kindness and sensitiveness the needs of sick Russian children, and the requirements of the Russian Red Cross. Owing to your knowledge and experience and kindhearted attitude many Russian children have recovered their health in the hospital under your direction."

The enormous services and efforts of Dr. Katherine MacPhail in Yugoslavia during the First World War and in the post-war period were not unnoticed in her own country, where in 1928 King George V awarded her one of the highest British orders bestowed on women, namely an O.B.E. However, as Katherine could not travel to London when the orders were awarded, it was formally presented to her in the British Embassy in Belgrade instead of in Buckingham Palace.

During these years, when the post-war crisis had passed and the situation in the new state had considerably improved, and the hospital was functioning smoothly according to a now well-established rhythm, Katherine had time for various other activities. She was a member of the Red Cross Committee and the Voluntary Women's Society for Child Welfare, and took an active interest in their work. Apart from that she took a very active part, first in the establishing, and then later in the work of the Anglo-Serbian Club in Belgrade, which later developed into the Anglo-American Yugoslav Club, the activities of which attracted considerable attention. In the premises of this club, as in those of the Belgrade Motor Club, of which Katherine was also a member, a variety of fund-raising performances took place over the years, and annual sales for the benefit of the children's hospital. In addition to intensive work and a lively social life, Katherine liked to travel and take photographs. She often travelled to Great Britain, mainly in order to collect funds for the hospital and to visit her family. In addition, wherever she could, she travelled in various parts of Yugoslavia (Figs. 52 and 53). On her travels she often took photographs, mostly of the countryside and towns in Macedonia, Montenegro and Bosnia, and also of national costume that obviously fascinated her, since her collections contain many such photographs. One of Katherine's favourite places, which she often visited, was Sremska Kamenica, where Darinka Grujić then lived, with whom she had maintained close friendly ties. In addition, Vasa Srdić with whom she also had a close friendship, lived in nearby Temerin. Since she liked Sremska Kamenica so much, at the end of 1925 Katherine bought a house there, and a quite a large plot of land with an orchard and a small vineyard. She paid for it with the money her late mother left her. The house, or "villa" as it was called, was quite big: it had four spacious rooms, a wide verandah, a garden, orchard and vineyard, with a hut; it had a lovely situation, on a hill on the outskirts of the village, with a marvellous view of the Danube, the endless plains of Bačka across the Danube, and spurs of the Fruška Gora hills. At first Katherine mainly used this house on her visits to Sremska Kamenica for restful week-ends, and often stayed there with her friends and guests. One of her dear and well-known guests was Flora Sandes. She was famous as the Englishwoman who had fought with Serbian Army during the war, and became a sergeant. She was extremely popular and there were many stories about her; Katherine recalled one in her memoirs. When Flora was demobilised, it happened that it was Christmas time and she was invited together with the other members of the British colony in Belgrade to the traditional British Minister's Christmas party. The problem just then was that she had only a few women's clothes, so Katherine and one of her nurses took great trouble to see that she was properly dressed. Or so they thought, for to their horror, as she stepped out of the car on their arrival at the Embassy, they saw that under her evening dress, she was still wearing army boots! But the British Minister, Sir Alban Young, who knew her very well and saw their confusion, just said calmly: "Come on in, Sandes, it really doesn't matter." Flora Sandes spent a whole year in Katherine's villa writing one of her books about her wartime experiences.[58]

The enormous number of children who passed through the hospital provided indisputable evidence of the popularity of this institution, and the confidence that the parents had in the work of the hospital, which, for them and their children, was a place of hope and comfort (Fig. 54). In addition to the most up to date treatment and irreproachable care, every effort was made to help these small patients in various other ways (Fig. 55), for which one of Dr. Katherine MacPhail's "stories from the classroom" provides evidence: "Little Alexander, a mite of three years, lay for months in the surgical ward with a painful tubercular knee which always gave him great pain when his dressing was done. Every day as I went into the ward I could see from his face, by the anxious look and tremor of his lips, whether his dressing was over for the day or not, and it became such an ordeal to him that he trembled all over when it came to his turn to go into the dressing room. To try to cheer him up I gave him a little mechanical hopping robin, which was a great joy to him, and he always carried the bird clasped in his hands as he went in to be done, but after a time he lost interest in the new toy and handed it on to some of the other children, and he became listless and dull and silent. One day I was asking the boy in the cot next to him to sing, for he had a sweet little piping voice, and as he was shy I offered him a *dinar* (a small coin) if he would sing, which he then did. The next day, by chance, I asked Alexander if he would sing, and to my surprise he piped up a song all of his own making, as he had lain silent and apart for weeks taking little notice of anyone, and I knew he had in his mind's eye the rewards of a *dinar* and the "bonbons" it could buy. From that day he brightened up, and I would find him sitting up in bed ready to sing to me unasked as soon as I appeared at the ward door, and he learned about three songs to sing in rotation. His whole aspect was changed; he was so pleased with himself. As I thought it wise not to encourage too much buying of "bonbons", I offered the children one day the cigarette cards sent out by some kind members of the Save the Children Fund office in London, and, as there was a full supply of prizes, the whole ward started singing. And the competition spread to the other wards, too, and so the day was made a little brighter and the children all had their much-cherished pictures to tuck away under their pillows with the hope of adding others to their collection." [59]

After more then ten years with a kind of temporary status, in 1931 the Anglo-Serbian Children's Hospital finally gained full official recognition. The Government of Yugoslavia officially recognised the hospital as a permanent independent private institution under the supervision of the Ministry of Health; as such it obtained regular financial support from government funds earmarked for the health service. This recognition was extremely important for the future work of the hospital, since in this way its future was assured, and significantly more stable sources of financial provision were guaranteed. The name of the hospital was then also changed as by the end of 1929, the Kingdom of the Serbs, Croats and Slovenes was officially designated as the Kingdom of Yugoslavia ("land of the south Slavs"); [60] instead of Anglo-Serbian, from then on the hospital was called the Anglo-Yugoslav Children's Hospital. On the occasion of this event Katherine explained: "After ten years' work it is a great satisfaction to know that we can look forward to a continuance of our efforts for the children of Yugoslavia; for it has not been an easy matter for what was originally a foreign and temporary mission to be transformed into a permanent institution of the country, retaining its own identity and working alongside the national institutions." [61]

The Anglo-Yugoslav Children's Hospital certainly deserved this recognition. In July 1931 the hospital published a 10-year report of its work, [62] showing the number of children treated each year; from this it is clear that from its foundation in 1919 up to the end of 1930 there were 6,838 children treated as inpatients, and 131,797 as outpatients; so altogether the hospital treated 138,635 sick children, which, bearing in mind the high standards of the hospital, was a most impressive number, that aroused great admiration. One very important aspect of the work of the hospital was the health education of the parents, which took place mainly in the outpatients' department of the hospital. About this Dr. Katherine MacPhail wrote: "The Outpatients' Department, besides its actual help in alleviating the suffering of the little ones, does an inestimable piece of work in teaching the mothers how to observe symptoms in their children and in the treatment of simple complaints, as well as in laying stress on the necessity for paying great attention to personal cleanliness and hygiene. The value of this teaching from a child welfare point of view cannot be over-estimated. [62]

The hospital gained an immediate advantage from its official recognition. Immediately after the announcement of this fact, the *Nikola Spasić Foundation*, on the occasion of the opening of the Foundation's new headquarters, donated the hospital a notable tribute. In his accompanying letter the president of the foundation explained that the board had decided to make this contribution "in appreciation of the humanitarian work of the hospital, instead of following the traditional custom observed among our people, of blessing every new building by preparing a quantity of food and giving a banquet to which important citizens and others are invited, and on which large sums of money are spent to do honour to people who have abundance of everything in their own home." For this reason the board presented 20,000 dinars (about £ 80.00) to the hospital "for the Board consider that this sum of money will help to dry the tears and save the lives of many innocent children, whose parents live in misery, material and moral." [61] It was indeed an unusual gift, accompanied by an uncommon explanation, and, as always, very welcome to the hospital. In fact, in spite of regular government help which covered half of the expenses, and regular assistance from the *Save the Children Fund* in London, and also other donations, the hospital was always short of funds; for this reason parents who could afford to do so made a small contribution to the expense of their children's treatment. Sometimes the help given was connected with sad circumstances, and Katherine recalled one such occasion. A little girl of eight years old amused herself while lying in hospital, as did the other children, by collecting cigarette cards and then selling them to other children. As she was seriously ill, beyond medical help, when she died her mother gave the hospital 600 dinars that the little girl had earned by selling the small pictures.

The greatest benefactor of the hospital was certainly the SCF as Katherine wrote about it: "Besides the help given by the Government and the money received from the patients, the largest and most constant subscriber to the hospital has been *The Save the Children Fund, London*, which has given us every possible support from the very early days when the work was most urgent and when they had large responsibilities elsewhere in Europe. Without their encouragement and support we could not have continued our work and brought it to its present issue. The Hospital Committee, which is a sub-committee of the Fund, has done much to help and encourage the work of the hospital during these last years, and *The World's Children* has helped to keep up general interest by publishing articles from time to time." [62]

The hospital had also been receiving the donations from various sides, and an interesting form of help was the maintenance of a bed in hospital. "Beds are supported yearly by friends of the Serbs, *viz.:* *The Hon. Elsie Cameron Corbett, St. George's Girls' School, Edinburgh*, and *Mr. John Frothingham. The British Legion* supported a bed for one year" wrote Katherine in 1931. [62] To make it known a plaque with the name of the donor was put on the wall above the bed.

The enormous expense of maintaining the hospital in Belgrade, which increased from year to year, probably influenced Katherine, among other reasons, to think of moving the hospital somewhere outside the capital, where the expense would be considerably less.

Katherine first spoke about plans, which eventually led to the opening of a new hospital at Sremska Kamenica, in the official journal of the *Save the Children Fund*: "The World's Children" in March, 1931: "My great ambition is to increase our work among crippled children and tubercular children, of whom we have an endless stream coming to the Hospital, only one-fourth of whom we can take into the wards. So much can be done in the way of preventing deformities which would cripple a child for life, if only treatment is begun early enough." [61] As an experienced physician, Dr. Katherine MacPhail clearly noticed in good time that the form of illness in children had changed, that there was an increasing number of chronic tubercular patients who also needed help, whose treatment required a longer period of time, and which necessitated a radical change in the work of the hospital. She wrote about this at some length: "After twelve years of work among the children in this country, it seemed to me that one of the greatest needs at present time was to provide an open-air hospital for sick children who need a long time in the country, and especially for children suffering from tubercular disease of the bones and joints and from deformities due to other causes. Children have continually had to be turned away from the hospital who, if given medical supervision, fresh air, and good food over a considerable period of time, would have had a chance of having their wounds healed and their deformities arrested if not corrected. During the past year about

200 children treated at this hospital have been put in plaster, all of whom have been sent home, at once or after a short stay, and have had to lie, sometimes for months, in plaster at home. Many of them have to return to hospital two or three times, often from long distances, to have their plaster changed and their deformities readjusted. In a special open-air hospital for such cases they would have constant medical care and nursing over a longer period, and their general health would benefit by the open-air treatment. At the same time they would be removed from the proximity of their brothers and sisters, to whom they must be a continual danger through lack of cleanliness and attention and because of the inadequacy of the space available in their own homes. These children must live their lives in misery and suffering through lack of proper provision. There is no place for them in the general hospitals, since these are full of more curable cases, and there are not enough sanatoria to provide for the large number of cases. The only sanatorium existing for such children is a state institution at Kraljevica on the Adriatic coast." [63]

Katherine had probably been preoccupied with these problems for some time, and had obviously discussed them with Professor Leonard Findlay when he visited Yugoslavia, since he later wrote on this subject: "Dr. MacPhail has wisely devoted her energies to, and provided facilities for, the most important branches of pediatrics, *viz.*: medical diseases and orthopaedics. The latter deals with treatment of deformities and surgical tuberculosis, and this is the only special branch of surgery pertaining to childhood. For its efficient development convalescent homes are *sine qua non*, and I know it is Dr. MacPhail's ambition to develop her work along these lines. Needless to say, the country is eminently suitable for this kind of work, the climate being dry and there being a super-abundance of sunshine." [62]

At the beginning of the thirties Katherine began an active search for a suitable place outside the capital, but not too far from Belgrade, in open country, with plenty of fresh air and sunshine. At first she thought of buying one of the abandoned monasteries in Fruška Gora, [64] that seemed to her to be suitable for this purpose. However, when she approached the relevant ministry, where she obtained a list of empty monasteries, she was warned that these monasteries were very isolated, and that the roads leading to them were bad, so that she would be faced with practically insoluble problems as regards transport and obtaining supplies; this, naturally, raised considerable doubts in her mind. However before she finally abandoned this interesting idea, Katherine decided to ask the advice of her old friend Darinka Grujić, who at that time was still running her orphanage at Sremska Kamenica, so she thought that she would know everything about the Fruška Gora monasteries. In the spring of 1932, when all this happened, Darinka Grujić advised Katherine to abandon the idea of buying a monastery, but to try and find a suitable building, or even build a new one, at Sremska Kamenica, which, in view of its natural conditions would be a most suitable place for this purpose. Since Katherine anyway liked Sremska

Kamenica, in which she already had a holiday house, she liked this idea and immediately began to make plans to found a new hospital.

Since her villa in Sremska Kamenica was mainly empty and suitable for moving in, Katherine had the idea to begin by establishing a new hospital there, so she moved 25 children's beds into the building, with the intention of using this space for convalescent children from the Belgrade hospital. Her elder sister Annie who, after the death of their parents no longer had any permanent obligations, came from Scotland, and she ran this small hospital as a voluntary worker, with the help of two Serbian nurses and a cook from the village, which functioned throughout the summer of 1932. However, it was soon apparent that this place and this building were not suitable for a permanent hospital; there were many difficulties, especially in bad weather, so Katherine had to abandon this idea. "When the weather was bad and rainy there was very little room inside and endless mud outside", Katherine explained vividly. The one car they had was needed in Belgrade, so that in Sremska Kamenica they had no means of transport for going to the nearest market, obtaining food, or transporting children from the railway station in Novi Sad, the town across the river. For these reasons this small convalescent home was closed in the autumn of 1932, and the villa once more became a private cottage, used for week-ends visits and rest by Katherine and her friends and the staff of the hospital. Her old friend from the Salonika Front and the post-war days in Belgrade, Nan McGlade, spent some time recovering there after a serious operation; she had returned to Belgrade after living for some years in China. Later Katherine recollected how she and Nan McGlade would sit on the verandah of the villa watching the sunset in the distance over the Danube River, making plans to build a hospital in Sremska Kamenica, which would be a symbolic memorial to the British women who had worked for many years in Serbia during and after the First World War. Sadly, Nan McGlade did not live to see these dreams realised, since a few months later she died in the Children's Hospital in Belgrade, where her old friends looked after her right up to the end.

It would seem that during these days Katherine abandoned the idea of opening a new hospital in a monastery, and finally decided to build a new one somewhere in Sremska Kamenica. This village, with its gentle surroundings, in between the hills of Fruška Gora and the Danube, obviously attracted her very much, and she decided to stay there. In addition, it was an interesting area historically, which had been settled over the centuries by people of different origin and nationality, including some Celtic tribes, whose graves were to be found throughout the Danube valley; indeed the name of that mighty river was of Celtic origin, and Katherine, as she said herself, wondered whether she had been influenced by some atavistic notion which caused her to settle in that very place, in Sremska Kamenica. Whatever the reason, she then began to search for a suitable place in the neighbourhood of the village where she could build a new hospital; it would have to be in the country, away from a settled area, but not too far away; on a hill, where there would be ample fresh air and sunshine, since at that time these were the basic conditions for locating a hospital intended for the treatment of tuberculosis.

As well as Sremska Kamenica itself, to which she had become very attached, and where she spent nearly all her week-ends, at that time Katherine had become very close to someone who was already an old friend, namely, Mr. Vasa Srdić, who was then living in Temerin, a place some 6 miles across the Danube. He was the same Vasa Srdić who, at the beginning of 1920, when he was an officer in the Serbian Army serving at Zelenika in Boka Kotorska, had enabled Isabel MacPhail to select equipment for the "Villa Bravačić" in Dubrovnik from an abandoned Austrian hospital; from then on he had been a close friend of the MacPhail sisters. After the war Vasa Srdić, as a qualified agricultural engineer, obtained some land in Temerin where he settled and occupied himself with agriculture and fruit growing (Fig. 56). Since Vasa Srdić was involved in all Katherine's plans, he looked for a suitable site, and soon discovered that on Čardak Hill, immediately above Sremska Kamenica, there was an abandoned vineyard for sale, which would suit Katherine's plans. The approach to this patch of land was quite difficult, by way of a steep and ill kept road racked with potholes, that turned off from the main road to Fruška Gora not far from the outskirts of the village, and wound uphill right to the top, where this piece of land was situated, and then continued into the depths of the mountain.[65] From this piece of land there was a wonderful view of the village situated a little way beneath the hill, then on the mighty Danube, which flowed between Sremska Kamenica and Novi Sad in a north-easterly direction towards the Petrovaradin Fortress [66] which stood out in its magnificence and beauty on the right side. On the other side of the Danube the endless Bačka plain stretched as far as the eye could see; to the south and south-west there stretched the wooded hills of Fruška Gora, from which there came a constant stream of fresh air. Undoubtedly when Katherine first climbed up to Čardak, she was delighted with the situation of the place itself and its surroundings. As well as the main road that led to the hill, there was also a footpath which ran through vineyards belonging to a rich merchant from Novi Sad, which led in a north-easterly direction to a neighbouring hill at the foot of which was Katherine's villa. The vineyards were full of peach trees which came to the edge of the road along which they were walking; and in that early summer of 1933 the golden-red peaches already ripe, gleamed in the full sunshine; and Katherine, as she herself later related, felt that she had at last found the place which she had been seeking for so long. "I have chosen this site in the Fruška Gora from the point of view of good air, good position, easy communication, and accessibility for medical supervision", Katherine wrote later.[63] Without much further reflection Dr. Katherine MacPhail bought this piece of land, which on August 1st, 1933 was officially registered in her name; she then immediately began to make preparations to build a hospital.

Working in accordance with Katherine's ideas, and with the help of an engineer from the Hygiene Institute in Belgrade, an elderly Russian architect drew up plans for a three-winged building with a central courtyard, and a long terrace adjoining the north and west wings of the building, so that the children could be carried out and exposed to the sun throughout the day. Katherine immediately sought approval for the project from the Ministries of Social Security and National Health, and permission to build from the appropriate Ministry of Works. Assuming that obtaining permission would be a pure formality, and quickly achieved, and in order not to lose valuable time, work was begun on the building. Naturally, the main organiser of all this was the irreplaceable Vasa Srdić who engaged a contractor with 40 workers, who immediately, before the end of the summer of 1933, began levelling the ground, digging foundations and bringing up material (Fig. 57). The weather was favourable, the work proceeded quickly, but permission to build had not arrived. Katherine wrote letters, tramped from ministry to ministry, from official to official, patiently explained, sought, begged, and received promises, but bureaucracy moved slowly and proved difficult to master. One factor influencing this situation was the frequent change of ministers and other officials with authority through whom the decision had to be made. The Ministry of Social Policy and National Health passed the matter to the Ministry of Works, who passed it on yet again to the Technical Department of the *Dunavska Banovina* (the Danube District, a regional unit of the Danube area ruled by a *ban* or governor in Novi Sad), [60] which approved the project at the end of September 1933. However, even this was not enough, and on November 12th Katherine approached the municipal authorities in Sremska Kamenica, with all the necessary documentation; actually she only sent the documentation through the Municipality of Sremska Kamenica to the Danube District Administration, which had the authority to grant permission to build. However, notwithstanding administrative difficulties, the work of building the hospital was proceeding successfully, and the builders had already reached as far as the roof, but permission had still not come through. The situation was already dangerous, since the fines for such violations were very high, so Katherine finally decided to turn to her former protectress, Queen Maria, who in any case kept up her interest in both the work of the hospital in Belgrade and in the building of a new hospital in Sremska Kamenica. When the queen heard about the problem of the building permit she was really worried, since this involved a serious breach of the law. She at once involved herself in this situation, through her own channels; and, naturally, this intervention bore fruit, and a permit was signed within two days, so that the work could be continued in peace.

Another considerable problem that Katherine had to face was the financing of the building work. Her original plan had been to sell the hospital in Belgrade and use this money to build and equip a new hospital in Sremska Kamenica; however, as she did not wish to interrupt work in the Belgrade hospital before one in Sremska Kamenica was ready, Katherine obtained a loan from the bank, using the building and land in Belgrade as a pledge; and with this resource she paid for all the building expenses, which continually increased. In the course of building many problems appeared which Katherine could not even have dreamed of earlier. One of these was the problem of water supply. For this purpose a well was dug near the building, but this was not sufficient; so a new well had to be dug about 300 feet lower down, at the foot of the hill, from which water had to be pumped into a cistern at the top of the hill, from which it flowed into the water supply system of the building itself. Then it was necessary to bring electricity from the village about one mile away, and to obtain a transformer. Yet another problem was a huge quantity of excavated earth, which they did not know what to do with. Since in any case they needed a large number of bricks, Vasa Srdić had the idea to make bricks from this earth; so he brought some master brickmakers from Bačka, who also brought with them their families with whom they lived on the actual building site in huts. A man and his wife could make 1,000 bricks a day between them (Fig. 58); these were then dried in the sun and later baked in improvised kilns on the actual site (Fig. 59). These bricks were used to pave the courtyards, and to build garden walls, the garage and other out-buildings; in this way the cost of building material was considerably reduced. Thanks to Vasa Srdić, who found good builders and engaged plenty of workmen from the actual village who worked with a will, the work proceeded quickly, and in the autumn of 1933 the building was already under its roof. When the roof construction was already under way, according to an old custom, a new shirt was hung up for the chief builder, and a feast prepared for all the workmen. Tables improvised from scaffolding were set up in the courtyard, with food for 40 workmen, and also for Katherine, her sister Annie, and Agnes Hardie, and Alice Murphy, who came from Belgrade for this occasion. However, news of this celebration soon spread through the village, and many uninvited guests turned up so that soon there were about 100 people. To the great sorrow of Vasa Srdić, who had of course prepared all this, there was not enough food for all the guests, but it seems that there was plenty of wine since, as it was afterwards related, the celebration ended in great merriment.

By then it was quite certain that the building would soon be completely finished, and that the hospital would soon be moved from Belgrade to Sremska Kamenica, as had already been reported in the newspapers. Throughout this time the Children's Hospital in Belgrade had worked normally without interruption, despite the fact that Katherine had been extremely busy with administrative and financial business connected with the building of the new hospital, and also with constantly supervising the building work, which meant that she often had to be absent from Belgrade. However, the work in the hospital had been so well organised and regular during the preceding years that even without her presence it was carried on without a hitch, and the hospital continued to be visited by many guests (Fig. 60). Thus, it is on record that over Easter 1933, the hospital was visited by the young princes Alexander and Nicholas, the sons of Princess Olga and Prince Paul, who brought presents for all the sick children. As Katherine, who received them, related afterwards, the young princes were very pleasant, and talked to the children about their illness, and expressed a special wish to see the X-ray department and the operating theatre.[67]

At that time in Belgrade there were already well-established state institutions for the protection of children, such as the Pediatric Clinic of the Faculty of Medicine, established in 1925, so that the need for a general children's hospital, such as the Anglo-Yugoslav Children's Hospital, was much less; and for these reasons, in addition to increased financial problems, the number of beds in the hospital had been reduced by half, but the Outpatients' Department continued to work to its full capacity. Notwithstanding the considerable development of the health service during these years, the problem of chronic patients, especially those suffering from tuberculosis, was still very great; and for this reason, among others, Dr. Katherine MacPhail decided to move her hospital and change the profile of its work. She herself explained this as follows: "I have undertaken this development because I feel the time has come to transfer the activities of the hospital, which filled an urgent need in the years after the war, from general to special work, because there is such a large field of work for crippled children waiting to be dealt with." [63] This idea of Katherine's had the agreement and strong support of Queen Maria, the Ministry of Health and the Save the Children Fund, which made it possible for her to perform this great task successfully. One of the weightiest transactions from this point of view was the sale of the Anglo-Yugoslav Children's Hospital in Belgrade to the Ministry of Health. This procedure took some time and was not without difficulties. When the agreement was already concluded, Katherine could not receive the money for the sale until she had paid all the dues and taxes, which amounted to 85,000 dinars. As she had already spent nearly this amount on building the new hospital she did not have this money, and there was really no one to whom she could turn for help. Finding herself in this difficult situation, she tried once more to talk to the head of the Hospitals Department in the Ministry of Health. He was very sympathetic and suggested that she should go with him to see Dr. Dušan Stojimirović, a well-known specialist in Belgrade, who would perhaps be able to lend her this money. Katherine did not know this doctor, so it was very distasteful for her to approach him with such a request, but as she had no other way out she finally went and asked for his help. Dr. Stojimirović received her very cordially and listened to her story and then, to her great surprise, went to his cash-box, took out 85,000 dinars and gave them to Katherine without any further formalities; she, of course, promised to repay him as soon as she received the money from the Ministry of Health. Katherine was deeply touched by this generous and unselfish action. But this was not the only friendly gesture on the part of Dr. Stojimirović. When the hospital in Sremska

Kamenica was completed he sent five children's beds, the contribution he had promised, "as a sign of acknowledgement and gratitude for the generosity of the British people at a time when my homeland and my fellow-countrymen were faced with great misfortune." When she had secured the money for taxes another problem arose: in all the documents connected with the sale of the hospital, Katherine's surname was written as "Makfel", whereas she always signed herself "MacPhail". Because of this the bank did not wish to pay out the money, and Katherine's lawyer had to expend much time and effort to resolve this "trifling matter", and to prove that this was the same person. However, in the end the money from the sale of the Belgrade hospital was obtained, debts were repaid, and the outstanding finance secured to finish and equip the new hospital. In addition Katherine managed to buy a small flat in Belgrade, which she used for her frequent visits there, after she moved to Sremska Kamenica.

At that time the villa in Sremska Kamenica was a kind of staff-headquarters for building the new hospital, and here Katherine spent all her week-ends, during which time she went round the building site (Fig. 61), supervised the work and paid the workers. Apart from the workers who were staying there temporarily there were a number of local people who came to work there from the village; as one contemporary recalled: "A lot of people from the village earned good money there." They all greatly respected and valued Katherine, as is clear from an incident which she later recalled with pleasure. In the spring of 1934 Katherine asked the workmen to clear the courtyard and the garden round the villa of nettles and various wild plants. When she returned to the villa the next Saturday, to her great surprise and annoyance, she noticed that the workmen had cleared the courtyard so thoroughly that, together with the weeds, they had removed a row of young acacia bushes which she liked very much. This made her so sad and depressed that Vasa Srdić and his workmen immediately noticed. The next morning, when Katherine got up and went out onto the terrace, she could not believe her eyes: all her acacia bushes were in their place, as though no one had touched them. The explanation was simple. When Vasa Srdić saw how upset Katherine was he went out into the forest very early in the morning with some other people, and found some young acacia shoots which he then planted in Katherine's courtyard, alongside the fence, exactly in the places where they had been before. "I had no words to thank them," Katherine related later. "It was a real gesture of apology and sympathy. I don't think that many people would have thought it worthwhile to take so much trouble, but would have just hoped that I would forget it." But not Vasa Srdić, who was clearly a very considerate, well-meaning and honourable man. According to the stories of his contemporaries, he was popular and respected among other people, because he was kind, friendly with everybody and knew how to conduct himself properly. He was conscientious, good at everything, and always available; in this respect he was exceptionally useful to Katherine, indeed irreplaceable. He was a true source of strength, thanks to which the new hospital in Sremska Kamenica was built, which, at that time, under those conditions, in such a place and in such a short time, was indeed a real achievement. It is a fact that Vasa Srdić highly valued and respected Katherine and her work, that he was very attached to Katherine who had been his friend over many years, especially during the time when she was in Sremska Kamenica; then they were often together, visited each other and spent a lot of time together. It is also a fact that Katherine liked Vasa Srdić very much and had a high opinion of him, and that over many years he was her right hand, and a dear and irreplaceable friend. Probably a contributory factor in this mutual attraction was the origin of Vasa Srdić, whose mother was a Scotswoman; because of this he spoke English fluently, and Serbian with a "Scottish accent", as Katherine remarked in her memoirs; because of this Katherine and her close friends familiarly called him Mac Srdić. Probably because of all this some of their contemporaries asserted that they were having a love affair; and one of them, Mrs. Julka Skrjaga, who, as the wife of Katherine's chauffer Vasilj, [68] was certainly familiar with many of the details of this period of Katherine's life, said of them: "They were like husband and wife." It was also said that the house in which Katherine lived was known as "Srdić's villa", since it was generally thought that he was the owner of the house, which certainly was not the case. Naturally it is impossible to establish the true character of their relationship; but in view of the fact that they were both single, that there was a long-standing attraction of many years between them, the situation in which they found themselves, and other circumstances, it is quite possible and completely understandable that their relationship was very intimate, indeed that they were lovers, as it seemed to be assumed at that time in Sremska Kamenica.

Whatever the situation the tireless Vasa Mac Srdić and his men began to move towards the end of their work on the new hospital in the spring of 1934. In accordance with Katherine's special wish, a mosaic of the Scottish lion was made for the floor of the entrance hall. The drawing of a red lion with blue claws rearing upwards was made by one of Katherine's friends, the Scottish artist Stewart Orr; the actual mosaic was made by craftsmen from Temerin, found by none other than Mac Srdić (Figs. 62 and 63). Also in accordance with Katherine's wish, above the main entrance from the courtyard there was a carved relief, the figure of a child, actually a replica of the "Bambino" relief made by the famous Italian sculptor Andrea della Robia from Florence (Fig. 64). Katherine set this symbol in place in memory of her parents, and in recognition of the work of the *Save the Children Fund*, since this was their emblem. It was also placed above the entrance to the wards (Figs. 63 and 68); however in the course of the subsequent renovation of the building these reliefs were removed. Then there followed the arrangement of the courtyard and the small park, where flower beds were planted, mainly roses and petunias; and in the small park behind the inner courtyard trees were planted and paths constructed. The orchard and vineyard below the hospital building were also cleaned and put in order. The person responsible for these tasks was the capable Dobrosav, a master of all trades from the Belgrade hospital, who moved to Sremska Kamenica with other members of the staff. At that time most of the staff were Yugoslavs; the only people remaining from the British staff were Dr. Katherine MacPhail, the matron or head sister Agnes Hardie, and the irreplaceable secretary Alice Murphy. One of the interesting individuals who also moved to Sremska Kamenica with Katherine was her faithful chauffeur Vasilj, [68] who moved there permanently and worked with Katherine right up to the end of her stay in Yugoslavia. Another person who continued to be connected with Katherine and the new hospital was Dr. Svetislav Stojanović, who had already worked with her for some years in the Belgrade hospital as a surgeon, and continued to work with her for many years as the chief surgeon of the hospital in Sremska Kamenica (Figs.69 and 98).

In the summer of 1934, when the new hospital in Sremska Kamenica was ready, the Anglo-Yugoslav Children's Hospital in Belgrade was closed, after 14 years of work, and the building in Višegradska Street was handed over to the Ministry of Health, which transferred there the Eye Department of the State General Hospital. In 1938 this department moved into a new bigger building that was constructed on the same site, and in 1947 it was amalgamated with the former Eye Clinic into a unique Eye Clinic of the Faculty of Medicine in Belgrade, which is still there on the same location.

During its 14 years of work the Anglo-Yugoslav Children's Hospital in Belgrade certainly had a very important role. During this period it treated 8,600 children as inpatients, and over 170,000 were examined and treated as outpatients. At one time it was the only children's hospital in Serbia, and for many years it exercised the function of the one surgical unit for children, which later developed into the Children's Surgical Clinic. The first training school for medical sisters in Belgrade developed within the framework of this hospital and later a few hundred nurses received their practical training here. Four outstanding doctors who worked and gained experience in that hospital later became well-known professors in the Faculty of Medicine in Belgrade. In addition a large number of other doctors gained years of valuable experience in treating children's diseases, and in the organisation of modern methods of child protection in this same exemplary institution, since for a long time there were no others. The great services of Dr. Katherine MacPhail for all this were publicly acknowledged, and when the hospital was closed she was awarded the Order of St Sava, third class, for her work in Belgrade up to that time; Agnes Hardie and Alice Murphy were also decorated for their devoted work in Yugoslavia.

Katherine certainly had good reason to be proud, and it is not surprising that she felt very sad and full of regret when the hospital in Belgrade was closed, since this meant the end of a very rich period of her life. But it was also the beginning of a new era, in new surroundings, with new work, so Katherine certainly had no time for nostalgic thoughts or regrets; she was now faced with new challenges.

111

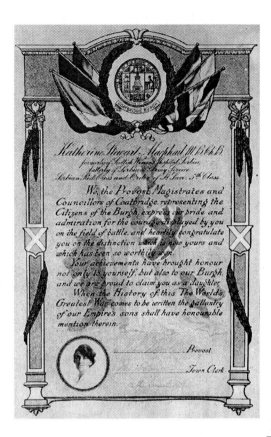

Fig. 29 A certificate granting Katherine MacPhail honorary citizenship of her native town of Coatbridge, issued on August 15th, 1918.
(Courtesy of Mrs. E. Biggs)

Fig. 30 Dr. K. MacPhail, with a group of sick children, in front of the barracks in Studenica Street, Belgrade, in which she established her first children's hospital at the beginning of 1919.
(Courtesy of Mrs. E. Biggs)

Fig. 31 The Topchider pavilion for convalescent children from the hospital; summer of 1919. (Dr. K. MacPhail's collection, courtesy of the Serbian Medical Association Museum, Belgrade)

Fig. 32 Patients and staff in the Topchider pavilion in the summer of 1919. (Isabel MacPhail is the second on the left in the top row) Courtesy of the SMA Museum)

Ever yours sincerely L. MacPhail.
Katherine

Fig. 33 A photograph of Dr. K. MacPhail taken late in 1915 or the early months of 1916 in Glasgow; Katherine gave this photograph, with its greeting, to Miloš Ćirić on May 5th, 1919, as is written on the back of the photograph.
(Courtesy of Dr. Milan Ćirić)

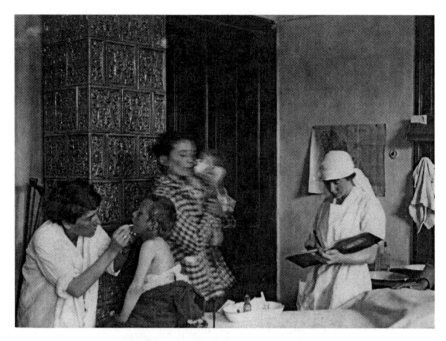

Fig. 34 Dr. K. MacPhail examining a sick child in the hospital in Prince Miloš Street (c. 1920). (Courtesy of Mrs. E. Biggs)

Fig. 35 Dr. K. MacPhail (wearing a white coat, in the centre of the picture) with a group of children and members of the staff on the terrace of the "Villa Bravačić" in Dubrovnik (c. 1920-21); the second on the left in top row (wearing a white dress and head-scarf) is Katherine's sister, Annie MacPhail. (Courtesy of the SMA Museum)

115

Fig. 36 Dr. K. MacPhail (crouching), and Annie MacPhail (standing), with the children in the "Villa Bravačić" in Dubrovnik (c. 1920-21).
(Courtesy of the SMA Museum)

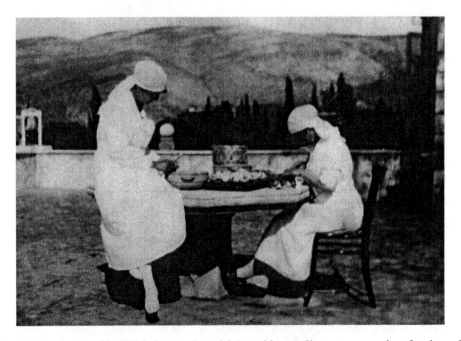

Fig. 37 Annie MacPhail (sitting at the table) and her colleague preparing food on the terrace of the "Villa Bravačić" in Dubrovnik (c. 1920-21).
(Courtesy of the SMA Museum)

Fig. 38 The park of the "Villa Bravačić", a photograph made from a water-colour painting by Katherine's father, Dr. Donald MacPhail, painted in the summer of 1920.
(Courtesy of Mrs. E. Biggs)

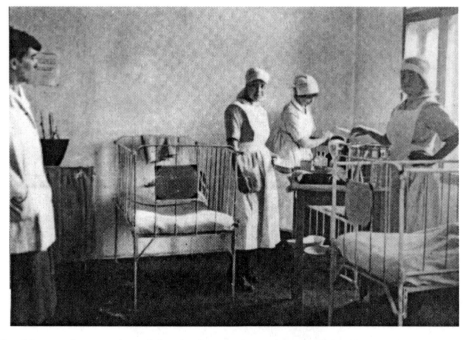

Fig. 39 Local nurses in training in the Anglo-Serbian Children's Hospital, under the watchful eye of Dr. K. MacPhail (on the far left).
(Courtesy of Mrs. E. Biggs)

Fig. 40 The building in Višegradska Street, number 20, in Belgrade, where the Anglo-Serbian, later Anglo-Yugoslav Children's Hospital was accommodated from 1921 to 1934. (Courtesy of the SMA Museum)

Fig. 41 The facade and entrance to the Anglo-Serbian Children's Hospital in Višegradska Street, Belgrade (c. 1921-22). (Courtesy of the SMA Museum)

Fig. 42 Transport of patients to the Children's Hospital in Višegradska Street in the winter of 1922. (Courtesy of the SMA Museum)

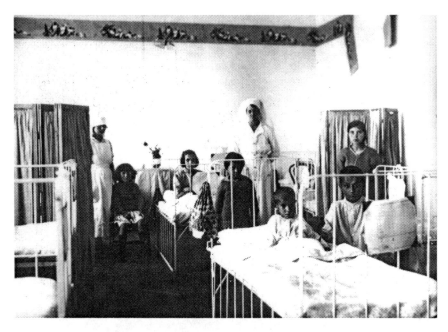

Fig. 43 The surgical department of the Children's Hospital in Višegradska Street; Sister King (the tall lady), is standing among the children; the name of the other sister is not known. On the wall are drawings based on Russian fairy tales.
(Courtesy of the SMA Museum)

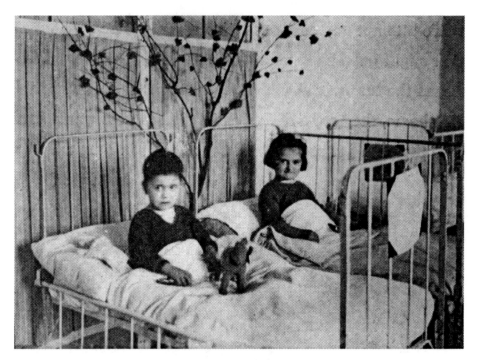

Fig. 44 Small patients in the internist section of the Children's Hospital in Višegradska Street, Belgrade (c. 1921). (Courtesy of the SMA Museum)

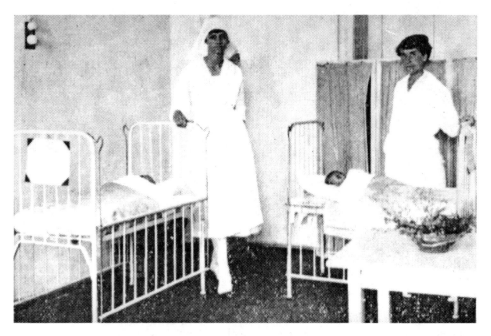

Fig. 45 The maternity ward, c. 1921; Dr. K. MacPhail (bare-headed), and Sister King. (Courtesy of the SMA Museum)

Fig. 46 The maternity ward at Christmas time, c.1921 or 1922; Sister Risely (seated), and Sister King, holding the babies.
(Courtesy of the SMA Museum)

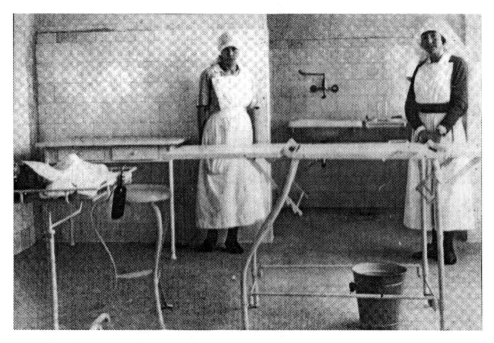

Fig. 47 The operating theatre in the Children's Hospital in Višegradska Street, Belgrade (1921). (Courtesy of the SMA Museum)

Fig. 48 "Myself with English & Serbian Staff" wrote Dr. K. MacPhail (third from the left in the front row) on the back of this picture taken in front of the Children's Hospital in Belgrade in 1922. Sister Matthews is standing on her right, and on her left Dr. Vida Perry, Nurse Jealous and Sister King. (The names of the other people in this photograph are not known) (Courtesy of Mrs. E. Biggs)

Fig. 49 Dr. K. MacPhail (standing, second on the left), with outpatients and those accompanying them, 1921; on her right is Dr. Vladimir Bogdanović, standing, and among the patients Sister O' Rorke, also standing. (Courtesy of Mrs. E. Biggs)

Fig. 50 Dr. Agnes Salmon and Miss Alice Murphy (c. 1930) in Belgrade. (Courtesy of Mrs. E. Biggs)

Fig. 51 Dr. K. MacPhail with her three nieces: Ann (sitting down), Jessie (the tallest) and Elspeth, in Benderloch (c. 1923). (Courtesy of Mrs. E. Biggs)

Fig. 52 Travelling in Montenegro; Katherine is riding on the first horse (c. 1925-30). (Courtesy of the SMA Museum)

Fig. 53 After a voyage down the River Drina by raft; Katherine is sitting in front, in the first row (c. 1925-30). (Courtesy off the SMA Museum)

Fig. 54 Dr. K. MacPhail (wearing a white coat), with the ward sister, seeing off children and their parents from the hospital (c. 1922).
(Courtesy of the SMA Museum)

Fig. 55 Christmas in the Children's Hospital in Belgrade, 1922.
(Courtesy of Mrs. E. Biggs)

Chapter 6

Sremska Kamenica, 1934 – 1941

At the end of May 1934, when the final work on the new hospital in Sremska Kamenica [69] was already completed, Dr. Katherine MacPhail sent a written request to the authorities of the Danube District in Novi Sad asking them to send a commission to inspect the building and to approve the opening of the hospital and the beginning of its work. In a document issued on July 3rd, 1934, the Danube District set up a commission of three members, headed by Dr. Jovan Popović, deputy director of the Institute of Hygiene in Novi Sad, to examine the building and other arrangements, and to submit an appropriate report. While this administrative procedure was being carried out, the hospital was completely built and equipped, and ready to start work. The first patients were admitted on August 1st, 1934; they were mainly tubercular patients transferred from the hospital in Belgrade, or those who had for some time been awaiting admission.

The commission of the Danube District set up to examine the hospital met on August 11th, 1934, made a thorough examination of the hospital and its surroundings, and then issued the following report:

"The main building is a ground-floor construction, situated on the spur of a hill which descends from the peak elevation 297 towards Kamenica; the place is healthy, dry and porous, exposed to the abundant and useful effects of the fresh air and sunshine. The building consists of a main frontal section, facing south-west, with two wings symmetrically attached to it. In the main part of this building there are three inter-connected rooms for the accommodation of mobile and non-mobile patients, a main entrance hall, an operating theatre, examination room, pharmacy, a room for sterilising instruments used for operations, an isolation room in case of an outbreak of infectious diseases among the patients, an office and a store room for medicines and instruments."

"In the wings there are administrative offices, a kitchen with a pantry, a dining-room for nurses and children, and kitchen nearby for preparing milk, tea and other light refreshments and two bedrooms. In the attics under the roof of the wings there are four rooms to accommodate the doctors and nurses. In the wings there are cellars for storing the necessities of life."

"There are four bathrooms with toilets, very conveniently situated in the wings of the building."

"The building has been constructed according to a very fine and professionally designed plan, as regards both treatment and the living conditions of patients and staff....In front of the west and south sides, part of the courtyard is paved with bricks for the reception of beds with their patients.... The entire courtyard is fenced in, and access allowed only to specific persons" (Figs. 65 and 66).

On the basis of this report the Danube District authorities, on August 21st, 1934, formally approved the opening of the Anglo-Yugoslav Children's sanatorium, which was thus formally and officially established and recognised. Then preparations began for the formal opening of the sanatorium, fixed for September 23rd, 1934. On September 21st, 1934, this news was announced in the daily newspapers, together with an invitation to the ceremony:

"Under the high patronage of H. M. Queen Maria, the Anglo-Yugoslav Children's Sanatorium in Sremska Kamenica will be officially opened on Sunday, September 23rd, at 11 a.m. The celebration will be attended by dignitaries of the Serbian Orthodox Church, representatives of English circles in our country and various other organisations. The management of the sanatorium invites all interested friends and organisations to accept this invitation to the ceremony. A train will leave Belgrade for Novi Sad at 7.55, returning to Belgrade at 16.20. Transport from Novi Sad station to Kamenica will be by car."

Sunday, September 23rd, 1934 was a beautiful September day, and there was a great celebration on Čardak Hill above Sremska Kamenica, described by a journalist from *Politika*, a leading Belgrade daily newspaper, in the following words:

"Today the ceremonial opening of this fine sanatorium was formally celebrated; built on a hill above numerous vineyards, open to the sun on all sides, it is extremely suitable for the treatment of tuberculosis. Many citizens attended the formal opening of the sanatorium not only from Novi Sad but also from Sremska Kamenica and other places in the neighbourhood. This hospital is under the patronage of H.M. Queen Maria, and is called the Anglo-Yugoslav Children's Sanatorium. The entrance to the sanatorium was beautifully decorated with greenery, and with the two flags of Yugoslavia and Great Britain. Cars and horse-drawn cabs carrying guests began to arrive at ten o'clock. Among the first to arrive was Mr. Henderson, the British Ambassador at our court, and the British commercial attaché, Mr. Sturrock. They were accompanied by the *ban* of the Danube District, Mr. Dobrica Matković. Then there came the bishop of Bačka, Dr. Irinej Ćirić, and Mr. Milutinović, the secretary, representing *Matica Srpska,* (literally, the "Serbian Queen Bee", a prestigious Serbian literary and cultural organisation; translator's note), a large number of Novi Sad doctors headed by Dr. Jovan Nenadović, president of the Medical Association, and Dr. Adolf Hempt, director of the Institute of Hygiene; from Belgrade came doctors who had worked with Miss MacPhail for several years: Dr. Dušan Stojimirović, Dr. Vladimir Bogdanović, Dr. Siniša Radojević, and Dr. Milan Sokolović from Nish. Also present were Miss Flora Sandes, an Englishwoman wearing the uniform of a Serbian infantry captain, first class, Mr. Branko Avramović, Member of Parliament, and many other eminent representatives of our public life."

"Just before 11 o'clock there arrived representatives of H.M. Queen Maria, Mme Dundjerski, matron of honour, and Mme Olga Lozanić, representing

Her Highness Princess Olga. In the crowded hall, beautifully decorated with a large portrait of H.M. the King, and H.M. Queen Maria, patroness of the hospital, and with greenery, the ceremonial opening of the hospital was blessed by the archpriest M. Milić, assisted by a member of parliament, Rev. B. Avramović. After the religious ceremony Mme Dundjerski, representing H.M. Queen Maria, formally declared the sanatorium open in a few warm and well-chosen words."

"There were many speeches on this festive occasion, including one from Mr. Henderson, then the British Ambassador in Belgrade. 'The opening of this sanatorium', he said, 'shows the continuing cordial relationship between Great Britain and the Kingdom of Yugoslavia, and is a sign that these connections will become even stronger. This gives me great pleasure, and I sincerely rejoice that relations between our two countries are so close. Yesterday I had the honour of a formal audience with H.M. Queen Maria, and on that occasion H. M. the Queen asked me to express in her name her regret that she could not be present at this festive ceremony, as she had originally wished to be." [70]

"Then Dobrica Matković, *Ban* of the Danube District, made a fine, cordial speech, including the following words: 'This imposing occasion expresses the gratitude and joy, not only of Novi Sad, but of the whole of this country, that we have obtained such a fine and unusual institution, which fills a great gap in our state, of which we are well aware. For this we owe a debt of gratitude to Dr. MacPhail, a great friend of our country."

"Speaking of the firm bonds of friendship between the two nations, Mr. Matković then said in a jocular tone: 'Relations between Great Britain and the Kingdom of Yugoslavia might well become strained because we, like the English, have a great affection for Miss MacPhail; in fact no one knows who likes her most, ourselves or the English. I would venture to say, and Dr. MacPhail will confirm this, that the Kingdom of Yugoslavia is her second homeland.'

'It certainly is!' exclaimed Dr. MacPhail.

'I greet Miss MacPhail', continued *Ban* Matković, 'and I hope that she will continue her humanitarian work, and I say: Long live Dr. MacPhail'

All those present cried loudly: Long live Dr. MacPhail!" wrote our reporter.

After numerous speeches the guests looked round the hospital thoroughly, and visited the small patients who, as the weather was fine, had been carried out onto the terrace in their beds for their usual treatment (Fig. 67). About the hospital itself, a newspaper reporter said:

"The sanatorium with all its equipment is worth over two million dinars; it has 36 rooms, including four large wards for the patients; a large operating theatre, an X-ray department, a room for X-ray equipment, and other things. At present there are about thirty children in the sanatorium. They pay for only the basic expenses, as in a state hospital, and poor children, of whom there are at present 15, are treated completely free. In fact the sanatorium could accept as many as 60 children."

"After the formal ceremony, light refreshments were prepared for visitors from Belgrade, and for official guests," the reporter concluded in his lengthy description.

And so Dr. Katherine MacPhail's new hospital began its work. This institution was a so-called special hospital, and as Dr. MacPhail herself explained at a meeting of the Council of the *Save the Children Fund* in London, in January 1935, "it has been specially built for orthopaedic cases...The treatment is specially directed against tuberculosis of the bones and joints, infantile paralysis, rickets, etc., and comprises surgical intervention when necessary, fresh air, sunlight, good food, extensions, rest, massage, cleanliness, immobilisation in plaster, and other means." [71] (Fig 68) As such, this hospital was a unique institution in Serbia. At that time, in the whole of Yugoslavia, there was only one other similar institution, in Kraljevica, on the Adriatic Coast in Croatia. And so, once again Dr. Katherine MacPhail embarked on a pioneering task in these areas, which naturally was not at all easy. The main problem was, of course, the financing of the hospital, which was "intended mainly for the children of really poor parents." Children who provided proof of poverty were treated completely free; others paid 25 dinars per day, though the real cost was about 40 dinars daily. The expense of treating poor children, and the difference in price for the others, had to be met from other sources. The hospital accepted children up to the age of thirteen, and in summer could accept 50 children, and 32 during the winter. At the end of 1934, for example, there were 31 children in the hospital, of whom 13 were from poor families and did not pay anything towards their expenses. The Sanatorium received a subsidy from the Ministry of Social Policy and Health, and also from the Save the Children Fund, and also other donations and gifts, but this was not enough for its maintenance, so Dr. Katherine MacPhail had to engage constantly in fund-raising. Among other things, on October 14th, 1935, Katherine sent to the *ban* of the Danube District a detailed and very interesting letter, in which she gave a report on the first year of work in the sanatorium, and also a financial report, with a request for financial help. This was the first report on the work of the sanatorium, during which 68 patients had been treated in the hospital, and 45 as out-patients, in the first instance for tuberculosis of the bones and joints. The hospital ended this year with a deficit of 150,000 dinars, so Dr. MacPhail requested the *ban* to approve this sum as an annual grant from the local budget for 1936-37 on condition that the hospital reserved ten free beds for poor children from the Danube District. This request of Katherine's proved fruitful. In the same document found in the archives of Vojvodina there was a note from an authorised official stating that the *ban* had ordered that all the outstanding debts of the hospital should be paid. At the same time the grant from the Danube District was increased to 150,000 dinars a year, instead of the current payment of 50,000 dinars. Other people took action on behalf of the hospital too, notably Dr. Branko Manojlović, then working as a village doctor in Sremska Kamenica, a great friend of Katherine's, and collaborator in the work of the sanatorium. In October 1935 he published a long article in the Novi Sad local paper *Dan* (To-day), in which he wrote:

"This hospital every year saves at least fifty children in our area from the unhappy fate of becoming cripples. There is no other hospital of this type in our area at all, and none in the whole country except the one in Kraljevica. The hospital has got into difficulties because it is supporting a large number of children from poor families. Its director, Dr. MacPhail has not had the heart to send these poor children away from her institution, even when she has exhausted her own resources and those from the local grant (she has a subsidy from the Danube District and from the Ministry of Social Policy and Health, which does not exceed 50,000 dinars per annum). This institution is indeed most essential for these children, since they must become capable in some way in order to support themselves and not become beggars. The hospital was founded for them in the first instance, and if it can serve them it indeed fulfills a very significant social purpose. The hospital in Sremska Kamenica is a gift to our people, the gift of a Scottish doctor, who has spent nearly two decades among our people, and who, as a doctor, has seen what is most lacking, and what is most needed. Through this hospital, and the work and love she and her English sisters and nurses have shown our small cripples, we do indeed see a truly unselfish love for our people, something which in our present materialistic age cannot easily be understood."

Dr. Manojlović then appealed for help for the sanatorium, suggesting various ways in which this could be given: "And our society could give more help to this institution, as well as those English benefactors whose names we see above some of the beds of our small patients. So far there is not a single one of our names to be seen there. This institution will welcome small contributions from less well off people as well. The newspaper *Dan* will take on the task of collecting contributions, and the names of contributors will be published."

There were indeed some beds in the hospital dedicated to deserving benefactors. For instance there was a bed dedicated to Elsie Cameron Corbett, then one to Eglantyne Jebb, one to John Frothingham and one to Lilian Vidaković.[72] This was one way of attracting donors to the hospital, and also of expressing permanent gratitude for their help; probably Dr. Manojlović had this in mind when he wrote the article cited above.

Dr. Branko Manojlović established very cordial and friendly relations with the sanatorium, which in time became an integral part of Sremska Kamenica and from time to time he came himself to work in the hospital and treat its children. Similarly, once a week one of the sisters would go from the sanatorium to the village to help him in his weekly out-patient clinic for children. This co-operation and friendship lasted for many years, throughout the time of Katherine's residence in Sremska Kamenica.

Queen Maria, as patroness of the hospital, in spite of her own considerable troubles, remained a great friend of the sanatorium and maintained a regular interest in the work and problems of the hospital. At the very beginning of its work, she gave the sanatorium 100,000 dinars (about £ 500.00), as her personal contribution; in addition she regularly gave 10,000 dinars to the hospital funds, as well as from time to time sending presents for the children. At the beginning of October 1935 Queen Maria paid an official visit to the sanatorium during which, accompanied by Dr. Katherine MacPhail and Dr. Svetislav Stojanović (Figs. 69) she visited the small patients and gave them presents. This was a great event for the hospital and for Sremska Kamenica, which was talked about for a long time. According to an eye-witness account, Queen Maria and her suite came from Belgrade by car without any special security, and the Queen greeted everybody and showed herself to be a very pleasant person. The protection of Queen Maria and other members of the court were clearly exceptionally useful for Katherine and her work. The fact that she had "very good relations with the court", as one contemporary remarked, opened many doors, and helped to solve many problems that would otherwise have been insoluble.

One of her "highly-placed connections" at the court was Princess Olga, [73] with whom Katherine had very cordial relations right from the day the princess came to Belgrade; Katherine was drawn to her by the so-called "British connection", and she and her sons had frequently visited the Children's Hospital in Belgrade, and this friendly relationship continued when the hospital moved to Sremska Kamenica, where Princess Olga and her sons were frequent guests. One such visit Katherine recalled with particular pleasure. At a meeting with the British Ambassador in Belgrade, the latter told her, as if by chance, that on a certain day Princess Olga would come to Kamenica with her lady-in-waiting, Mme Olga Lozanić, to visit the hospital, and that they planned to arrive about 12 o'clock. Katherine at once asked whether they intended to have lunch in a hotel in Novi Sad, to which the ambassador replied that they did not, but that they wished to have lunch with her in her villa. As Katherine lived very simply, she did not have at home the means of entertaining such highly placed guests; so she was very confused and frightened, and again tried to dissuade the ambassador from this idea, saying that it would be much better for them to have lunch somewhere in Novi Sad. However the ambassador insisted that they wished to have lunch with her, and Katherine, realising that she had no choice, agreed to be hostess. Fortunately at that time she had a Russian cook, whom she begged to give all she could on this occasion; and the cook, realising that this was an important task, prepared an exceptionally fine *borschtch* (Russian thick soup), asparagus from Katherine's garden, and *Vienna schnitzel* (breaded veal cutlet), so that the lunch, accompanied by the famous local Kamenica wine, passed in a very pleasant atmosphere, exceeding all expectations. After lunch they all sat on the terrace over coffee until half-past three, when they moved over to the hospital, where the Mayor of Novi Sad and his wife, and the staff of the hospital, officially welcomed the high guest. Princess Olga went round the hospital and gave presents to all the small patients who, naturally, were more than delighted by the visit and everything about the event.

At the end of 1936 an official report of the first two years of the hospital work was published in English and Serbian, [74] and the activity of the sanatorium was described in detail, with a number of photographs. According to present-day standards, the number of the hospital staff was astonishingly small for such an institution. The medical superintendent was Dr. Katherine MacPhail; the visiting surgeon Dr. Svetislav Stojanović, a specialist from the General State Hospital in Belgrade; the matron was Miss Agnes Hardie, and the secretary Miss Alice Murphy; there were also two sisters and five nurses, and a teacher, all Yugoslavs. And that was all, apart from some other helpers.

Dr. Svetislav Stojanović (Figs. 69), a colleague and friend of Katherine's from her Belgrade days, came once a week, every Thursday, when he made visits, performed operations, and also out patient examinations. In fact that was the only out-patients day, as can be seen from the report: "Besides the work of the Hospital, we hold an out-patients once weekly where we see our old cases from time to time after they have returned home, and examine other cases either for admission or for treatment as visiting cases." According to the recollections of Svetislav Novaković, known as Šajnović, from Sremska Kamenica, one of the helpers working in the hospital at that time, Dr. Stojanović often came with his French wife Germaine, and as they both liked grilled meat, on Thursday Šajnović usually grilled ćevapčići (small grilled meatballs somewhat lengthened, made from minced meat, which is a local specialty) on vine shoots, at which he was a great expert. According to Šajnović Dr. MacPhail also was fond of ćevapčići and often asked him to make them for her guests, most often for those from Britain. On these occasions she also took pleasure in drinking a glass or two of wine. Vasa Srdić liked his ćevapčići too, and was a frequent guest.

As the report states: "During these two years the Hospital has been able to show results which have fully justified its existence, though the scope of work has been restricted through the limited number of beds." The sanatorium began its work with 32 beds; by the spring of 1936 there were 46, and plans were made to increase the number to 100, since the pressure of patients continually increased. "Unfortunately", the report says, "there is never enough room for them all in our Hospital and many are turned away, denied the chance of becoming the straightened happy children we ultimately send home." During this two-year period 115 patients were treated in the hospital as inpatients, and a further 160 as out-patients. The number of 115 inpatients was relatively small for a period of two years, but it must be borne in mind that these were patients who, because of the nature of their illness, had to stay a long time in hospital (23 even spent between 12 and 24 months there). The greatest number were those suffering from tuberculosis of the hips, spine, and knees; in addition there were children suffering from various other diseases of the bones and joints; so in fact it was a question of a real children's orthopaedic hospital; as such it was the first and only one in Vojvodina and the surrounding area. During that time 25 operations were performed, 194 punctures, 84 plasters applied, and 113 X-ray photos taken, which was certainly an admirable achievement. Fifty-two patients were released from the hospital as cured, 12 in an improved physical condition, and 7 in the same state, sent home for various reasons soon after they were admitted, while others remained for further treatment. According to this report, the hospital in Sremska Kamenica "has been built for the purpose of treating children suffering from bone tuberculosis, and fills a gap in the scheme the State is trying to undertake in the general fight against tuberculosis which is a veritable scourge in this country." This treatment of tuberculosis of the bones and joints, or osteo-articular tuberculosis (abbreviated to OAT), which was then carried out in the sanatorium in Sremska Kamenica, was very contemporary and on a world-class level; Dr. Katherine MacPhail was specially concerned about this, and she had previously visited some of the best known European centres for the treatment of OAT. At that time so-called "open-air hospitals" were established all over the Great Britain, and, as it was published in *The World's Children* in February 1938, "she confessed that in planning it she had in mind such institutions as the Lord Mayor Treloar Homes at Alton, the Agnes Hunt Hospital at Oswestry, and Dr. Rollier's Clinic at Leysin. The latter two, at any rate, started with only a few beds and were now world-famous." [75] Dr. A. Rollier in his Clinic at Leysin in the Swiss Alps, since 1904, had treated OAT by means of heliotherapy in areas with a continental mountain climate, combining this therapy with the appropriate training of those confined to bed for longer periods. In Sremska Kamenica Dr. Katherine MacPhail followed strictly the method and pattern of treatment used by Dr. Rollier, which she described in a paper written at the invitation of the *Medical Review*, a journal of the Medical Association of Vojvodina, which appeared in Novi Sad in 1960.[76] There she stated that after visiting a number of well-known European institutions for the treatment of OAT, she "had proceeded to open a similar institution on the hills of Fruška Gora at Sremska Kamenica, in a place with maximum exposure to sunshine, and at the same time a constant breeze of clean fresh air from the hills of Fruška Gora." (Figs. 70 – 73) The fact that this place was not chosen by chance, but after detailed investigation, is clear from the following information in the same article: "Because of its geographical situation, Sremska Kamenica has a moderate Pannonian climate. This is characterised by moderately hot summers and moderately cold winters, and also a small quantity of rainfall. During winter the cold is increased by the eastern wind, which does not appear very often or last very long, but can be extremely strong. From information supplied (by Dr. Manojlović in Sremska Kamenica), the average annual temperature is 12°

centigrade, the average maximum temperature 16.5° and the average minimum 7.5°. The highest summer temperature in July is 38°, the lowest winter temperature rarely less than minus 15°. The hottest month is July, with an average temperature of 23°, and the coldest month is January, with an average temperature of 0.5°. The average annual rainfall is 596 mm, rain falls mainly during the spring months. Fog rarely occurs in Sremska Kamenica, and when it does appear it does not reach as far as the hospital. During the period of greatest heat, which occurs in the Pannonian plain, [77] Kamenica always enjoys a current of fresh forest air from Fruška Gora, which is the main climate characteristic of this region. A sufficient amount of sun and the constant breeze provide the best possible conditions for our patients with tuberculosis of the bones and joints." This correct estimate of the geographical and climate conditions suitable for such institutions is undoubtedly confirmed by the subsequent erection of a large Institute for Tuberculosis in Vojvodina on an adjacent hill, in the immediate vicinity of the Anglo-Yugoslav hospital, which was opened in 1960.

The methods of treatment for tuberculosis of the bones and joints at that time, before the discovery of antibiotics and anti-tubercular drugs, consisted mainly of increasing the patient's resistance and included: a specific diet and hygienic regime (good food, rest, quiet, cleanliness), aero-therapy, sun-therapy (natural and artificial) and immobilisation, together with minor surgical interventions.

One of the main elements in the treatment was exposure to the sun (heliotherapy) and fresh air (aero-therapy), about which Dr. Katherine MacPhail remarked: "In order to obtain the best and widest results of sun and air therapy, the children on their arrival in hospital were immediately freed from their plaster appliances and bandages which cover the greater part of their bodies; then, released from these devices we can expose them to the pleasant and refreshing influence of the sun and fresh air, immobilising them in special light extension devices, or by placing them in open linen vests which were fastened to the sides of the hospital beds. During the treatment they are exposed to specific periods of heliotherapy in accordance with Rollier's principles and practice. On fine days the patients are exposed to the influence of fresh air on special terraces, and on very hot days the patients were sleeping out all night exposed to the constant breeze from the hills of Fruška Gora, and indoors in the heat of the day, having their sun treatment in the early morning, over by 9.30 a.m. (Figs. 70 – 74). On days when there is no sun, and during the winter, artificial heliotherapy is used, with the help of a quartz apparatus for both general and local application; apart from the individual treatment the collective treatment of all the patients in a single room was also possible using a special device for collective quartz-treatment." [78]

Much attention was paid to good, nourishing food, and the children had to take regular doses of cod-liver oil, which was not very popular with them, but was extremely important, and at that time the main source of vitamin D, which was essential for strengthening bones and preventing rickets. Cod-liver oil was obtained in barrels, and, as a contemporary remarked, "the entire hospital smelt of cod-liver oil." Similarly, great attention was paid to the children's cleanliness and hygiene, and to the good order and cleanliness in the hospital. All the visitors were fascinated by the tidiness of the small patients, and of the hospital itself. One of the visitors made the following comment: "The children were bathed every day, and neither their finger nails or their toenails were ever black." Food was served punctually, and every afternoon, between one and three o'clock they had to sleep, "and any child who didn't sleep had to keep his eyes shut." Those most responsible for the exceptional state of cleanliness and order in the hospital were Agnes Hardie, the Matron (Fig. 69), and her closest colleagues, Sister Milka Batić (Fig. 77) and Sister Anica Škvorc, who worked in close agreement with the other members of the staff, so that the work was accomplished smoothly and without problems. The matron, "Miss Hardy", as they all called her, had a particularly important role; Katherine had a very high opinion of her and considered her faultless both in her work and her understanding of the children. "I never met a better organiser, nor anyone with more sympathy and understanding," said Dr. Katherine MacPhail, in acknowledgement of Agnes Hardie and her devoted work.

One of the most important and, as it was considered, integral aspects of the treatment during a long-time stay in the hospital was the children's schooling. There was a school within the framework of the hospital, which was a branch of the local elementary school at Sremska Kamenica, in which the hospital always had its own separate teacher. All children of school age had lessons every day between 8 a.m. and 12 noon, and after this they had lunch. When the weather was fine they had lessons on the terrace; the children were carried out there at the beginning of the lessons, and in bad weather they were taught in their rooms. They had four hours of teaching each day, and worked according to the official standard programme for elementary schools; the children were examined and given marks as they were in other schools, and at the end of the year they obtained a certificate from the elementary school at Sremska Kamenica. In fact every aspect of life in the sanatorium was conducted according to the rules of school life; the time-table of the hospital was arranged in accordance with the time-table of the daily lessons; this was very important, since the regular teaching in the hospital assured an exemplary state of order, which was very useful for the medical treatment. The children liked the school and it was for them a kind of entertainment; there was no question of anyone refusing to attend school. Dr. Katherine MacPhail would often come to the lessons, encourage the children, give them a pencil or some other small thing they had dropped, since all the children were in bed (Fig. 75). For the smaller children, under school age, a kindergarten was organised where they learnt songs and poems with their nurses and teachers. In addition, as a vitally important part of occupational therapy, "they all had, large and small, a course in artistic drawing, painting and handiwork, which was undertaken as an experiment by a voluntary worker, who had experience in such work, along the lines of the Čižek School in Vienna, [79] and this proved a great interest to the children. Besides occupying them, this showed that many of them had real artistic talent which if cultivated, might prove useful to many of them in their sometimes forcibly restricted lives." (Fig. 76) As the great majority of children were of Orthodox religion once a week an Orthodox priest from the village came to give them religious instruction. There was also a library in the hospital, with plenty of school books and books for children; they also had piles of toys which they often received as presents from visitors on festive occasions. A present-day villager, then aged ten, recalls that the small patients often threw their toys from the terrace where they were lying in the sun, and then he and other children from the village would come up secretly and collect the abandoned toys, which were of great benefit to them. For the children each day was filled with work, study and entertainment, so that they were contented and happy, as was obvious to all the visitors. To the great pleasure of the small patients, it often happened that on various festive occasions they had special performances. The most important of these took place in accordance with the express wish of Queen Maria on January 19th every year, which was the birthday of her second son Tomislav. That day a large group of performing artists always came from Belgrade to entertain the children; this was a great event, to which the children looked forward for months ahead. There was always a big Christmas celebration organised in the hospital, when the children and members of the staff received many presents; and according to a tradition dating from the Belgrade days, and in the spirit of Anglo – Serbian friendship, Christmas was celebrated on both the Christmas dates, December 25th and January 7th.

"The results of the treatment were satisfactory and encouraging, especially at a time when not much was expected from medical treatment," said Dr. Svetislav Stojanović, the hospital's surgeon, speaking at the first Yugoslav Pediatric Congress held in Belgrade in 1937; he produced statistical evidence, and the results of treatment in the sanatorium for the first three years of its work, from September 1934 to September 1937. During that period, 458 children of both sexes were treated, either in the hospital or as out patients, from the age of one to thirteen years. The average period of treatment was two years and three months, which explains the relatively small number of patients treated, many of whom returned home healthy and happy, with strengthened limbs, able to take their place with their brothers and sisters in school and play. Most of the patients successfully treated for tuberculosis of the bones and joints were serious cases, with deformities, with festering collections and fistulas, but 80 – 82 % of these patients were sent home cured. (Figs. 77 and 78)

Undoubtedly the sanatorium at Sremska Kamenica functioned very successfully at that time, and was a prestigious institution from every point of view. This was certainly due to the staff of the hospital, which worked with great devotion and efficiency, as well as to Dr. Katherine MacPhail herself. Miss Agnes Hardie, the Matron, was responsible for the internal organisation, a task that she undoubtedly performed with great commitment and effectiveness, about which Katherine wrote: "There was always a qualified person responsible for supervising the hospital staff and their work. The authority of the most senior sister, the supervision and continual instruction of the medical personnel ensured both the care of the patients and the good relationship of the staff, which guaranteed the successful work of the hospital." According to the evidence of contemporaries, Agnes Hardie was a very energetic person, who, as one of the former workers in the hospital said, was "God and stick" (a Serbian expression meaning to be the sole ruler) in the hospital, where she lived and occupied herself with everything. Most of the staff lived in the hospital itself, in a subsidiary building in the courtyard and in a building on the other side of the road, where the hospital garage occupied the ground floor; it now bears the house number 56. In the building in the courtyard there was a communal dining room where they all had dinner together (Fig. 99). The hospital provided food for all the staff, and it was the custom for them all to gather together round a large dining table for their communal lunch as soon as the children had settled down for their afternoon rest. Katherine then served them all with their food, and, as a contemporary remarked, she gave generous platefuls, and "she was not miserly in that." The local cooks prepared the food, so that they had mainly local dishes from Vojvodina, which Katherine liked. All the staff, without exception, had a very high respect and regard for Dr. MacPhail, who behaved towards them with great consideration and understanding. "She was quiet, gentle and modest and never raised her voice," according to one of her contemporaries, "she was very pleasant to her staff and behaved in a friendly way." From everybody she demanded conscientious and orderly work, and in working hours there was strict discipline, but during free time she behaved to everybody in a cordial and amiable way. When the nurses went to Novi Sad in their free time, either for shopping or to go to the theatre, whenever it was possible they had a car to take them there. The hospital had a car at its disposal driven by the permanent and faithful driver Vasilj, who brought provisions and other necessary things and acted as Katherine's chauffeur, and if necessary drove members of the staff. The affection which everybody in the hospital felt for their doctor is clear from an episode from those times which Katherine later recalled with pleasure. On the occasion of the silver jubilee of King George VI, Katherine and Agnes Hardie and Alice Murphy were invited to a formal function in the British Embassy in Belgrade; when they returned to the hospital, to their great surprise, they found the staff gathered together, who invited them to take part in a celebration which they had arranged for this occasion. "We were invited to eat delicious meat – a kid roasted on a spit behind the garage with wine to toast the King. Then Dobrosav, our handyman, stepped out playing the *gajde* (a sort of bagpipe), which he had speedily made out of the skin of the kid we were eating; he was followed by a neighbour from the farm next door who carried a long pole topped by a bunch of syringa and declaimed a long poem in Serbian composed by him in honour of the occasion. So we had two equally enjoyable celebrations."

Miss Alice Murphy (Fig. 50) was responsible for the financial and administrative aspect of the hospital's work; she was clearly very skilled at this, and Katherine had great confidence in her. About this she said: "Miss Alice Murphy, the hospital secretary, worked out the complicated system of payments. Her sincere feeling for and interest in the children and their parents, her patience when difficulties arose contributed much to keep the hospital financially stable. The rational purchase and distribution of food did much to keep the daily expenditure within reasonable limits." The collection of money and daily expenditure certainly gave rise to problems and required great skill. In this task Vasa Srdić, an old friend of the hospital who managed a model estate in Temerin, which included agriculture and fruit growing, and the care of livestock, was of great help, as he supplied the sanatorium at Sremska Kamenica with these agricultural products. However, although the hospital was often in financial difficulties, some extra food was always prepared, especially hot soup, which was distributed to homeless people and day-labourers in the neighbourhood, who would gather together at the hospital, sitting on benches in front of the kitchen, waiting for their usual rations.

The annual cost of maintaining the hospital amounted to 500,000 dinars, and the only permanent and secure source of income were the annual grants from the Ministry of Social Policy and Health (50,000 dinars) and of the Danube District Authorities (150,000 dinars). The difference between these sums and the total needed, i.e. 300,000 dinars, had to be obtained from the parents of the sick children who were able to pay, various hospitals funds, and contributions from private individuals in the country and abroad. The Belgrade Municipality paid a seventy per cent maintenance grant for each poor child coming from Belgrade; then insurance societies, the Railway Worker's Fund, and various other societies paid for children whom they sent; but quite a large number of poor children who did not belong to any of these categories had to be paid for by the hospital itself, which was not easy to guarantee. The Anglo-American Yugoslav Club in Belgrade also helped by giving their premises and assisting in the hospital's annual sale, and also the members of the Belgrade Auto-Club who had been organising yearly concerts on the behalf of Katherine's sanatorium. Help from abroad gradually decreased until only the Save the Children Fund continued to make an annual contribution of £ 480.00 (about 10,000 dinars); in addition occasional gifts were received from time to time. It happened that at the beginning of 1939 Princess Olga invited Katherine to tea, and on that occasion gave her a cheque for £ 250.00 (about 5,000 dinars), which was a pleasant surprise; she explained that this was money raised at a fund-raising concert in London in aid of the sanatorium, organised by her sister Marina, Duchess of

Kent. [73] Since Queen Maria, the official patroness of the hospital, began to suffer from ill-health at this time and often travelled abroad for treatment, and was in fact living in Great Britain from 1938 onwards, H.R.H. Princess Olga more or less took over her role towards Katherine and her sanatorium. Princess Olga loved children and had a high regard for Katherine and her work and helped her whenever she could; she frequently came to Sremska Kamenica on unofficial visits, bringing her own children with her, and always some presents for the small patients.

As the sanatorium at Sremska Kamenica was not far from Belgrade, and situated in the attractive region of Fruška Gora, various visitors came quite frequently, including those sent by the British Embassy (Fig. 79). One such caller, a young man named Michael Tippett, according to Elspeth Biggs, was unlucky enough to fall ill with scarlet fever while he was there, and Katherine had to keep him in her children's hospital, and isolate him and nurse him in a separate room and looked after him until he recovered. He felt very awkward about this and kept apologising, but he was of course very grateful. Later he became a famous conductor and composer, well-known throughout the world. "I wonder if he remembers that?" wrote Elspeth from St Andrews in 1987. "He was here a few months ago, as Sir Michael Tippett, conducting one of his own symphonies with the Scottish Chamber Orchestra." (see Appendix 1).

The members of the Dušmanić family in Belgrade were frequent guests at Kamenica; Katherine had with them a long-lasting friendship. Constance "Con" Dušmanić, a Scot married to a Serbian officer, [80] was a close friend of Katherine's from the time of Salonica Front and her Belgrade days; and she and her four children were among her most frequent visitors, and they spent nearly every Christmas together in the hospital. They all called Katherine "Doc" and treated her as one of their family. Constance's children, especially her daughter Dana Dušmanić (later Stanković), had happy memories of these visits; she later recalled how as children they had made piles of paper hats every Christmas and taken them to the hospital, together with packets of sweets for the small patients. Another frequent guest was Katherine's old friend from the Salonica Front, Dr. Miloš "Miša" Ćirić, who was then working in Novi Sad as a specialist for lung diseases. They often visited each other, and on these occasions Dr. Ćirić also brought his children. His son Milan Ćirić remembers these visits to the sanatorium at Sremska Kamenica, where he used to go as a child. While his father was drinking tea and talking to Dr. MacPhail, he would run around the courtyard and play with the children; the main attraction, as he recalls, was the hospital wheel-barrow. Miša Ćirić helped Katherine whenever he could and wherever it was necessary. It so happened that at the end of 1935, when the hospital was in financial difficulties, he did a great deal to solve this problem. First of all he arranged that the Anti-tuberculosis League of the Danube District should allot the hospital a significant sum of money by way of immediate help; this did not give rise to any great difficulties since the president of the League

140

was Dr. Jovan Popović, the vice-president Dr. Miloš Ćirić and the secretary and treasurer Mr. Dejan Lazić. Dr. Jovan Popović, who was then deputy director of the Hygiene Institute in Novi Sad, was a great friend of Dr. Miloš Ćirić from the time of the Salonica Front; he also had a great regard for Dr. Katherine MacPhail and her work, and he also helped her whenever he could. According to Mr. Dejan Lazić Dr. Ćirić and Dr. Popović managed, through their influence, to arrange that the grant from the Danube District should be increased from 50,000 dinars to 150,000 dinars per year from the beginning of the financial year 1936-37; this significantly improved the financial position of the hospital. In addition, there was a permanent link between the Hygiene Institute in Novi Sad and the sanatorium, since the Hygiene Institute in Novi Sad kept records of all the tubercular patients; so they often came to the sanatorium, at first Dr. Jovan Popović and Mr. Dejan Lazić together, then later Mr. Lazić by himself; since he was an official of the Hygiene Institute, through these frequent contacts he had the opportunity to get to know the situation in the hospital at close quarters, and also Dr. MacPhail herself, about whom he said: "Dr. MacPhail is a lady in the best sense of that word: dignified, but not proud and unapproachable, full of love towards the children and sympathy for their sufferings, a mother and older sister to all the staff, from whom she required discipline regarding the children and their prescribed medical treatment. She observed everything, but never raised her voice, even when some mistake had been made. It really was a large family, filled with love and respect towards their work and duties. Dr. MacPhail dressed well, but not luxuriously. Everything about her suggested modesty, ease of approach, and frankness." According to the recollections of yet another contemporary from this time (1937), Katherine was "short in stature, about 5 feet 6 inches tall, quite thin, with broad hips, a long mild face, and short dark hair combed to one side (Fig. 80). She dressed modestly, mainly in a sporting style, and usually wore dark clothes. She was always kind, frank and approachable. She spoke Serbian well, but with a definite foreign accent; however she sometimes had difficulties in talking to people, because she was hard of hearing." Her deafness was the result of the typhus she had suffered in 1915, and this gradually got worse over the years, which caused her considerable difficulty.

Katherine lived in her villa, which was about 1.2 miles from the hospital; she usually came on foot, along a field path which, of course, was not paved, and which still exists; "she walked briskly, and liked to walk," according to one of her contemporaries. However, Katherine spent most of her time in the hospital, where she had her meals with the other members of staff, and where she stayed until late in the evening. She had a nice office on the ground floor of the right wing, which had its own door leading directly from the courtyard. It was a large room, with fine furniture. "There she received official visitors, and friends who came to see her," and during the rest periods she would sometimes walk in the vineyard or in the orchard below the hospital. The villa in which she lived was in an outlying part of the village, which was at that time quite empty; the house was

141

spacious, but simply furnished. On the side facing the courtyard she had a fine terrace, facing west, with beautiful views of Fruška Gora, the hill slopes of which were covered with vineyards and orchards; her hospital could be seen at the top of the hill (Fig. 81), and also the Danube with small islands. Katherine would often sit on this verandah, enjoying the truly lovely view of the sun setting over the Danube. The courtyard was spacious, and had a well; also there was a separate building where Lacika lived, a worker who looked after the small garden in the courtyard, and also the hospital park and vineyard. When she had time Katherine would relax in this courtyard (Fig. 82), and she derived much amusement from her two dogs, of which she was very fond (Fig. 83). But these dogs were not just for amusement, they also provided protection for Katherine, especially late in the evening, when it was her custom to return home from the hospital.

Dr. Katherine MacPhail was extremely popular and well liked in Sremska Kamenica, and today many of the older inhabitants of the village remember her and speak of her with great respect. As she was frank and approachable, she enjoyed contact with people, and made many friends and acquaintances among the people of the village. She accepted invitations and visited the homes of the peasants on various festive occasions, especially when they had a *slava*; she would then drink a glass of *rakija* (a strong brandy made from various fruits, most often from plums, when it is called *shlivovitza*) or wine from the Fruška Gora vineyards; she also liked the local food. She took part in a variety of village activities, particularly in the work of the Red Cross in Sremska Kamenica. Mrs. Milica Ćirić remembers a course for the first aid assistants in the village organised by the tireless Dr. Branko Manojlović where she acted as secretary and in which "Doktoritsa MacPhail", as everyone in the village called her, also took part. In Novi Sad at that time there was a so-called "Anglo-American Yugoslav Club" which was founded in 1931, [81] and in whose activities Katherine took an active part, together with her old friends Darinka Grujić and Vasa Srdić, who were also members of this club; it was connected in some way with the club of the same name in Belgrade, of which Katherine had indeed been one of the founders.

During these years Katherine often went to Belgrade, where she had a small flat in the centre of the town. She also regularly visited Great Britain, where she would go to see her family, with whom she was in constant contact, and also old friends who helped her in her work. As Katherine and her work were well known in Great Britain, on these occasions she was almost always invited to visit various societies and institutions and talk about her work. This is quite clear from an article in the journal of the SCF in February 1938, which reports that Dr. Katherine MacPhail attended a meeting of the Yugoslav Society of Great Britain on January 3rd, 1938, where she gave a lecture on the work of the sanatorium in Sremska Kamenica. The chairman of the meeting was none other than Dr. Louise McIlroy, Katherine's old friend from her days in Glasgow and at the Salonica Front, where she was then the head doctor of one of the Scottish Women's Hospitals, stationed first in France, then in Salonica, where Katherine's younger sister Isabel worked for a time; later she became professor of Obstetrics and Gynaecology at the Royal Free Hospital School of Medicine for Women in London. In introducing Katherine, Dr. McIlroy said: "At a time when there were a great many neglected children in Serbia, she took care of many of them and she developed one of the greatest pieces of work that any man or woman has ever done in that land. We are extremely proud of what she had done." After Katherine's lecture, accompanied by many slides Miss Nina Boyle, the novelist – who was in the audience – remarked after the lights had gone up again: "It is a perfectly wonderful work", one in which the Save the Children Fund (she spoke as a member of the Council) was proud to have a part. "We congratulate Dr. MacPhail on her success and on her heroic efforts to save these children" said Miss Boyle – and she added that she was glad to notice, over the portico of the Hospital, the emblem of the Bambino, which was the symbol of the Save the Children Fund all over the world. And in bringing the meeting to a close Dr. McIlroy concluded: "I feel there it is something far more than medical work that Dr. MacPhail is doing. She is doing real service in the cause of peace and friendship between Yugoslavia and Great Britain. She is keeping the British flag flying in that land through devoted humanitarian service." [75]

These were enjoyable and peaceful years for Katherine, filled with devoted work and successful achievements. Her sanatorium functioned faultlessly, and represented a real oasis, surrounded by vineyards and orchards (Fig. 84), which resounded with the joy and merriment of children who felt themselves to be in safe hands, and who were gradually returning to life. Katherine loved children; above all she understood sick children and concern for them filled her life with joy and contentment. She was happy and she felt that these years at Kamenica were a "golden age" in her life and work.

Unfortunately heavy war clouds, which were once more beginning to hover over Europe, also began to threaten this oasis of peace, joy and happiness with a feeling of the coming menace. In the annual report of the Save the Children Fund for 1939-40 Katherine said: "Things are difficult, but we are trying to carry on as normally as possible." However she was aware that, from the military point of view, the sanatorium was in an extremely unsatisfactory, exposed position, in the first line of defence if an enemy attack should come from the north, which was by far the most likely possibility. Moreover throughout the autumn and winter of 1940, the Army had been digging trenches and gun emplacements on the banks of the Danube and all round the countryside; in the immediate vicinity of the hospital some twenty of these fortified positions were established, which must have caused great alarm and, naturally, greatly increased Katherine's anxiety for her hospital and her small patients. For this reason she several times during these months consulted with the appropriate authorities in the hope of finding a solution. In the summer of 1940 the army health authorities decided that, in the event of war, they would take over the sanatorium and turn it into a military hospital for orthopaedic cases, but later they abandoned this idea, as they considered the hospital inadequately secure for this purpose. Some months before the outbreak of war, the Ministry of Health worked out a plan for evacuating children from potentially dangerous areas; however, there was clearly considerable confusion with regard to this, and Katherine was unable to obtain any clear answer to questions about it. She later described this situation in the following words: "We had been told that our children were to be evacuated to one of the health resorts in the mountains. This in the end was reserved for military purposes and we were then told that they would be sent to a convalescent home in the interior near Nish. This was then found impossible, it being wanted for children evacuated from the neighbouring district. Ultimately the authorities could not give me any advice, as they had not made any provisions for the children. So after consulting them several times I and our visiting surgeon decided to evacuate the children to their own homes and we advised the parents to take them into the villages in the mountains." [82] This was quite a difficult time for Katherine, when the burden of responsibility for the children in the hospital clearly weighed heavily upon her. "These weeks of indecision (as to what to do) lay like a load on my heart", wrote Katherine later.

However, in spite of the severe strain and considerable uncertainty, the sanatorium continued to function normally, and on January 19th, 1941 there was the usual hospital performance on the occasion of Prince Tomislav's birthday, which remained vivid in Katherine's memory, probably because of the circumstances in which it took place, and because it was the last event of this kind. A year later, when she was already in Great Britain, Katherine described this occasion in detail, and quite nostalgically: "It was a day of bitter, freezing wind and heavy snow. The hospital was far out in the country and it seemed impossible that any one could reach us in such a blizzard. The children were full of fear that the artists would not be able to come, but to the joy of everyone, a telephone message came through in the early morning to say that all were coming and that everything was to be ready. Then the excitement began. At the end of the largest ward a stage was erected with decorations, flags and curtains, like a real theatre stage. Then a piano appeared, brought in a military lorry by ten stalwart soldiers, while outside a snow plough drawn by great horned oxen cleared the road mounting the hill to the hospital. All day the nurses and staff worked to get ready. The children had to be dressed in their best jumpers and everyone arranged comfortably in their places, so that each could get a good view of the stage – no easy task, as many of them were fixed in their beds or were in plaster of Paris, and only a few could sit up. However, everyone was soon comfortably settled: at the back, the spine cases turned over and propped themselves up on their elbows; in the middle, the hip cases lying down; and in the front, all the knee cases sitting in a row. Excited whispers came from the children. Djura, our oldest hip case, was heard to whisper to his neighbour: 'Matron says, Spines at the back, hips in front. *Hvala Bogu* (Thank God) I'm a hip.' At last, all were settled, fifty eager and excited children. As three o'clock came near, guests began to arrive in cars, sleighs and even lorries, all thankful to get into the warmth from the blizzard outside. The Queen's lady-in-waiting arrived in good time with an attendant armed with a shovel, in case her car should get stuck in a snowdrift. She brought gifts of sweets for each patient as a birthday remembrance from Prince Tomislav. Then came the artists, and soon the show began. The troupe of artists were a strange collection of people, old and young, and the head of the party a wonder and delight to all the children. To them he was the greatest magician of all, for does he not first of all produce a grand piano and then the nimble-fingered Kapellmeister of the Royal Guards Band to play for them? And then beautiful ballerinas in shimmering dresses, gypsies playing sweet-toned zithers, lithe gymnasts twisting and turning in wonderful rhythm, acrobats who jump to the ceiling and then tie themselves into knots? Then comes a magician who brings hot cakes out of an empty pan and lovely white doves out of an old hat; next an old gardener who makes beautiful bird calls, the hoot of the owl and the cooing of the wood pigeon. Each in turn enthralls the children who sit quiet as mice, aches and pains forgotten. The show lasts two hours, all too fleeting. If only it would go on all night! If only there could be three birthdays instead of one each year! But now comes the last but the most beloved of them all, *'Chiro'*, the ventriloquist doll, who sings to them and calls them each by name. More battered every year, he always comes back. The concert would not be complete without him. The concert ends with his being packed away in his wooden box screaming at the pitch of his voice, 'I want to stay here, I don't want to go home'. Then the head of this wonderful band of artists tells the children some stories and he promises them that he will come back next year. At the end, all with one voice unite in 'Three cheers for Prince Tomislav! Long live Queen Maria!' The show is over and the weary artists settle down to well-earned refreshments before starting back on their long, cold journey to Belgrade. The guests depart and the hospital settles down for the night, the children to dream of lovely bird calls, sweet music and the free, easy movements of the gymnasts." [83]

Sadly, the progress of events at the beginning of 1941 obliged Katherine, in view of the hesitations of the government and the uncertainty of the general situation, to take definite measures to evacuate the children and arrange for them more secure accommodation. With great regret, at the end of February and the beginning of March 1941, all the children were placed in plaster casts and sent home; their parents were promised that, if all went well in the end, the children would be returned to the sanatorium as soon as possible. Three weeks before the outbreak of war, all the children were evacuated and the hospital was empty. The subsequent development of events showed how right Katherine had been to take these steps, since later, when a massive mobilisation began and a state of wartime chaos prevailed, it would have been very difficult to send the children home, since for most of them their homes were a considerable distance away.

All the staff were given indefinite leave; the hospital's surgeon Dr. Svetislav Stojanović was called up for military service. The head sister Agnes Hardie, who was on holiday in Great Britain when war broke out between Britain and Germany, had stayed there and volunteered for war service, so that only Katherine and Alice Murphy remained in the hospital, which suddenly become empty. "It was so sad to see the hospital so quiet and empty", Katherine wrote later. However, it did not remain empty for long; a few days after the children and the staff had left, an anti-aircraft battery with eight officers and 120 men was billeted in the hospital grounds and buildings. The situation was clearly becoming increasingly serious, and the British Embassy advised all British subjects, especially women and children, to leave the country as soon as possible and go to Turkey. However, Katherine and Alice Murphy decided to stay in Yugoslavia to the end, in order to show good faith in the people and provide help wherever they could. "Once our responsibility to our children was ended, and as our services were not to be used by the local military authorities, our hopes were to be able to go down to Dalmatia and await the moment when we could organise some work for refugees there or attach ourselves to a military medical unit", explained Katherine later. [82]

Then began long days of waiting and anxiety, about which Katherine wrote later: "The officers of our battery used to come every night to our sitting room and listen to the news from London in Serbian. On their Belgrade station they could only hear news that was allowed by the Germans. The news from London they could believe. How bitter they were in their souls that their country was ready to sign away their freedom! When the pact [84] was signed there was a strange silence in the hospital, not a single officer or man came to listen with us to London. They were ashamed, as were all the Serbs, but still in their hearts, defiant." [82] These were indeed strange days, full of uncertainty, fear and painful forebodings.

The British embassy again demanded that Katherine and Alice Murphy should leave the country as soon as possible, but they were determined to stay: "We felt somehow that if we left we would be abandoning to their fate our friends who believed so much in Britain, and actually as long as we were there the people round about us felt somehow that things must come right", wrote Katherine. "It was on March the 25th that the pact was signed. I went up to Belgrade many times during these days as I wanted to keep in touch with our own Legation and with the few British people left, as many by now had gone. The gloom was indescribable; something seemed to be in the air, nobody knew what, till suddenly on the night of March 26th-27th the *coup d'état* took place." [85]

It so happened that Katherine was in Belgrade that very night; the previous day she had had meetings with her Yugoslav and British friends, with whom she had talked about the situation, the rumours, the possibility of a *coup d'état* and the future development of events, then late in the evening she returned to her small flat in the town which was in the immediate vicinity of the Ministry of War and the Ministry of Internal Affairs. By a trick of fate, or probably because of the nearness of these ministries, during the bombardments of April 6th, 1941 her flat was completely destroyed by a bomb that directly hit the building. That night, as soon as she had fallen asleep, Katherine was awakened by strange sounds: "Suddenly in the stillness of the night I heard the tramp of soldiers, and beneath my window I saw a small gathering of officers and men. At first I did not realise what was afoot until I heard the salute and the signal for action, 'Long live King Peter' and the answer, 'Long live the King'. The sentries guarding the Ministries were then disarmed and a cordon of soldiers were placed across the street thus barring all ways to the Ministries. Quietly and with the swiftness of lightning, heavy field guns, machine guns and small armed tanks were brought out from the courtyard behind the Ministry of War and mounted in the streets facing in all directions, thus isolating the main Ministries, which were quickly taken possession of by the military. During this brief time the Commander of the Royal Guards had been captured, and the Guards regiments surrounded in their barracks. The Royal Palace was surrounded and one by one the Ministers who had played a part in betraying the country by signing the pact were seized and put under arrest. As the officers and men who were taking part in this passed beneath my window they seized each other with wild enthusiasm, kissing each other as free men and beside themselves with joy. Quickly I realised that this was an overthrow of the Government and that a handful of officers and a few picked troops had taken power into their own hands. All night and into the morning young enthusiastic officers guarded the Ministries until they were taken over, tanks decked with the Yugoslav flag paraded the streets; all other traffic, cars, buses, wagons and pedestrians were turned back as they entered the town. Without one drop of blood being shed the change-over had been achieved and by dawn lorries drove through the surprised town distributing leaflets with the declaration of King Peter 'that he had decided to take the Royal power into his own hands' and calling on all citizens and authorities to fulfil their duty to their king and country. He announced that three Regents had resigned and he appealed to the people to rally round the Throne." [82]

Katherine learnt later that the *coup d'état* had been carried out by a group of Air Force officers under General Dušan Simović with the support of the Royal Guards and other Army units. Early in the morning that critical day the young King Peter drove through Belgrade to broadcast to his people. "Serbs, Croats and Slovenes", he proclaimed, "at this moment so grave in the history of my people, I have decided to take the royal power into my own hands. My loyal Army and Navy have at once placed themselves at my disposal and are already carrying out my orders. I appeal to all Serbs, Croats and Slovenes to rally round the throne. Under the present grave circumstances this is the surest way of preserving internal order and external peace. I have charged Army Corps General Dušan

Simović with the formulation of a new Government. With trust in God and the future of Yugoslavia, I appeal to all citizens and all authorities to fulfil their duties to king and country."

In such a situation, so full of exciting and fateful events, there was, of course, no thought of further sleep, and Katherine could scarcely wait for the morning, when she wished to go to the British Embassy to talk to someone there; however, as things turned out, this was no easy task. The streets of Belgrade were already crowded with excited and joyful people who publicly condemned the signing of the Pact, and greeted the young king and freedom. It was the wildest rejoicing that Belgrade had ever seen. The British Embassy, when Katherine finally arrived there, was surrounded by a mass of people who had spontaneously gathered there, and were impatiently waiting to cheer the British ambassador. In the embassy itself there was a celebration. All the staff were gathered together, and quite a lot of people from the neighbourhood. Bottles of champagne were opened to the accompaniment of popping corks, and drunk in large quantities. Everybody congratulated everyone else, and all thought that the British had supported the *coup d'état*. At any rate, if they had not organized it, they had known in advance that it was being prepared, and had given active assistance, through their special services.

The revelling went on all day in Belgrade and throughout the country. The Yugoslavs had chosen to defy Germany even though they knew that the price was high. David Walker, a newspaper correspondent in Belgrade at the time, described the atmosphere there in the following way: "A whole nation laughed and drank and sang in the shadow of its own destruction."

After the celebration and conversation in the embassy and a short walk through the seething Belgrade streets, Katherine returned to Sremska Kamenica, where she also found a different atmosphere. "I returned that day to Kamenica to find our Battery completely transformed, and with these young officers for whom an awful fate was waiting we drank the health of King Peter, Queen Maria his mother, Yugoslavia and Great Britain. The Battery left in a few days to take up a position in the mountains further south, and a young officer in charge of a searchlight company with thirty or forty soldiers remained quartered in hospital."
82

After the enormous excitement, celebration, and outpouring of exuberant joy, which gripped the country on March 27th, there followed difficult days of uncertainty, waiting and conjecture. "The days which followed were days of horrible excitement. Everyone was uncertain what was going to happen, mobilisation was hastened up and information as to what was going on was almost impossible to get;" thus Katherine described the situation. "During the confusion of these last days we packed up the hospital things and made preparations to leave." By that time Katherine obviously realised that the situation was really serious, and that she would have to leave everything behind and go away, so she began intensively to make preparation. The Red Cross

Society had promised to look after the hospital in the event of her departure, naturally as far as they were able to do so; however their headquarters was in Novi Sad, while the hospital was far out in the country on the other side of the Danube. Then she sought permission from the military authorities to travel by car to the frontier, though it was by no means certain that this would be possible. In the British Legation she had been advised that, if she decided to leave by car, she should try to get through to Greece, or else go to the Dalmatian coast, which was what she planned to do, as she hoped that at least that part of the country would be defended, and that she would perhaps be able to stay there and organise some kind of help.

And then, suddenly, it all began. On Sunday, April 6th, 1941, Katherine and Alice Murphy, who had recently been staying in the hospital and sleeping there, saw from the hospital terrace, from which there was a splendid view across the Danube to the plain of Bačka and Novi Sad, the bombardment of Novi Sad aerodrome. Katherine described this in the following words: "On the sixth of April we were awakened by planes flying over the hospital. We thought they were Yugoslav planes exercising. But as we watched them we saw bombs being dropped on the local aerodrome across the Danube and fires started in Novi Sad, our nearest town. Then we realised that war had begun. When we heard from our searchlight company officer that Belgrade was being bombed we knew it was time to pack up and go." [82]

Although General Dušan Simović and his new National Government acknowledged its neutrality and declared Belgrade an open city, early in the morning on April 6th, 1941, eight hundred German bombers had flown over the city to fulfil Hitler's orders that Belgrade must be destroyed, and more than twenty thousand men, women and children were killed in this ruthless act of destructive vengeance on an almost defenceless city. David Walker, who was in Belgrade at the time, describes how "when the bombing began people ran out into the streets to curse the Germans. They stood there, waving their fists at them while the volume of bombs steadily increased. There were no adequate shelters and no defence measures of any kind. Within an hour of the first bombardment there was no water, light or communications. Burning buildings were left to burn. The dead were left in the streets where they lay while a few inadequate Red Cross ambulances tried to collect the wounded." The city was not only practically undefended but totally unprepared. Germany had not made a declaration of war and Belgrade had been proclaimed an open town. Nevertheless, for four days German bombers systematically attacked the city and then left it for dead.

That grave morning the final preparations for departure were made in feverish haste. All the hospital equipment which was still in use was packed up and put away in the cellars, where it would be protected if the hospital should be bombed, but some equipment was sent to the village for a Red Cross first aid station containing twenty beds, which had been quickly set up by Dr. Branko

Manojlović. Katherine and Alice Murphy then went to the village and obtained a written permit to leave, without which they would not have been able to travel; then they packed those of their personal possessions which they were able to take with them, and were ready to depart. Finally they paid their remaining staff, locked the hospital and left the keys with Mrs. Julka Skrjaga, the wife of their chauffeur Vasilj, who had decided to stay in Sremska Kamenica whatever happened; then they said good-bye to the searchlight officers and the company and set off by car at three o'clock in the afternoon, driven by their faithful chauffeur Vasilj, for Slavonski Brod, a railway junction on the way from Belgrade to Sarajevo, some 125 miles from Kamenica, where they intended to take a train to Sarajevo, and from there south to Dubrovnik.

Fig. 56 Mr. Vasa Srdić on his estate in Temerin (1930s). (Courtesy of Mrs. M. Ćirić)

Fig. 57 Transporting material to build the hospital in Sremska Kamenica (1933).
(Courtesy of the SMA Museum)

Fig. 58 Making bricks on the building site of the hospital in Sremska Kamenica (1933-34). (Courtesy of the SMA Museum)

Fig. 59 Baking bricks on the building site of the hospital in Sremska Kamenica (1933-34). (Courtesy of the SMA Museum)

Fig. 60 Dr. K. MacPhail (second on the right, without a hat), with an official delegation, in front of the Children's Hospital in Belgrade (c. 1933). (Courtesy of Mrs. E. Biggs)

Fig. 61 Dr. K. MacPhail (standing), with a visitor, on the terrace of the hospital in Sremska Kamenica (c. 1934). (Courtesy of Mrs. E. Biggs)

Fig. 62 Panel with the mosaic of the Scottish lion, made in Temerin (1934).
(Courtesy of the SMA Museum)

Fig. 63 Mosaic of the Scottish lion set in the floor of the entrance hall of the hospital in Sremska Kamenica; above the door of a hospital room is the carved relief of the "bambino."
(Courtesy of the SMA Museum)

Fig. 64 Relief of the "bambino", with the words "Save the Children" (in Latin: "Salvate parvulos"), placed above the main entrance to the hospital in Sremska Kamenica. (Photo by B. Lučić)

Fig. 65 One of the first photographs of the hospital in Sremska Kamenica, surrounded by vineyards, taken by Dr. K. MacPhail in 1934. (Courtesy of the SMA Museum)

155

Fig. 66 The hospital in Sremska Kamenica, immediately after its completion in 1934; view from the eastern side. (Courtesy of the SMA Museum)

Fig. 67 The hospital courtyard on September 23rd, 1934, when the formal opening of the hospital was celebrated. (Courtesy of Mrs. E. Biggs)

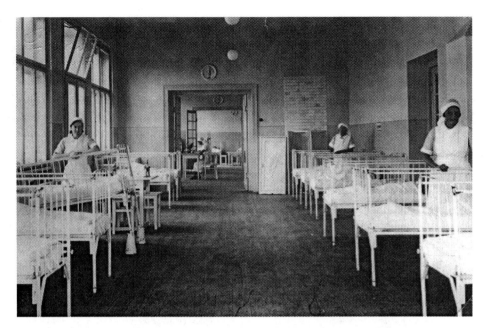

Fig. 68 The interior of the hospital in Sremska Kamenica (1934-35); the relief of the "bambino" was placed above every door. (Courtesy of Mrs. M. Ćirić)

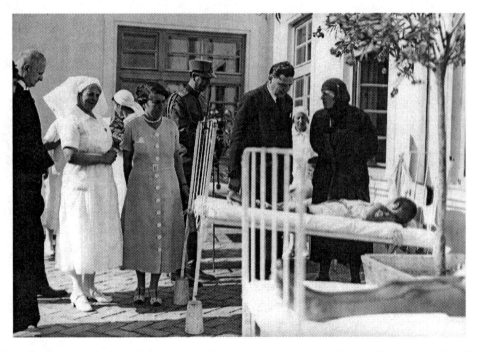

Fig. 69 Queen Maria of Yugoslavia, in deep mourning, and her suite on a visit to the hospital in Sremska Kamenica in October, 1935; Dr. Svetislav Stojanović, the chief surgeon to the hospital, is standing on her right, and with them are her adjutant in uniform, and Dr. K. MacPhail; beside her is the matron, Agnes Hardy. (Courtesy of Mrs. M. Ćirić)

Fig. 70 The hospital in Sremska Kamenica and its inner courtyard (c. 1936). (Courtesy of the SMA Museum)

Fig. 71 Children lying in the fresh air (areotherapy) and in the sun (heliotherapy) in the inner courtyard of the sanatorium in Sremska Kamenica (c. 1936-37). (Courtesy of the SMA Museum)

Fig. 72 A child with a diseased spine, on a so-called "extension", in a bed in front of the entrance to the sanatorium (c. 1936-37). (Courtesy of Mrs. E. Biggs)

Fig. 73 Children resting in the afternoon sun on the western terrace of the hospital; in the distance is the Danube (c. 1936-37). (Courtesy of the SMA Museum)

Fig. 74 Children in plaster casts learning to walk in the courtyard of the hospital in Sremska Kamenica (c. 1935). (Courtesy of Mrs. E. Biggs)

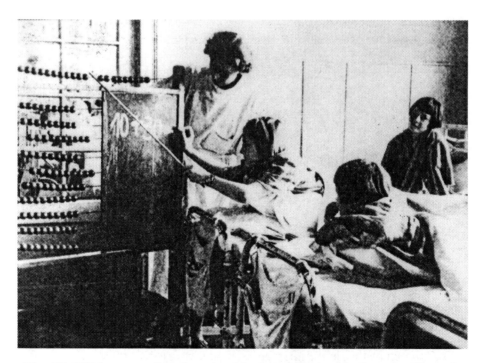

Fig. 75 Children attending the school in the sanatorium in Sremska Kamenica (c. 1936-37). (Courtesy of Mrs. M. Ćirić)

Fig. 76 Small patients engaged in hand-work in the hospital courtyard (c. 1936-37).
(Courtesy of the SMA Museum)

Fig. 77 Sister Milka Batić with a nine-year old boy admitted to the hospital on
November 3rd, 1934. (Courtesy of Mrs. E. Biggs)

Fig. 78 The same child, cured, and about to be sent home on August 12th, 1936. (Courtesy of Mrs. E. Biggs)

Fig. 79 Dr. K. MacPhail (looking towards the camera) with some friends in a café on the bank of the Danube (c. 1936-37). (Courtesy of Mrs. E. Biggs)

Fig. 80 Dr. Katherine MacPhail (c. 1935).
(Courtesy of Mrs. E. Biggs)

Fig. 81 View of the Fruška Gora hills from the verandah of Dr. K. MacPhail's villa in Sremska Kamenica; the sanatorium can be seen on the left, at the top of Čardak Hill. (Courtesy of Mrs. E. Biggs)

Fig. 82 Dr. K. MacPhail, in a rare moment of relaxation in the courtyard of her villa in Sremska Kamenica (c. 1935). (Courtesy of Mrs. E. Biggs)

Fig. 83 Dr. K. MacPhail with her dog in the courtyard of the hospital in Sremska Kamenica (c. 1935-36). (Courtesy of Mrs. E. Biggs)

Fig. 84 "The hospital at Kamenica in 1937, surrounded by vineyards and maize fields"; description written on the back of the picture by Dr. K. MacPhail.
(Courtesy of Mrs. E. Biggs)

Chapter 7

The Second World War, 1941 – 1945

When they left Sremska Kamenica Katherine and her fellow-travellers soon realised that their journey would be neither easy nor simple. The roads were already blocked; endless columns of military vehicles transporting soldiers came along one after another, while many civilian vehicles, with agitated and nervous drivers and passengers, were moving in all directions. Soldiers were on guard at the bridges and railway stations, and the peasant guards, composed of armed and nervous civilians, who examined the car and their documents, stopped them at villages on the way. Everywhere there was unrest and uneasiness; everybody was hurrying away somewhere and it seemed as though the whole country was on the move. What Katherine feared most was that some military unit or peasant guard would simply requisition their car for military purposes, which would make their journey much longer and more difficult. However, this did not happen, and to their great relief they arrived late in the evening at Slavonski Brod railway station. There they said good-by to Vasilj, who immediately set off on the journey back to Sremska Kamenica, while Katherine and Alice Murphy took refuge in the house of the stationmaster, where they had to wait for the morning train to Sarajevo. The station was already crammed full of people, including some refugees from Belgrade, who talked about the horrors of the recent bombardment; most of them had nothing with them but the clothes they stood up in. At 5 o'clock the next morning. Katherine and Alice boarded the train for Sarajevo and set off on a journey that lasted two days and two nights. The train was already packed out at the start of their journey, and at every little railway station there were crowds of young men who had been called up and were hurrying to join their units, so that their journey was very hard and extremely uncomfortable; there was no question of sleep. However, even in this situation Katherine was obliged to perform her duty as a doctor. When they were approaching Sarajevo someone announced that a woman had just given birth in the train, so Katherine went to see the situation and give what help she could. When she reached that coach she found the pale and exhausted mother with the baby in her arms; beside her there was another small child, and her sick husband sitting helplessly by. The woman told Katherine that her husband was seriously ill with tuberculosis; a few days before he had been discharged from hospital, because they had to make room for the wounded, and during the bombardment of Belgrade their house had been destroyed, and they had nowhere to go but her husband's native village in the mountains of Bosnia. Unable to do anything else, Katherine woke up a strong soldier who had slept through all the time in the compartment, and asked him to give up his place to the young mother. Since Katherine always behaved firmly and energetically in such situations, so that no one could refuse her requests, including this soldier, he willingly got up and enabled the woman to lie down and recover a little. Later Katherine saw this woman; she was then a little better, as were her family; they left the train at a wayside station, and prepared to continue their journey to a village in the mountains.

Katherine and Alice arrived in Dubrovnik on the morning of April 9th, 1941, and with the help of an old Russian friend they settled near him, where they could rest and wait to see how events turned out. Apart from various rumours there was no news, and in fact no one knew what was happening in the country, so they still hoped that they would be able to stay and form a medical team that could help the army or the Red Cross. However, these hopes were soon dashed. Meanwhile they had reported to the British Consul there, who also knew nothing about what was going on – and so several days passed with little news of what was happening. When Katherine again visited the consul on April 14th to ask for news, he told her that they must be ready to leave in half an hour, since all British people in that area had been ordered to leave Dubrovnik and proceed to a small town further south, down the coast. So they packed their few things and were taken by the Consul to the little town of Herceg Novi, which was in Montenegro. There they found "a strange collection of British people who had come from every direction", and there they heard that the British Minister and the Legation staff were expected to arrive over the mountains at Kotor that evening, some twenty miles further down the gulf from Herceg Novi.

Later Katherine herself described those days and their events in the following words: "Herceg Novi was already crowded with people who had escaped from Belgrade, many waiting to see how things would go before leaving for some remote mountain village. There was little food and everyone had to forage for themselves. That day and the next we wandered about meeting friends and gathering news, then on the evening of the second day we met a messenger from our Legation who brought the dreaded news that the Yugoslav army had capitulated to an overwhelming force and that we were to leave at once and meet our Minister and all the other British in a small village near Cattaro (Kotor), as it was hoped there would be a chance of us getting off on a British destroyer. Getting there was not so easy this time and after a twelve hours' wait we managed to requisition a military lorry and arrived at our destination, to be told by our agitated Consul that there was no room for us in the village and no food, and possibly a long wait. However we found a room and food, bad though it was, and were prepared to await our fate, which, we still hoped, would be the destroyer. The Minister was still able to get contact with the outside world as they had a receiving set, but they could not send out messages and so it was difficult for our authorities to keep in touch with us. However, in the afternoon to our great surprise two Sunderland flying-boats slipped quietly into the bay and everyone wondered if this would be our chance of escape. Cars from our Legation hurried past, and high Yugoslav officials. We saw people embarking and then the Minister returned with an empty car and the Sunderlands sailed off with their passengers. The Minister had sent off some of our people who had been wounded in the bombing, some wounded airmen, and some high officials of Yugoslav and other nationalities who were implicated with the British, and had returned himself to protect the rest of us and to share our fate." [82]

Unfortunately it was not the only disappointment that Katherine, together with a considerable number of other refugees, experienced during those days. In fact a significant number of people of different nationalities and occupations had gathered together in the small town of Perast on the gulf of Kotor, all fleeing from the occupying forces. There were about 100 British people, together with the remaining embassy staff, including the courageous and exceptionally conscientious ambassador, Sir Ronald Ian Campbell; also a number of Yugoslavs, Poles, Czechs and others who wished to flee from the country. All were relying on the help of the British, and hoped that by daybreak the long-expected British destroyer would arrive, which would take them all to some safe place. Katherine later described these events in the following words: "As the night drew on we settled in our strange quarters to wait, and some went to bed and others sat about on top of their suitcases. We had no light and were scattered about in dark, poverty-stricken houses. The people were kind to us and shared with us everything they had to eat, which was a strange soup and black bread. Then at 11 o'clock at night we heard voices calling us to collect at once at the village inn, as we were to embark at once. We were to be allowed to take only one suitcase with us, those of us who had even that. We gathered together by the light of candles and then began our exit into the pitch dark night. We had four miles to go to the quay, cars which had brought our people over the mountains were there to take most of us along, and when we arrived at the quay we could dimly make out the rigging of two motor sailing ships which the Yugoslavs had put at our disposal to take us out to the open sea to meet the hoped-for-destroyer. We were embarked, crowded into a small space and many of those who had hoped to go with us had to be left behind, with many regrets. There were many who could scarcely bear to see us go as with us went their only chance of escape. Out of the darkness we heard voices shouting farewells. We reached the mouth of the Gulf by dawn but on the horizon there was no sign of the destroyer, which never came, and so we landed again et Herceg Novi, the little port which we had left the day before and resigned ourselves to be taken prisoners by the Italians who took possession of the town the next day." [82]

After the arrival at Herceg Novi the group of British people and their ambassador were accommodated in the "Boka" hotel; the owner's attitude towards them was friendly, but the hotel had been completely emptied, since it had to be prepared to serve as a military hospital; there were not enough beds for everybody, so about fifty of the men slept on the floor of the main hall. Also there was no food in the town, shops were shut, and everything that could be eaten had already been removed and hidden in good time, so the members of this unhappy group fed themselves by dividing the last remnants of bread and dry food which they had brought on their journey. "On the last day of our freedom we had visited the little seventh-century Greek Orthodox church of the monastery of Savinac on a quiet hillside out of the town," Katherine sadly remarked later.

On April 18th, 1941, the entire group was taken prisoner, when a motorised unit of the Italian army arrived by road from Dubrovnik further north. "We had to resign ourselves to being taken captive by the Italians, only thankful that it was not the Germans", said Katherine later. An Italian officer introduced himself to the British Minister, saying: "You are now our captives. There is the open air and the sea and the sun, please enjoy yourselves!" He allowed them to stay in the hotel. However this relative freedom did not last long. Two days later a more senior and officious officer arrived, who forbade them to leave the hotel. The fact that the Italians meant this seriously was confirmed by an unpleasant incident the following night, when they were wakened up by the sound of gunfire and explosions under the hotel windows; the next morning they learnt that one group of prisoners had tried to escape by motor-boat that night, but they had been rudely prevented. The following afternoon a British submarine suddenly appeared in the bay, bearing a flag of parley, probably in an attempt to evacuate the British Ambassador and other British subjects, but while it was waiting in the bay three Italian planes appeared and, despite the flag of parley, they began to drop bombs, and the submarine quickly dived and disappeared; and thus the last hope of evacuation completely collapsed. "And so ended my long sojourn in that country which had become my second home," Katherine concluded sadly. [82]

This group of captives, consisting mainly of British subjects, remained in Herceg Novi for a week, and relieved the boredom of staying constantly in the same hotel in various ways. As the company included two opera singers, an improvised concert was arranged, at which one of them, David Edge, sang arias from "The Marriage of Figaro" in a fine tenor voice, which delighted the Italian officers who were also billeted in the hotel, and which probably alleviated the conditions of their imprisonment, at least to some extent. "Edge will always sing us out of trouble", commented the ambassador optimistically. Then suddenly, early one morning at 3.30 a.m., all the captives were roughly awakened and ordered to be prepared to leave within an hour. As it was not difficult to get ready quickly under those conditions, they were all ready on time, but it was nearly midday before they left in buses and military lorries, travelling towards Durazzo in Albania. All the women in the group and some of the men were packed off in one bus; at Bar, a small place near the Albanian frontier, they were joined by a group of Yugoslav officers in a separate car who were supposed to show them the way to Albania. However when it grew dark the Italian driver of the bus lost sight of the accompanying car in front of him, and suddenly found himself on a narrow mountain road with a steep, sheer canyon on the right side.

Hoping to avoid this chasm he turned sharply to the left, after which the bus fell into the ditch alongside the road. Fortunately no one was hurt, and while they were waiting for help they managed to light a fire and prepare something for supper. After a few hours another bus arrived and took them to Durazzo, where the other members of the party, who had arrived earlier, were waiting in the one hotel available, which was already overcrowded. Because of this Katherine's group were taken to a camp outside the town and lodged in some dirty wooden huts with straw mattresses. However, when they returned to the hotel for supper a little later, the British Minister told the Italians that the women must be given accommodation in the hotel. At his determined insistence some rooms were made available, and Katherine and Alice Murphy finally obtained a room with comfortable beds, when it was already long after midnight. The ambassador, who had in fact shown them the greatest kindness and consideration during these days waited until he was sure that they and their meagre luggage were properly settled in their hotel room.

The week's stay in Durazzo was definitely the worst part of their imprisonment. The town itself, as Katherine succinctly explained, had "little water, hot weather, flies, mud flats and smells." The internment régime was stricter than it had been earlier, and they were only allowed out of the hotel in groups of six, accompanied by a guard, for half an hour each day; so, to keep up their strength, they took as much exercise as they could on the roof of the hotel.

The entire group of prisoners was removed from Albania and taken in Italian military planes to Foggia, and then by train to the little spa Bagni di Cianciano in central Italy with a view of a lake, *Lago di Trasimento*. The total number of prisoners, which was finally gathered together here, was one hundred and eleven, since the British citizens imprisoned in Dubrovnik were added to the original group. This party, headed by the British Ambassador Sir Ronald Campbell, consisted mainly of diplomats, mining engineers fleeing from the Trepča zinc and lead mines in South Serbia, teachers from the British Council, business people, marine officials, and a small swarm of journalists. In Cianciano, as in any spa, there were plenty of hotels, so the whole party was divided into three and accommodated in three different hotels, where they were quite comfortable and had proper food. Their freedom of movement was limited, but they were allowed to go out for walks and take exercise for two hours every afternoon, and they could if they wished go into the town, provided they were accompanied. As the imprisonment rules were not very strict, the sport-loving Britons soon began to play football and cricket, and to organise games of bridge and chess. Some of the journalists even managed to produce a newspaper entitled "Imperial Affairs", which they claimed, quite correctly, as the only British newspaper in Italy. Katherine, as a doctor, was allowed to visit any of the party who was sick, but she had to be escorted there and back by a guard.

Ever since the outbreak of war in Yugoslavia, Katherine's relatives had been extremely anxious about her, and fearful about her fate, since they did not know what had happened to her, even whether she was still alive, or where she was. "There had been weeks of worry and dread, and many articles in the press about her fate", recalled Katherine's niece Mrs. Elspeth Biggs. It was only when Katherine's group reached Italy that her family received a telegram from the Vatican, and learnt that she was alive and well, a prisoner-of-war in Italy; this was a great relief to them.

The period of internment in Italy proved to be reasonably pleasant, since everybody, both officials and local people, was very kind; it lasted for five weeks, during which time the American Embassy in Rome engaged in negotiations for their repatriation, which began on June 11th, 1941. That day all the prisoners were taken by bus to the nearby town of Chiusi; all the local people came to their departure, where the atmosphere was very cordial. "They hoped to see us back in better times and were certainly going to miss our trade in beer and cigarettes", commented Patrick Maitland, the experienced *Times* Balkans correspondent. The other journalist from that group, David Walker, later wrote: "It was impossible to believe that we were in an enemy country. Not one of us had been interrogated, not one of us had received anything but kindness at the hands of the Italian Foreign Office and the Italian people."

The "Belgrade Party", as they were called, were taken by train across the French Riviera to Spain, as far as Madrid, where they learnt that the British Ambassador Sir Ronald Campbell had been knighted. The ambassador and diplomatic personnel were taken by air from Madrid to Lisbon, and then by another plane to Britain; the rest of the "Belgrade Party" were taken to Gibraltar, where they had to wait for a boat to take them home.

Even when the long-awaited ship finally arrived, Katherine's troubles were not over. First of all, they could hardly get on the boat, which was overcrowded with two thousand passengers of different nationalities; then the very next night the ship was bombed. After that a rumour circulated on the vessel that on the previous day one of the passengers had released a pair of carrier-pigeons, and that this was perhaps a signal to the enemy. Because of this the sailors searched all the cabins and luggage, and found that one of the passengers had a radio-transmitter; the next day an enemy submarine attacked the ship, but fortunately without success.

Even here Katherine did not lack work. Under her leadership the members of the "Belgrade Party" formed a voluntary Red Cross squad, which put itself at the disposal of the ship's doctor, so that it could help him if necessary in the ship's hospital, or if the ship had to be evacuated. Naturally this offer was gladly accepted, but the ship's captain warned them that if something should happen they would have to act very quickly, since there were over two thousand passengers on board, and only 700 places in the life-boats; he also explained that, after setting the wounded in the lifeboats, it would be best to jump immediately into the water, since in these circumstances this would offer the best chance of survival! Fortunately there were no further incidents, but the ship had to make a wide arc round the British Isles, sailing north nearly as far as Iceland, and only then turned towards Ireland and a week later finally sailed into the River Clyde.

"At that time, my elder sister Jessie, by now a fully qualified nursery school teacher, was looking after 40 pre-school children who had been evacuated from Glasgow to a large house on the Clyde at Cove, and she saw the ship coming in, but didn't know that Aunt Kathie was on board, until my Mother phoned us all, that evening", wrote Elspeth Biggs, one of the Katherine's nieces, later.

When during the passport and customs examination the customs officer noticed a small box on top of the things in Katherine's suit-case, he asked what was in it; Katherine answered: "That's my O.B.E." The officer immediately shut her case and said briefly, with a smile: "Welcome home!" It was only then that Katherine really felt she had arrived home. "It was a long, long voyage!" So Katherine described it later.

After her arrival Katherine made for the nearest telephone and phoned her sister Janet in Chapelhall, who then informed the rest of the family, so that they were all at last able to relax. "The relief and happiness we all felt was one of the great moments of the war", was how Katherine's niece, Elspeth Biggs, later recollected that day.

Soon after her return to Scotland Katherine was invited to London by the BBC to take part in a broadcast to Yugoslavia. On this occasion she spoke in Serbian and addressed some words of comfort and encouragement to the people of occupied Yugoslavia, and also the hope that they would eventually be liberated. As "Radio London", as it was usually called then in Yugoslavia, was quite often secretly listened to there at that time, many people heard her message and rejoiced to know that she was alive, and in a safe place, as they later told her in 1945, when she once more came to Yugoslavia.

After the death of their parents Katherine's sister Annie had moved to St Andrews, where she bought a small house for herself and Katherine which replaced their parental home, and where the two of them intended to settle after their retirement. Although this house had already been prepared for Katherine, she nevertheless decided to stay in Glasgow where she moved in with an old friend, Dr. Ellen Orr, who was a surgeon in Glasgow Royal Infirmary. Soon after her arrival and recovery from the journey Katherine started work as a children's doctor in a child welfare clinic in the Lanarkshire villages, near Glasgow. In the course of this work she visited different places in the area, including her native Coatbridge, where she had an afternoon clinic for children. As all these places were near Chapelhall, where her sister Janet lived with her family, she was a frequent guest there, according to her niece Elspeth, and at one time regularly went to lunch there. For a short while she also stayed with them in Chapelhall, where her brother-in-law, Dr. McFarlane had a medical practice, since some cases of smallpox had appeared in that area, so Katherine helped him and accompanied him to his morning and evening surgeries in two different villages, to assist him in inoculating all his patients.

Since Katherine only worked for half a day in the children's clinics, she had plenty of time for her favourite activity of organising and collecting help for Yugoslavia, her second homeland. At that time Katherine had agreed to be chairman of the West of Scotland Committee of the Yugoslav Relief Society, a large body that included many former members of the volunteer missions to Serbia during the First World War. One of the leading members was Dr. Stephen George, originally named Stevan Djordjević. He was one of the children who, during the First World war, had managed to escape from Serbia through Albania; after this he was evacuated to Great Britain, where he studied medicine in Glasgow, married a Scotswoman, gained British citizenship and stayed on to work as a doctor in Glasgow. After the Second World War he went to work in Nassau, in the Bermuda islands. He was later decorated for his work, and remained there until his death. Dr. S. George and Miss Netta Wilson, the secretary of the committee, were the main source of strength and Katherine's most active co-workers on the committee, which arranged meetings and lectures and a variety of visits, at which they collected contributions for aid to Yugoslavia. Ministers from the Yugoslav government-in-exile, which had been established in London since the summer of 1941, attended these meetings regularly; Katherine later related an episode which occurred at one of these gatherings. One day there was a large meeting of this society in one of the Glasgow theatres, at which Milan Gavrilović, [86] one of the ministers of the government-in-exile, was a guest speaker; and next to Katherine, on the stage, sat the Duchess of Atholl, who was a patron of the committee, and seldom missed a meeting. When the Mayor closed the meeting she turned to Katherine, obviously dissatisfied, and protested that the meeting had ended without the national anthem. Katherine replied that there was no orchestra; then the duchess asked whether there was not at least a piano. Katherine then noticed that there was one in the orchestra pit in the theatre, so she said that there was a piano, but no one to play it. The resolute duchess then announced that she would play it, and immediately asked the mayor and the treasurer of the committee, who were in the theatre, to help her down from the stage to the orchestra pit where she immediately opened the piano and began to play "God Save the King". The audience that had begun to disperse, immediately stood still, and they all sang the anthem to her piano accompaniment; the meeting then finally ended, to the general satisfaction of all those present. This committee was really active and soon raised the first thousand pounds, which was handed over to King Peter of Yugoslavia when he visited Glasgow; later they raised £ 10,000 to help Yugoslavia.

Naturally, Dr. Katherine MacPhail's many activities could not pass unnoticed; her fame from the First World War increased, and the town council of her native Coatbridge, of which she was already an honorary citizen, confirmed this status and elected her Burgess of the Burgh of Coatbridge; on April 16th, 1942 the appropriate document was handed to her at a special ceremony (Fig. 85). This was not just an honorary distinction, but carried with it some unusual privileges. For example, the bearer of this title was at liberty to ride anywhere in the town on any form of public transport without payment, and also to free drinks in the local public houses. Naturally, Katherine never tried to exercise these privileges, but later she sometimes said jokingly that she regretted that she had not made use of her right to free drinks.

During these years, although it was wartime, there were obviously some happy moments when nearly all the members of Katherine's immediate family gathered together again. According to her niece Elspeth, the last of these gatherings was in the summer of 1942, when, after a long interval, Katherine's sister Janet with her family, and Katherine and Annie, spent the summer together in Benderloch, the traditional holiday resort of the MacPhail family. The only member missing was Isabel, who at that time, after being evacuated from China, was staying with her children in Canada. Elspeth, unfortunately, had only one week with them, as she was by then in the Navy, stationed at the Atlantic Headquarters in Liverpool.

At that time Katherine often travelled to London, where she attended meetings of the Yugoslav Red Cross Committee, of which she was also a member, and in this way she kept in touch with the numerous Yugoslavs who were then in Great Britain. In addition she regularly visited her old friends and sponsors from the Save the Children Fund, who were always glad to see her. Katherine was certainly very active during these years. She carried out her medical work most conscientiously, and in addition participated in the work of humanitarian organisations in Scotland and in London. However, she never abandoned the thought of returning to Yugoslavia and restoring her hospital.

At the beginning of 1944, when the outcome of the war was already clear, preparations were begun in the Allied countries to help the occupied regions of Europe; the Save the Children Fund, which in the spring of that year set up its first relief unit to help Yugoslavia, asked Dr. Katherine MacPhail to head this group; she, of course, accepted this offer since, among other things, she saw this as a good opportunity to return to Yugoslavia and to her hospital. So in the spring of 1944 Katherine was in London, where she established and prepared her unit for departure. From there she wrote to her sister Annie: "I am to be in charge of the party on the way out, 47 in all, 32 women and 15 men. They are British Red Cross, YWCA, Guides, Scouts, Catholic Relief Committee and Save the Children Fund....I hope we all get peacefully to our destination." This unit, of course, included Katherine's colleague of many years, Alice Murphy. This variegated group established by the Save the Children Fund (Fig. 86) was to operate within the framework and under the protection of UNRRA, [87] a United

Nations agency established to help liberated countries which had been devastated by the war. At that time the UNRRA headquarters for European countries was in Cairo, as was the Allied staff headquarters for the Middle East, so Katherine's unit from Great Britain had to be moved to Cairo. While she was waiting for a convoy in which to transport her unit, Katherine spent some time in London, where she found her niece Elspeth, who was a member of the Royal Navy, also waiting for transport to the Near East; she later wrote: "During the spring of 1944, both Aunt Kathie and I happened to be in London. I was waiting for a convoy to the Middle East, and she was doing likewise. We saw each other often, when I was off duty. One memorable occasion was a reunion with her cousin Ian MacPhail, who had just been repatriated in the first exchange of wounded prisoners of war. He had fought with the New Zealand forces and had been badly wounded and captured in Crete. I was so proud to march about London between them, one a tall army Captain with a limp and a walking stick, the other 5 ft., also in khaki, with rows of medals, and me representing the Navy, with my head held high!" Ian was the youngest son of Katherine's uncle Dr. James MacPhail, a missionary in India; Ian had moved to New Zealand where, in peacetime, he was a successful sheep farmer.

Katherine and her unit left Great Britain on June 8th, 1944, two days after the landing of the allied forces in Normandy. "I was glad that she had gone", her niece Elspeth wrote later, "as it was at that time that the German V rockets started to rain down, day and night all over London and the south of England, and it was ghastly."

When Katherine's unit reached Egypt, it was billeted in a camp near Cairo, on the edge of the desert, where they had to wait for transport to Italy. Since the wait in Cairo lasted a long time, some members of the unit, including Alice Murphy, began to work in field hospitals in the neighbourhood, and some drivers were sent to a large field hospital near Suez. Katherine herself stayed as near to headquarters as possible so that she could follow the course of events, but this wait in Cairo, in the scorching and dusty desert, got on all their nerves, as Katherine wrote: "There seem to be a good many obstacles, mostly political. The uncertainty, long continued, is making us all edgy and unsettled, so our military superiors are trying to keep us busy with exercises and lectures. We have been doing long two and three days trips, going as complete units, camping and trying out different situations which would be interesting if they were the real thing. We have been to Ismailia and camped on the shores of the Bitter lakes and another time to Aboukir on the property of King Farouk." However all this, and the beauty of the desert by moonlight, could provide no real compensation for "living in constant wind, blowing sand and flapping tents, and intense heat."

Of course there were more pleasant moments. Katherine again met here Miss Dana Dušmanić, the daughter of her old friend Constance Dušmanić; [80] Dana was a volunteer driver with the British Eighth Army in Egypt following the example of her mother who was a volunteer driver in the First World War. Dana then asked for a transfer, which she was able to do, so that she soon became a driver in Katherine's unit. Yet another person dear to Katherine was a driver in her team – Helen Gordon-Duff, the daughter of General Fortescue; [43] Katherine had been a friend of hers, and also of her father, from the time of the First World War. There was also a Quaker group stationed in the district whose members they often met. Katherine had been on friendly terms with this organisation ever since the time she had spent in France during the First World War. It is interesting to note that the Quakers whom Katherine got to know at this time included Chris Nickolls, the son of her old friend John Nickalls with whom she had worked in France and who had then wanted to marry her. However, Chris learnt this only after his father's death. [31]

A month after Katherine's unit came to Egypt, her niece Elspeth arrived; she was stationed in Alexandria. A few days later Dana Dušmanić arrived from Cairo to visit her sister Tatyana or Tinkle, as they called her, who was in the same unit, and also to hand over Katherine's letter to the commanding officer, in which she asked for leave for Elspeth so that they could see each other before she left for Italy. On receiving a day's leave Elspeth immediately travelled to Cairo where she spent a day with her beloved aunt, about which she later wrote: "It was only for 24 hours, but we managed to go to the pyramids, where I had quite a job keeping her from buying an Arab horse (!), have a meal and go to a concert that evening. I left next day, and by the time she came up via Alexandria a few days later, I was in hospital with jaundice, and she couldn't find me, so I didn't see her again for a long time." (Fig. 87)

After waiting for four months in the stifling heat of Cairo, at the end of October 1944 Katherine, together with a small group of civilian officials, was transferred to Bari in Italy, where at that time there were some field hospitals in which sick and wounded Yugoslavs, military and civilian, were being treated. "It is pleasant to be in a green land and a cool one once again", Katherine wrote to her sister Annie. "We are a large mission and I can't say that I enjoy being in such a crowd of strangers, but I hope we may get sorted out soon and break up into smaller groups." At that time Katherine's deafness, the result of the typhus she contracted in 1915, was gradually getting worse, and this began to cause difficulties for her in communicating with strangers who, unlike her regular colleagues, did not know about this problem; so because of this she missed her unit, which had stayed in Egypt. However, after her arrival she did have one unexpected happy encounter. Among the first people she met in Bari was her cousin, Dr. Dugald MacPhail, the second youngest son of her uncle Dr. James MacPhail of Indian fame; [1] Dugald was the first of the MacPhails to break away from the tradition of studying at Glasgow University, and had taken his degree in St Andrews; he had joined the Royal Navy as a doctor, and then disappeared into the special services. In this capacity he had been parachuted early in the war with a number of other British doctors into the liberated territory of Yugoslavia where he had spent some time working with the Partisan resistance units. This was a very pleasant reunion of two relatives, and a wonderful opportunity to have a long talk in which they were able to exchange news of the entire family.

During November 1944 the entire UNRRA mission destined for Yugoslavia, including Katherine's unit, was transferred to Italy and billeted in Bari and San Spirito; and there once again there was a long period of waiting throughout the cold winter. The reason for the delay was political. The new Yugoslav government, headed by Marshal Tito, refused to accept the large number of foreigners represented by the UNRRA officials. Material aid was welcome, but they did not want to accept foreign relief workers. While this problem was being discussed, the entire UNRRA mission destined for Yugoslavia was kept waiting in Italy. During this time almost the whole of Katherine's unit, apart from Katherine and a few others, found employment in the Italian UNRRA Mission in Bari. As waiting continued, at the end of November Katherine and a few of her colleagues took a few days' leave and travelled to Naples and Rome, where they visited many places where there had been battles between Allied and Nazi forces; later she described one of these scenes: "Cassino, especially the beautiful monastery on the mountain top, and the villages around were a sight never to be forgotten – total destruction – with the people still looking for their belongings and living almost without roofs over their heads in any shelter they can find. In the midst of the exquisite countryside of vineyards, olive and orange groves, and a backdrop of snow-capped mountains, the desolation seemed more awful….the people are certainly suffering a good deal – no heating, little lighting and little food," Katherine wrote to her sister Annie. "But it did us good to get away from this stand-still situation here – negotiations are slow."

And the talks between UNRRA and the new Yugoslav authorities were indeed unforgivably slow, in view of the wretched and poverty-stricken situation in the country at that time. The refusal of the Yugoslav communist authorities to receive the UNRRA mission, which was purely humanitarian, and whose help was so necessary for the suffering and devastated country, was certainly unreasonable and incomprehensible, and indeed inhuman towards their own people, most of whom had neither food nor clothes, to say nothing of anything else. The reasons for this refusal were obviously ideological. Although formally the connection with the wartime allies still existed, an ideological barrier was already being established against the free world; this was later known as the "Iron Curtain", and gradually led to a new division of the world into two opposing blocs, and to the so-called "cold war". The new government was extremely distrustful and suspicious of foreigners from the western countries; and in this atmosphere of distrust and fear, especially towards the Americans and the British, their propaganda constantly spread through the nation. Because of all this, foreigners from western countries were unwelcome, and, contrary to the situation after the First World War, the attitude towards them was one of considerable hostility and fear, of which the members of the UNRRA Mission in

Bari were well aware. However in the end Yugoslavia had to accept help from UNRRA, although official communist propaganda insisted that " behind this there was capitalist interest to speed up the establishment of a world market;" the simple reason was that the country was devastated and the people hungry. The help from UNRRA was enormous. In addition to food and clothing, distributed to the people in so-called "UNRRA parcels", Yugoslavia also obtained medicines and medical equipment, and agricultural and industrial machinery. Among other things, Yugoslavia received 66 locomotives (made in the U.K.), some 12,000 vehicles, 12,000 horses and mules, and about 3,000 tractors.[88] Because of this UNRRA and especially their "parcels" were extremely popular with the people in all parts of Yugoslavia at that very hard time.

It was only after four months of talks that the Yugoslav authorities finally agreed to accept one hundred UNRRA officials, who had to be specialists, and to act only as observers. When the process of selecting specialists to be sent to Yugoslavia began in Bari, Katherine felt desperate, and began to lose all hope that she would ever return again to Yugoslavia, her beloved second homeland, and to her hospital.

.

Fig. 85 Certificate of honorary membership of Coatbridge Municipal Council, awarded to Dr. K. MacPhail on April 16th, 1942. (Courtesy of Mrs. E. Biggs)

Fig. 86 Dr. K. MacPhail, wearing the uniform of the Save the Children Fund (S.C.F.), at the beginning of 1944. (Courtesy of Mrs. E. Biggs)

Fig. 87 Dr. K. MacPhail in Cairo, in front of a pyramid, in the autumn of 1944. (Courtesy of Mrs. E. Biggs)

Chapter 8

Communist Yugoslavia, 1945 - 1947

While Dr. Katherine MacPhail and her team were waiting helplessly in Italy, the hand of fate once again intervened in her life. Good luck, which had never yet abandoned her, once more came to her aid. This time the fortunate circumstance was the fact that the President of the Anti-Fascist Assembly of National Liberation in Montenegro was Dr. Niko Miljanić, Katherine's old friend and colleague from her Belgrade days. When he heard that Dr. Katherine MacPhail and her unit were in Italy waiting for permission to enter Yugoslavia, he immediately sought permission from the highest authorities that this unit, together with three Red Cross workers, should at once be permitted to enter Yugoslavia, since their presence in Montenegro was indispensable. It is interesting to note that his request went by way of the British military mission in Dubrovnik, which then sent a cipher telegram to the British military mission in Belgrade, which in turn sent a telegram to the Yugoslav government then based in Belgrade, since Dr. Niko Miljanić himself had then no means of communicating in this way.

Dr. Katherine MacPhail and her unit obtained permission to enter Yugoslavia, after four months of waiting; and they were the first humanitarian team, together with some UNRRA officials, to enter the new, communist Yugoslavia, in March 1945. Later another team from the Save the Children Fund obtained permission to work in Yugoslavia, within the framework of UNRRA. This team included Dr. Eleanor Singer, and some medical sisters stationed in Sarajevo. They worked with a maternity unit, which had been opened in November 1945, where they established a children's department; in addition on Sundays they visited the surrounding villages with a mobile clinic. The Society of Friends also worked in Yugoslavia within the framework of UNRRA, and it was mainly their drivers who transported valuable loads of food, clothing, medicines and other equipment.

Dr. Katherine MacPhail and her unit had arrived in Dubrovnik in March 1945, where they were very warmly welcomed by Dr. Niko Miljanić who saw to it that they were all cordially received and comfortably accommodated; this was not easy, since although the British and Americans were then officially allies, they were not at all popular. As soon as they were settled in Dubrovnik, Katherine immediately sought permission to travel to Sremska Kamenica to restore her hospital; the Ministry of Health quickly arranged for air transport and summoned her to Belgrade to discuss the future of the hospital. She and Alice Murphy then travelled to Belgrade, where they were unpleasantly surprised, and grieved, because the city seemed to them devastated and impoverished. In Belgrade they found their old friend Flora Sandes, who had spent the whole period of the occupation in Belgrade, and also Dr. Svetislav Stojanović, who seemed to them "older and worn out." He took them to see the state hospital, which seemed to be in poor state, lacking everything from bandages to bedclothes. The patients were lying in bed in their clothes, covered with blankets that they had brought themselves.

The British military mission in Belgrade then lent Katherine a jeep, in which she and Alice Murphy travelled to Sremska Kamenica to visit their hospital and see what state it was in. "We found the hospital standing, but entirely bare, the windows broken and the doors off," so Katherine described her first impressions as she went round the hospital, "an empty shell completely stripped of everything moveable, and all electric installations and water supply and fitments, wiring and water pipes and stoves." However, the inhabitants of Sremska Kamenica welcomed Katherine very warmly, as they had always done. Dr. Branko Manojlović, who had remained in the village during the war, gave them a friendly welcome and invited them to lunch; then they heard about everything that had happened. The saddest news of all, which greatly upset them, was that Katherine's close and dear friend Vasa "Mac" Srdić had been in a prison camp in Belgrade during the war where he had been killed; the whole village mourned him. Unfortunately it had been the fate of many. As regards the hospital, they learnt that during the occupation the government at that time had taken the keys, and also Katherine's car, which had been left with Vasilj Skrjaga; at one time the building was used as a hospital in which Dr. Daniel Slakal had worked; he had sympathised with the Partisan movement, so the Partisans from Fruška Gora had often come and taken away medicines, food, and bandages; on one occasion the hospital had been attacked. Because of all these circumstances the hospital had been moved into the premises of a brewery in Petrovaradin, and Dr. Daniel Slakal had moved into Novi Sad. After that the hospital had remained empty, and became more and more neglected; a contemporary recollected that as a child, during the war, he had gone with other children into the abandoned building and they had played there. Katherine's villa was undamaged, since during the war some people who had looked after everything had occupied it. After visiting Sremska Kamenica Katherine and Alice Murphy returned to Belgrade, where they were given only vague promises, after which they flew back to Dubrovnik where their unit was waiting.

While they were staying in Dubrovnik Katherine visited the "Villa Bravačić", where a convalescent home for the sick children from her Belgrade hospital had been accommodated in 1920-21. To her great disappointment she learnt that this building, which had once been a children's paradise, was used as a prison.

While Katherine and her unit were waiting for permission to enter Yugoslavia, and while she was in Dubrovnik, the Save the Children Fund in England was collecting funds for her mission. According to an entry in their periodical *The World's Children*, their office was visited in March, 1945 by King

Peter II and Queen Alexandra who, in the name of the Yugoslav Relief Society, of which they were joint patrons, handed over to the Fund a cheque for £ 5,000 towards the expenses of a special unit which the Fund had sent out to Yugoslavia under the leadership of Dr. Katherine MacPhail. On this occasion King Peter said: "All Yugoslavs remember with gratitude the great work which Dr. MacPhail and the Fund have done and are doing for the relief of my people." Dr. MacPhail, added the king, had now returned to Yugoslavia to continue her great work of relief with a unit of able and qualified workers under the auspices of the SCF, and that cheque, collected by the magnificent efforts of the Yugoslav Relief Society, was a token of respect and esteem for the work the Fund was doing. "May God bless their efforts", concluded the King. According to the same article, the Secretary of the Fund, in expressing thanks for this "noble gift", reported that the Fund had already sent a large quantity of children's clothing and food to Yugoslavia, and that it would shortly, with the help of the Canadian Red Cross, send yet another large quantity of hospital equipment and clothing.[89]

After they had been in Dubrovnik for some days an order arrived that Katherine's unit should move to Budva, a beautiful little walled town on the coast of Montenegro, where Dr. Niko Miljanić planned to open a children's hospital with a special department for tuberculosis of the bones and joints, similar to the one at Sremska Kamenica, in Queen Maria's summer palace at Miločer, a beautiful suburb of Budva right on the seashore. As equipment for such a hospital was not yet available, the team carried out only the preliminary work, expecting that the government would obtain everything that was needed for the work of the hospital. Meanwhile nearly all the members of the unit, especially the medical sisters, began to work in one of the Budva hotels which had been turned into an improvised hospital run by two Yugoslav doctors, but with great difficulty, since the building lacked the appropriate sanitary conditions. However, when one of the British officers fell seriously ill he was moved to this hospital where his life was saved; as soon as he was well enough he was evacuated to Italy, accompanied on his journey by Elsie Stevenson, one of the sisters from Katherine's team; she did not come back, since the local Red Cross immediately engaged her for work in Italy, and later in Germany; she was cordially welcomed everywhere, in contrast to the situation in Yugoslavia. This was a great loss for the team, and marked the beginning of the dissolution of Katherine's unit. They cooperated well with the Yugoslav doctors in this hospital, and mutually helped each other. One evening Katherine was returning from Dubrovnik to Budva in a car driven by Helen Gordon-Duff, when they suddenly heard the sound of a gun being fired, and noticed a stationary ambulance, obviously damaged, on the other side of the valley. As they did not know what was the matter, they were somewhat frightened and confused, but they turned off the road and drove round the valley; when they reached the ambulance they saw one of the doctors from their hospital, who had fired his gun to attract their attention; he was afraid that they had not noticed and would continue their journey. There was a seriously ill patient in the ambulance, and when everything had been explained they took the patient and the doctor in their car to the hospital in Budva.

In Budva Katherine's team was accommodated in a villa, the landlady of which had two small children; her husband had disappeared during the war, and she was perpetually very frightened. They had their meals in a military canteen where they came into contact with Partisan soldiers, and Katherine noticed a great difference between them and the Serbian soldiers in the First World War. "These men had been good fighters but they were rough and ill-mannered", wrote Katherine. "They obviously disliked us because of Trieste, [90] or I know not what. We ate in the same mess but they never greeted us, or spoke to us, and on Armistice Day they entirely ignored us – even though we were supposed to be allies. The head soldier, or officer, it was difficult to know which, would come in and sit down at our table without saying a word except to the landlady. Once he said he would need our *camion* the next day and when I said this was impossible as it was being serviced he left in a very angry and almost threatening mood. This didn't affect me after all, but terrified our landlady, who said I must always obey their orders. I think we were particularly unfortunate, as not all the soldiers were so ill-mannered and rude and we knew that in their hearts many felt we were friends – only politics separated us."

In spite of Dr. Niko Miljanić's efforts, preparations for opening a children's hospital in the summer palace in Miločer proceeded extremely slowly, since it was very difficult to obtain equipment and other necessary things; and Katherine became yet more convinced that a much better task would be the restoration of the hospital at Sremska Kamenica, on which she continued to insist. Meanwhile her team began to get smaller, since many of its members, already weary of waiting, began to leave, including Katherine's friends Helen Gordon-Duff and Dana Dusmanić, who returned to England to continue her studies. It also happened that at that time Dr. Niko Miljanić was transferred to Belgrade to take up new duties, so work on opening a children's hospital at Miločer practically came to a standstill and Katherine's new, greatly reduced unit was ordered in July 1945 to move to Belgrade where UNRRA was working at full capacity. It was then that discussions began about re-opening the hospital at Sremska Kamenica.

As living conditions in Belgrade were then very difficult, Katherine took the whole team to her villa at Sremska Kamenica; fortunately it was in good condition and they could all be accommodated there. The team now consisted of eight members. In addition to Katherine there was the matron, Marion Tew, the physiotherapist Doreen Kerr Jarrett, three male drivers, Alwyn Griffith, Tew and Robbie; then Beatrix Macartney, also a driver, and of course, the irreplaceable Alice Murphy. Sister Agnes Hardie from the old pre-war team was missing; she was then working in a Red Cross unit in Germany. The men put up some tents in the courtyard and the garden of the villa, while the women occupied the rooms in the house; so they were all satisfied and ready to work.

However, difficulties then began with the new authorities in the country. Since the members of this group had not been officially recognised as UNRRA officials, but simply as a separate unit of the Save the Children Fund attached to UNRRA, the authorities began to take a sharper look at this situation, and Katherine was soon summoned to the UNRRA headquarters in Belgrade, where she was told that her team would probably have to leave the country, leaving behind all the equipment they had brought with them, since the Yugoslav authorities decided that as few foreigners as possible should remain, and then only experts. This was a heavy blow for Katherine, who was full of hope, and longing to get to work. Katherine, shattered by this development, asked the UNRRA official if she could see the Minister of Health at once. When she came a few days later to a meeting that had been arranged, to her great surprise she discovered that the Minister of Health was an old acquaintance of hers, a young doctor who before the war had worked in the Police School in Sremska Kamenica, and had at that time often visited her hospital, where he had attended operations and the fitting of plaster casts and learnt a little English. Since during the war he had joined the Partisans and shown outstanding courage, he now occupied a high position in the new government. When Katherine appeared they both laughed and greeted each other cordially, but when she asked him whether it was true that her team's time in the country would be cut short, he tried to explain the attitude of the new government towards foreigners. Then Katherine, who was already upset and anxious, asked him what the Save the Children Fund in London would think if their team, which they had sent out with the best of intentions, was thrown out of Yugoslavia? And these people were very highly qualified professional specialists who had left their families and good jobs in order to help Yugoslavia? As regards herself, she said, she had spent so long in this country that she felt herself to be half Scottish and half Yugoslav! Then the minister began to hesitate, but he still emphasised his point of view, then Katherine produced her final argument: "Do you know, doctor, I think I was looking after your Yugoslav children before you were born, or when you were a very small boy, so you can't really look on me as an outsider in your country." After this the minister laughed and said that she had convinced him, so he would make an exception for Katherine and her team, who could stay in Sremska Kamenica and resume the work in the hospital. And so Katherine achieved yet another hard-won victory, of course, as time would show, not for long; and work on the restoration of the hospital could begin.

A year later, in 1946, Katherine related all this to her old friend Francesca Wilson, who was then a highly-placed UNRRA official, and who had come on a visit: "Our relations with the Government are very good. In 1945 the Ministry of Health allowed me to take over the hospital again and bring out three trained British workers with me, Matron, Secretary and a teacher of handicrafts. The hospital had been used for soldiers by the enemy, and was knocked about and stripped bare of all its equipment. We found some of its furniture in the neighbourhood, hidden away in people's cottages; UNRRA supplied beds, and I had linen and blankets sent me from societies in Canada and Great Britain, and the Vojvodina authorities did the repairs. They pay all the general running expenses and the salaries of the Yugoslav staff, which is, of course, very large, as the children are helpless. In fact, for a poor country, they budget for it generously. The Save the Children Fund supports the British staff and helps in a number of ways. It is a joint Anglo-Yugoslav activity [88] - the only one of its kind."

In fact the Health Department of Vojvodina Government [91] provided the budget for the upkeep of the hospital at that time, and this covered some of the general running expenses, repairs and the wages of the Yugoslav staff. The British staff was maintained and supported by the SCF, which had long-standing connections with Katherine MacPhail's work in Yugoslavia, and of which she had become a member when she was asked to take out their Unit in 1944. Most of the surgical materials, instruments, dressings and medicines had been supplied by various societies in Britain and Canada who wanted to help Yugoslav children. Sir Charles Hyde, a wealthy British industrialist, who had died some years previously, had bequeathed £ 5,000.00 for children's work in Greece and £ 5,000 for children's work in Yugoslavia; the Save the Children Fund was helping in this decision .The latter bequest was allocated to the hospital through the Foreign Office in London.

After an agreement had been concluded with the minister of the department for the protection of mothers and children in the Ministry of National Health in the Federal Democratic State of Yugoslavia, on August 15th, 1945 a document, no. 4332 was sent to the Health Department of the National Liberation Council in Novi Sad, worded as follows: "With the agreement of this ministry, Dr. MacPhail will once more manage a children's hospital in Sremska Kamenica. Dr. MacPhail is bringing with her both sanitary material and certain other things necessary for setting up the hospital. We request that you give Dr. MacPhail whatever help she needs. (Signed) Dr. Olga Milošević, head of the Department for Protection of Mothers and Children." A little later it was explained to Dr. MacPhail in Novi Sad that, in accordance with new regulations, the government would have to appoint a so-called administrative director for the hospital, as the person who officially issued the orders, and she was asked, if she so wished, to suggest someone whom she would like to occupy this post. Katherine then suggested Mr. Branko Bugarski, who was then head of the financial department in the Principal National Liberation Council of Vojvodina; she had known him before the war, and she considered he could be of assistance to her as a financial specialist. Her suggestion was accepted and, in accordance with the decision of the Presidency of the National Assembly of the Autonomous

Province of Vojvodina, no. 10632, issued on October 13th, 1945, Mr. Branko Bugarski was appointed to this post and began his work immediately.

Soon after concluding this agreement, with the help of Ministry of Health, Katherine started work on repairing the hospital building; the government of the Autonomous Province of Vojvodina [91] met this expense. The main problem was the renewal of the electric wiring, since both the transformer and the lines to the village had been destroyed. At the same time, in accordance with the recent agreement, Katherine promised to obtain equipment for the hospital. As much of the furniture from the hospital had been distributed throughout the village, she and her chauffeur Vasilj, who had come back to work at the hospital, spent several days going round the houses in the village where they found beds, stoves and tables and chairs from the hospital; most of these had been hidden in summer houses and the local people gladly returned them. A list made by the local wartime committee in Kamenica proved to be very useful in this task; so plenty of things were restored to the hospital. Almost all the equipment from the operating theatre was found in a military hospital in the nearby town of Sremski Karlovci. When Katherine went to look for her things the director of the hospital told her that he had known that the equipment came from her hospital, but that in the circumstances it had been a god-sent gift, and very useful to them. All the equipment was then returned to Katherine, with many thanks and apologies from the director. While she was still waiting with her team in Bari in Italy, Katherine had ordered a large quantity of medicines and bandages, which were beginning to arrive. UNRRA provided a large number of hospital beds and bedding, and a generous gift arrived from Canada, through their Red Cross. Florence Harvey (Fig. 27), her old friend from the Salonica Front and her days in Belgrade, sent 46 boxes of children's clothing and bedding through the Canadian Red Cross, so that Katherine was able to give clothing to the staff of the hospital as well as to the children there, and to poor children in the village and in other places. In his memoirs Branko Bugarski describes how Katherine then decided to give everyone employed in the hospital who had children two pairs of pyjamas for each child. One employee who had six children was given 12 pairs of pyjamas, and Branko Bugarski himself received 4 pairs of pyjamas for his two daughters. Katherine gave a large amount of this material to the Red Cross in Sremska Kamenica and other places. Among other things, Katherine had brought with her five vehicles: two small lorries, two passenger cars and a jeep, so that the hospital then possessed a "car park" such as it never had either before the war or later. Two drivers, Vasilj Skrjaga and Alwyn Griffiths, who was officially a handicrafts teacher, looked after the cars. If necessary, Branko Bugarski also drove the cars. However, although there were enough cars and petrol supplied by UNRRA, Katherine usually came to the hospital on foot, and rarely by car. At that time a dwelling house on the road from the village to the hospital became available, which was occupied by members of the staff of the hospital. The present address of this house is: 44 Dr. Katherine MacPhail Street.

Work on repairing the hospital proceeded well, and to Katherine's satisfaction, as can be seen from a report which she sent at this time to the Save the Children Fund: "I feel that we can look forward to getting the hospital opened before long. We are promised increased help from the Yugoslav Ministry of Health and 200-bed-hospital equipment has been allocated to us with a view to increasing our work as soon as possible – I should think next spring all being well. The 200-beds material has not yet been 'liberated', but when it is the Ministry wants me to use what we can now and to store the rest for future use so that it does not get dispersed. They are talking of putting up huts which I believe the Yugoslav Red Cross are getting from Italy and this may expand our capacity. I think we may begin with what material we have got, on a small scale without waiting for the UNRRA material to turn up, but we cannot do so until the electricity supply is assured, and they are now working on it." [92]

In a remarkably short time for these difficult post-war days the hospital was repaired, whitewashed and cleaned; also the electricity and water supply were finally established. As there was not enough furniture, the most essential things, such as wooden chairs, tables and shelves were made in the village, and together with a smaller number of old beds, the hospital was opened again on December 19th, 1945. Work began with five beds, as described later by Marion Tew, who was then working as the matron; the first five patients were: "Mileva, aged 12, who had been having treatment for three years for a T.B. hip, and is quite convinced that we shall make her shortened leg match the other. Savka, aged 15, has a T.B. ankle, not improved by her enforced camp life. She is a serious girl, very anxious to prepare herself for her final school examination and studying hard with the help of our senior sister. Her father, like so many others, 'disappeared' during the war, leaving her mother with five children to support. Marica, aged 17, was really over age, but could not be refused for she was so ill and her mother's only hope was in the 'English hospital'. She had multiple abscesses from her T.B. hip, diseased kidneys, and an affected heart, due no doubt to the heavy labour, which had been her lot - carrying bricks. To our sorrow Marica died, but her mother, who came as cook in order to be near the child, is still with us. Peter, aged 8, is a round-faced jolly little boy, suffering from a T.B. knee. Actually there is no 'suffering' in Peter's make-up. Our fifth patient was a girl of 10, Dragica, with a history of six years' illness. She was a mere skeleton and the size of a five-year-old child, with her back a mass of plaster sores and open wounds from her T.B. hip. She is, however, a very happy little girl with a charming smile and is hopefully resigned to her present life." [93]

An extremely severe winter, with a lot of snow, such as occurred that year, made the work of the newly opened hospital almost impossible. "Admissions were necessarily slow during the inclement weather, and we were not really sorry, for there was a serious shortage of water on account of the heavy snows, freezing the pipes, a frequent breakdown of the pump, etc., owing to the inferior materials used for repairs;" so wrote Marion Tew. Huge snowdrifts blocked the path to the hospital, making it impossible to get supplies, a problem that Katherine solved in a typical way. Branko Bugarski described one such incident in his memoirs: "It was the winter of 1946. The cart that brought us milk and other necessary things from the village became stuck in the deep snow caused by heavy snowfalls and a strong wind, which tore the telephone wires. When I reported this to the doctor she asked me: 'How many spades have you got, Comrade Bugarski?' Somewhat confused, I answered: 'I have 20 spades, and you gave me 18 winter coats, which I handed over to the storehouse keeper. 'Thank you', said the doctor, 'bring me a spade'. I had to obey her, so I brought her a spade. She then climbed up the hill and began, by herself, without anyone else around, to clear the snow from the path. I didn't say anything; I reported to the storehouse keeper, took a spade, stood beside her, and then I began to dig up the snow and clean the path. Believe it or not, within ten minutes 15 other people appeared; only one sister and the elderly cook, 77 years old, remained indoors. In an hour the path was cleared, and a cart with milk and other things was able to get to the hospital."

In the spring of 1946 the hospital already had 21 patients, and by the summer, when the equipment arrived, there were 60 beds available, and from October 1946 onwards, 75 beds, which were always occupied. As the number of children suffering from tuberculosis had increased considerably during the war, there was an enormous demand for treatment from all parts of the country, and there were always 50 sick children on the waiting list. In such a situation it often happened that a seriously ill child was sent home and put on the waiting list because there was no room in the hospital; this was always extremely unpleasant, both for the patients and for the hospital staff. Dr. Svetislav Stojanović, who was once more co-operating with the hospital, which he visited every week, when the discharge and reception of patients took place, usually performed this duty. A typical incident has been described by Francesca Wilson, who spent a few days in the hospital in September, 1946: "Mirko, aged three, was brought by his peasant father all the way from Leskovac, south of Nish. He had curvature of the spine and all the signs of acute malnutrition – pigeon chest, rough skin, flabby joints, huge abdomen and boils on the head. The doctor shook his head – there was no bed for Mirko. The father bowed and with that Serb gentleness that is so paradoxical and so disarming, said, 'Dobro, Gospodine', and started on his long journey home with his crippled baby. Then suddenly there was the Matron, running after him, waving her arms – she had found a cot. She seized Mirko, carried him back and put him into it. He responded by pinching and scratching her whenever she came to feed him or give him a saline bath and for a long time he spat out his milk and would only eat bread. Mirko had that old attraction that monstrous, misshapen children have for women. I was present when he made his first statement and smiled for the first time, and I felt it, too. Matron put a clean

191

overall on him. Mirko whispered, 'It's got a little pocket,' and smiled. It seemed an event of enormous importance." [88] The children accepted for treatment came from different parts of the country, and nearly all of them were poor, and possessed nothing. Francesca Wilson described one such patient whom she met during her visit to the hospital; it was Vojislav, a clever boy, twelve years of age, who came from Bosnia where the worst battles had been fought. "His mother won Dr. MacPhail's heart because when asked what possessions she had she replied: 'I have my soul and four children – nothing else." At the beginning, after the re-opening of the hospital, life was by no means easy; there was a shortage of equipment and it was not easy to obtain good food. "There is much to be done for them", wrote Marion Tew, "and the hundreds of others waiting to come, but our work is sadly hampered by lack of essentials, such as a weighing machine, quartz lamp and X-ray apparatus. Meanwhile, we can at least help to build up the children's resistance to T.B. by good food, fresh air and rest, and although their diet is not as varied as we could wish, we are able to give them eggs, milk and dried fruit. Fresh meat can usually be had once a week. Such items as eggs and cheese often have to be collected in 'penny numbers' from far afield, and the dried fruits are personal rations of the English personnel, which are handed over to the children. We have a good supply of cod-liver oil from England and Canada." [93] With the approach of spring and summer the situation as regards supplies improved considerably. A small farm was established beside the hospital, where pigs were reared for the needs of the hospital, and fruit and vegetables from the hospital's orchard and garden were regularly used to feed the small patients. "When I came there in 1946 the orchards and vineyards on the hills behind the hospital and right down to the river at its feet were heavy with golden apricots and muscatel grapes. The air was fresh up there, the sun strong and healing", wrote Francesca Wilson. And there were all the children, whenever the sun was not too strong, lying outside in their beds in the courtyard or on the terrace, chirping like sparrows and eager to tell me their stories. I need not have travelled far and wide in Yugoslavia; they came from all over, and from them I could get a very concrete picture, not only of the age-long pattern of its life, but of what Yugoslavia had suffered in the war and what it was doing now in the peace. When I went to the boy's ward I wondered that I had spent so much time with the girls – they had so much to tell me: there was no question of looking for subjects of conversation. They all knew exactly what they wanted to be. Only one, a Macedonian and the son of a priest, wanted to be a teacher – the others were all engineers, lorry-drivers or air-pilots. Looking at them lying on their backs or with disease of the hip or knee, this seemed fantastic, but Dr. MacPhail told me that the majority recover and live a normal life. When I expressed surprise at this, Dr. MacPhail said, "Well, look at Phyllis. Her father was British, and worked at the Belgrade Consulate. She came to me with disease of the hip, and went out cured. And in this war she parachuted down to Tito in the mountains and had all sorts of adventures.' I had seen Phyllis in the British

Consulate at Split, rattling away in Serbian, quick and light in her movements as a bird. It was most encouraging to think that cures were so complete." [88]

The children in the hospital were happy and contented, and, in spite of the difficulties, the atmosphere in the hospital was cheerful and joyful, and the small patients chattered and sang and laughed all day long (Figs. 88 and 89). The recollections of one of the patients at that time provide convincing evidence of how the children felt, and what the situation was like in the hospital at that time: "In the spring of 1946 I came to stay with my aunt in Novi Sad, and, on her doctor's advice, she placed me for treatment in the children's hospital in Sremska Kamenica. I was then twelve years old. When I came for treatment I was frightened about what would happen to me. The hospital was very clean and tidy, and Dr. Katherine (as we called her) wore a white coat with a veil over her head, like religious sisters. Her appearance aroused fear and respect in me and other children....Dr. Katherine came to visit us every morning at 8 o'clock and talked to every patient and encouraged us all. She made a similar visit in the afternoon or evening. There were children here for treatment from all parts of our country. There were some troublesome children, and the doctor was strict and warned them to obey the instructions about their treatment; she spoke in Serbian, with a few words in English, which were translated for us, and said that anyone who did not want to be treated would be sent home. She was strict with the staff too if everything wasn't clean and tidy on time. Her appearance, her smile and her gentle words filled me and the others with the belief that we would get well, but we must do what we were told....The conditions of treatment were excellent, the food was plentiful and varied, At least once a week the nurses bathed us (they moistened and soaped a small towel, washed us with this, then put on our pyjamas or nightdress). During the summer months we were taken out into the courtyard or terrace to sunbathe. While we were sun-bathing we were given caps for our heads with a shield and dark glasses. If there were not enough of these protective devices they fastened a cotton cover to the bed behind our heads, covering half of our bodies, depending which part of the body was affected by illness. Behind our heads, fastened to the bed, we had a cotton bag in which we kept our towels and toothbrushes and other things. We had a school in the hospital, and teachers came to us every day from Sremska Kamenica, either in the morning or in the afternoon, and gave us lessons and set us homework; then teachers gave us marks based on our answers and written work.....Dr. Katherine often came to see us, and her appearance, during her morning and afternoon visits, was like a plaster on a wound for us patients....she poured strength into us, and the belief that we would get well and go home....I have no words to describe her kindness and concern for every patient, because she watched over us with a mother's love for every one and tried to find the best way of helping us."

During the summer of 1946 it seemed as though everything was going well; the hospital was working at full capacity, its activities were developing without major problems, they were co-operating well with the government, and

Katherine was in a very optimistic mood. In July that year she travelled to London, where the Yugoslav Society of Great Britain arranged a reception in her honour, at which Captain L.H. Green, chairman of the Society, in welcoming her said: "Nothing but her intrepid determination to get her own way could have achieved under present conditions, what she has accomplished in Yugoslavia." Katherine, in her speech, stressed the fact that the re-opening of her hospital, in a country in which no private initiatives in the field of social activity were allowed, could be regarded as significant recognition of the value of that institution. "When I returned I found the hospital absolutely vacant, like a desolate monastery, the garden a desert, but I recovered some of its own furniture and secured equipment and reconstructed the work with the help of the Yugoslav authorities, who had borne the whole task of repairing the building. They realised that work for children was one of the most important things a country could undertake", explained Katherine. And she also emphasised the fact that the hospital, which then had 60 beds, would increase this capacity to 200 beds in the course of a few months. "There was no reason why it should not go on increasing. They must leave politics out of the question. Eighty per cent of the people of Yugoslavia were friendly to Britain, and they looked to us more than to any other country for help", added Katherine.[94] Katherine also discussed these plans with Francesca Wilson in September 1946. "The trouble is that these patients need care for a long time after they return home – good food, rest and sun, and often their families are too poor or too ignorant to give this. We try to get the parents to bring the children back every three months to make sure they have no relapse, but the pressure on the hospital is so great. There are fifty on the waiting list now and hundreds more who should come. Children are often put into plaster and sent home when they should stay. Since TB has increased disastrously with this war, there is an urgent need to build and have at least 200 beds. We have plans. The Government is very eager to see the hospital expanded", Katherine told her. And Francesca Wilson concluded: "The abstracted conspiratorial look of the seasoned Scots pioneer came into Dr. MacPhail's eyes, and she added, 'I think I know of a site for it.'"[88]

The need for a bigger hospital was certainly great, and the new government was undoubtedly interested in the welfare of children; but at that time there was considerable tension between Yugoslavia and the western powers over Trieste,[90] and other unresolved questions, so that it was exceptionally difficult to secure any kind of co-operation between Great Britain and Yugoslavia, even in such a mutual enterprise as the maintenance of a children's hospital.

As in the pre-war days, the sanatorium attracted the attention of many visitors who often came to see this truly unique institution. Nearly every week-end there were visitors from Belgrade, mainly from the UNRRA headquarters and the British embassy; as a rule they were pleasantly surprised by the atmosphere which prevailed in the hospital, and one UNRRA doctor, after his visit, said it was the "singingest" hospital he had ever seen. One of the most frequent guests was the British Ambassador Sir Charles Peake who, immediately after his arrival in Belgrade, visited the hospital. He arrived in Belgrade on a Saturday and descended with some of his staff on the hospital on the Sunday, saying he wanted the hospital to be the first place he visited in Yugoslavia. After this Sremska Kamenica and the children's hospital were his favourite place for excursions, which he often visited with his wife. In this way they both became friendly with Katherine, whose work they greatly valued and appreciated, so that they became great champions of the hospital. That autumn Katherine, probably as an attempt to revive and continue a pre-war tradition, arranged a party to celebrate the grape harvest, to which many guests were invited, including, naturally, Sir Charles Peake and Lady Peake. Roasted sucking pig was prepared, and wine in abundance, and there was music, singing, and dancing the *kolo* round the fire in the courtyard. It was a joyful and lively celebration that lasted until the small hours of the morning and to a great extent revived the spirit of the long past pre-war times.

This party, however, was the last one, and, in one sense, a farewell celebration for Katherine and her colleagues, since the days ahead were filled with uncertainty, suspicion, unpleasantness and even open hostility. There were many signs of this, and Katherine was aware of the situation. Right from the beginning of the post-war work of the hospital the organs of the new government in Vojvodina had appointed a so-called administrative director of the hospital, whose duty it was to supervise the funds allotted by the state for its upkeep. This person was Branko Bugarski who, according to his own admission, had been suggested by Katherine herself, and who was very kind, patient and friendly in his attitude, and, as he himself affirmed, not a member of the ruling Communist Party, though Katherine did feel that he was a *commissar*, "who had been sent to watch and report everything that went on at the hospital." The telephone line between her villa and the hospital was cut, and at that time a medical sister was sent from Belgrade with orders that she was to be employed in the hospital; and it soon became clear from her behaviour, and her excessive curiosity, that she was a spy and a secret police informer. There came an order at that time to put in the hall, a large photo of Tito shaking hands with Stalin, but Katherine, typically, as her niece Elspeth Biggs remarked, somehow found a photograph of Tito shaking hands with Winston Churchill which she put in the hall too; so, after that the matter was solved by mutual agreement, and both photographs were removed. Katherine soon became aware that everything that happened in the hospital was regularly reported to the local committee of the Communist Party. An atmosphere of distrust and doubt gradually developed in the hospital, which was in fact typical of the whole country at that time. It was a time of fear and suspicion, and many of her friends disappeared. However, the hospital in Sremska Kamenica was obviously attracting special attention from the appropriate organs of the government, because it was frequently visited by guests from the British Embassy and also other foreigners, mainly British and American; the communists, paranoically xenophobic anyhow, were particularly sensitive about this fact, and they openly showed it to Katherine who was under constant observation. The extent to which the communist government of that time was suspicious about Katherine and her team is clear from the fact that Vasilj Skrjaga, her chauffeur for many years, was imprisoned in Novi Sad for three months in 1948, that is after her departure from the country. He was considered to be a spy, and to have collaborated with Dr. Katherine MacPhail, who was also affirmed to be a foreign spy. While in prison he was tormented and cross-examined about all Katherine's movements, about what she did and whom she mixed with. However, nothing could be proved, and Vasilj was not condemned, but simply discharged from prison and left in peace.

In spite of all this unpleasantness and increasing distrust, the hospital continued to function properly because it was under the protection of UNRRA. However, the work of UNRRA in Yugoslavia was coming to an end, and in September 1946 Katherine received a letter from UNRRA in which she was officially informed that from November 1st, 1946 onwards their responsibilities for any kind of voluntary, humanitarian or social activity would cease in Yugoslavia. Thus Katherine lost a powerful protector, and as she foresaw what was going to happen, she was extremely worried about the future of the hospital. Realising that under the new conditions she would not be able to stay and work as she had done formerly, Katherine formed a plan whereby the sanatorium could be integrated into the new state system of social security. She proposed to the Ministry of Health that the hospital should be changed into a rehabilitation centre for children left handicapped as a result of tuberculosis or other illnesses, where they could become qualified for various useful occupations; in particular she planned to establish workshops to make orthopaedic aids and devices, where grown-up invalids could also been employed. "In this way the hospital building would be a social training institution, fulfilling a useful purpose as a special rehabilitation centre", Katherine wrote in a letter to the Ministry of Health; but she never received an answer. Realising that under the new social system she would not be able to continue her work, Katherine wanted to leave Yugoslavia and return home, but the British ambassador continually persuaded her to stay as long as possible in the hope that the situation would improve. "There is very little interest still surviving in Yugoslavia", Katherine wrote home at this time. "This is regretted by a great many people and just on that account our presence here has been of even greater significance that it was before. Officially the country is in the process of taking up a definite policy and attitude to our country and we are no longer considered to be friends and Allies as we had always been. I told you that our Ambassador is deeply interested in the hospital, and I have told him many times I could not go on any longer, but he always persuaded me to continue a little longer to see how things went. Whatever happens we have done a good piece of work and the place has real value."

Meanwhile Agnes Hardie, Katherine's former companion and head sister from pre-war days, managed to return to the hospital; she now replaced Marion Tew as matron, who returned to Great Britain. All the remaining British subjects had also gradually left the hospital, so that only Katherine and her two old and most faithful teammates remained – Agnes Hardie and Alice Murphy. The work in the hospital continued as usual, but in a gloomy atmosphere of uncertainty and fear. "It was quite clear at that time that a genuine communist régime was being established in Yugoslavia", wrote Katherine, and she realised that the communist ideology was beginning to affect the children too. "Even the children in the hospital have changed, especially the older ones," she reported later. "It used to be the custom in the hospital that about 7 o'clock, after supper, the children would say their prayers, room by room, while the sister on duty visited them; after this she would put out the light. However, one evening the older children refused to say their prayers, and after that the habit gradually ceased." From the time of its formation it had been the custom in the hospital in Sremska Kamenica that on Christmas Eve a Christmas tree would be set up in every ward, and in the evening the sister on duty would light candles and the children would sing Christmas carols and receive presents. However, at Christmas in 1946, which for Katherine and her colleagues was their last Christmas in Yugoslavia, when the candles were lit as usual, the children began to sing Partisan songs about Marshal Tito. Katherine, who was in the hospital, put a stop to this singing, and said that they were not celebrating Tito's birthday, but the birthday of Jesus Christ. Then she turned to the oldest girl in the ward, who was the leader, and she simply shrugged her shoulders and said she did not believe in that. Later, after that night, there was no more singing in the hospital in Sremska Kamenica. It was a sad Christmas for Katherine and her two British associates, to whom it was clear that their mission in this country was over, that new conditions prevailed to which they could not adapt themselves, and that it was time to go home. The one thing that held them back was their sense of duty towards the sick children, and the constant pressure from the British ambassador that they should stay and continue their work.

And the work did continue until May 1947, when Dr. Uroš Jekić, who was then Minister of Health and later professor of psychiatry at the Faculty of Medicine in Belgrade, came to Sremska Kamenica to visit Katherine and to tell her that, according to the spirit of the new régime, all hospitals must be nationalised; and that in accordance with this principle the Anglo-Yugoslav Hospital in Sremska Kamenica must be handed over to the Yugoslav authorities by the autumn of 1947 at the latest. Dr. Uroš Jekić, who was an old acquaintance of Katherine, patiently explained to her the plans and ideas of the new régime, and thanked Katherine and the two remaining members of the British staff for their valuable services, and for the way in which they had helped to maintain cordial and friendly relations between Great Britain and Yugoslavia, which would always be remembered. Although Katherine and her co-workers Agnes Hardie and Alice Murphy were expecting something like this, it was still for them a sad and heavy blow. After so many years of sacrificial work and service to this nation, they were simply deprived of everything, denied any kind of hospitality and ordered to leave the country for which they had done so much, and which they regarded as their second homeland.

The hospital buildings in Sremska Kamenica and the entire estate had been registered in Katherine's name, as her private property, and in a conversation with the minister she had reached an agreement about some form of letting out the hospital to the government, on condition that it would continue to work as it had done up to that time, naturally without any British staff, for the next two years, and that Katherine would be allowed to return in 1949, when the hospital and its estate would be finally handed over to the state. This was clearly just a formal agreement, since the process of nationalisation in the new Communist Yugoslavia was, for the most part, proceeding relentlessly. There were some attempts to exempt the hospital in Sremska Kamenica from this process, but without success. Branko Bugarski, who was at that time the administrative director of the hospital, made the following comment: "Many people in Yugoslavia, and particularly those of us who lived in Kamenica, were extremely sorry that Dr. Katherine MacPhail had to leave the hospital, which was also ours, in 1947 because of nationalisation. I personally went to Belgrade three times and begged the relevant authorities to make an exception in this case, and to allow Dr. Katherine MacPhail to stay in Sremska Kamenica, and to leave the hospital when she wished." However, nothing could stop the new government from carrying out their programme to introduce a communist social system, and Katherine, who realised this, soon began to prepare to go home to Scotland. She managed to send home to Scotland some furniture, and some valuable items from her villa, such as a big *ćilim* (Turkish carpet), three Bosnian chairs, two copper plates, and a large Turkish *mangala* (brazier); but most of her personal possessions and books were distributed to her friends as parting gifts. The vineyard with its own house, situated just below the villa in which Katherine lived, was sold to Julka Skrjaga, the wife of Vasilj Skrjaga, who had been her chauffeur for many years, and had continued to live in Sremska Kamenica with his family. Katherine let the house in which she lived to temporary residents until the question of the hospital's future was definitely solved. However in August 1948 this house with its courtyard was also nationalised, and became the property of the local people's council in Sremska Kamenica. For her this was a sad end of everything; she was brutally deprived of her hospital and her foundation, her work, her estate, her way of life, and her second homeland, which she had loved so well, and separated from those for whom she had done so much. Later she herself wrote: "It was with a heavy heart that I left the work which I had begun, then carried on for so many years." However, in one sense, she felt it was a great relief that after so many months of uncertainty, suspicion and fear, everything was now ended. "All three of us were nevertheless glad that this sad and painful situation was at last over", Katherine remarked later.

When all the preparations and formalities were finally completed, Dr. Katherine MacPhail, Miss Agnes Hardie and Miss Alice Murphy left Sremska Kamenica and Yugoslavia in June 1947, this time finally, without any hope of return.

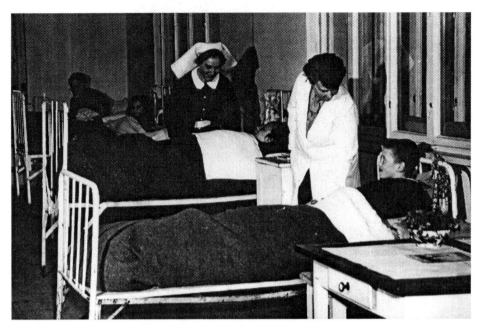

Fig. 88 Dr. K. MacPhail and the head sister, Marion Tew, during a visiting round in the hospital in Sremska Kamenica in 1946.
(Courtesy of Mrs. E. Biggs)

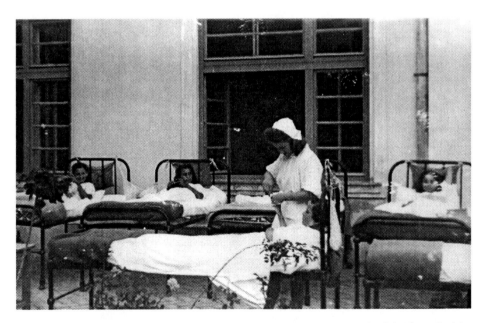

Fig. 89 Looking after the small patients lying in the courtyard of the hospital in Sremska Kamenica (photograph taken by Marion Tew in 1946).
(Courtesy of Mrs. E. Biggs)

Chapter 9

Scotland, 1947 – 1974

During the journey home to Scotland, towards the end of June 1947 Dr. Katherine MacPhail reached London, where the Yugoslav Society of Great Britain arranged a large welcome party for her. This took place at the Goring Hotel on June 25th, 1947, as soon as "a most unexpected guest" arrived from Yugoslavia, "under not the happiest circumstances", as the president of the society put it in his speech of cordial welcome. According to an article in the journal *The World's Children*, Dr. Katherine MacPhail told those present that "the cause of her return to England was the decision of the Yugoslav Government that everything must be nationalised. Moreover, officially, the country did not want foreigners, though the man in the street did not seem to share this prejudice. The Government had offered to buy or to lease the hospital, but Dr. MacPhail had countered this with the offer of a loan of the premises for two years, which she deemed more appropriate to the traditions of the hospital as a link between the people of Britain and the people of Yugoslavia." [95]

After her return to Scotland Katherine settled in St Andrews, "the old grey city by the sea" on the east coast of Scotland, where some members of her family already lived, and where her sister Annie, who was also unmarried, had already bought a house for the two of them before the war, where she had lived since that time. It was a pleasant, convenient house, with two storeys above the ground floor (Fig. 90); the address was 4 Kinburn Place, and it was here that Katherine lived for the rest of her life. At that time Katherine was extremely tired and unhappy after all her years of hard work and everything she had gone through; also her deafness had increased and she certainly needed a long rest. St Andrews, a small, quiet university town on the coast, and the comfortable home where she lived with her elder sister Annie provided excellent conditions for rest; and here Katherine soon recovered, surrounded as she was by the care of her relatives. Fortunately she had no financial problems, since her father, Dr. Donald MacPhail, had taken care of the situation in good time. He had left a considerable sum of money in the bank for his two unmarried daughters, Annie and Katherine, which provided a regular income on which they could live without any anxiety.

Katherine spent the first few months resting and "putting our house in order", as she wrote to an acquaintance from the Save the Children Fund. However, as she was not used to remaining long without work, she soon began to think of new ideas and projects, about which she wrote in a letter: "But I have always an urge to keep in touch with children's work. I have been making efforts to procure a place which would make a home for children from Germany, but the problem of finance for its upkeep proved too difficult and I have not pursued that further. The SCF asked me recently to go to Palestine with their unit but I felt I

201

was not strong enough nor young enough to stand such a tough task." Katherine continued to keep up all her connections with colleagues, and with many individuals and organisations, and especially with the Save the Children Fund, and she often travelled to London where she met friends and representatives of this humanitarian organisation, with which she had been connected for so many years. She was a member of the Cowdray Club, which was situated in a large old building in central London, which Lady Cowdray had left to the club exclusively for the use of women doctors and medical sisters. That was her base there and she always stayed in this club during her frequent visits to London.

Katherine kept in touch with her colleagues from the hospital, and also corresponded with some of their friends and acquaintances from Yugoslavia. In a letter to Branko Bugarski, dated February 8th, 1948 Katherine wrote: "I am going to London for a few weeks tomorrow where I will see, I hope, Miss Macartney and Miss Tew (who will be home on leave). Miss Murphy is busy in Poland." Katherine had not stopped thinking of Yugoslavia, and especially of Kamenica, and in the same letter she writes: "Here we have had very little snow and winter is nearly over. Kamenica will be beginning to look lovely now and soon the fruit trees will be in blossom. I listen to Belgrade quite often on the wireless." Obviously Katherine remembered Yugoslavia with considerable nostalgia, and was once more making various plans to help Yugoslav children. In a letter to an official of the Save the Children Fund at the beginning of 1949 she says: "I still have some money which I can use for Yugoslav children," as she wondered whether there was perhaps some project in any European country. "I may be going out to Yugoslavia this spring or summer to finish up all my affairs there", Katherine wrote on the same occasion, "and so could possibly spend some time in Italy or France to have a look round".

The visit to Yugoslavia did indeed take place in October 1949 when Katherine, accompanied by her old and intimate colleague Alice Murphy came once more to Sremska Kamenica, to arrange the handing over of the hospital, as had been agreed, and also to deal with other tasks connected with her estate. The political mood in Yugoslavia at that time, after the break with the Soviet Union, had already changed considerably, and, notwithstanding a certain amount of suspicion, foreigners from western countries were not automatically regarded as enemies; and Dr. MacPhail and Miss Murphy were cordially welcomed as friends in Sremska Kamenica. In the hospital they found quite a few members of staff who had known them in previous years, and who were sincerely glad to see them again, and asked them when they would come back to the hospital. They also came across some small patients who had already begun their treatment in Katherine's time, and whose happy smiles made it clear that they recognised their "doktoritza Katarina" ("Doctor Katherine"). "The hospital looked beautiful and bright in the autumn sunshine", wrote Katherine, not without sadness.

"Newly painted outside and in it shone in the midst of the golds and browns of the surrounding vineyards. Looking round it all seemed the same; the children having their lessons in the sheltered courtyard; daily dressings being done in the dressing room; office staff filling in endless lists; and nurses running about the wards. Nothing seemed changed. The women squatting in the kitchen peeling potatoes; newly washed clothes fluttering in the breeze and the sound of wood being chopped in the yard. And yet I felt a difference".

There certainly were differences; the hospital was overcrowded, since there were over a hundred children housed in a nearby auxiliary building; there was not enough hygienic material, and a feeling that there were not enough qualified staff. Katherine immediately noticed that the children were pale, a sign that they were not sufficiently exposed to the sunshine, which was still at that time a very important part of the treatment. "Instead of lying immobilised, fixed to the bed in good comfortable positions, the children sat or lay without much attempt to straighten their deformities", wrote Katherine as she described her impressions. "The staff said this was because they had no materials to make the corsets or extensions which were essential for this work, and being untrained they had made no attempt to improvise the necessary apparatus. The beds were packed together, leaving no space for bedside lockers where the children used to keep their treasures, and there were no toys to be seen. This was not surprising as there are no toys to be had in the shops any more and so the children have nothing to play with, and no material for embroideries and knitting to keep them busy and happy as before. As I looked at the rows of beds it seemed as if all the gaiety had gone from the hospital," wrote Katherine sadly.

Undoubtedly the quality of the work and life in the hospital had deteriorated considerably since the departure of Dr. Katherine MacPhail and her team. The specialist level of the work had inexorably fallen considerably; there was no longer strict control or discipline, nor efforts to maintain European standards of treatment and care, and the considerable financial support and help from abroad was no longer available. All this had a very disagreeable effect on the sick children, who were aware of the situation; this is clear from the recollections of one of the patients who was treated in the sanatorium at that time: "While Dr. MacPhail was in the hospital, and controlling its finances, the conditions of treatment were like a fairy tale – food, hygiene and everything else. But after her departure, when the hospital became public property, the conditions of treatment deteriorated, and the hospital was abolished as a place for treatment of children's diseases and became part of the Regional Hospital".

But in spite of everything Katherine was glad that the hospital was still working, although she felt that she could still have done a great deal to help, and felt sad about this: "Two years have gone past since we left, but it is still known as the Anglo-Yugoslav hospital and I should think will always remain so in the minds of the people. And the Bambino is still over the entrance to the hospital", wrote Katherine sadly on a later occasion. "I am glad the work goes on, but how?

A few of our own trained nurses, some more material, another pavilion to take in more and more children, and how much we could still do to help them with their burden of crippled children".

The final handover of the hospital to public ownership, as had been agreed in 1947, was simply an empty formality, an illusion, since meanwhile laws had been passed authorising the nationalisation of all private organisations, including "all sanatoria, hospitals, public baths, spas, and treatment centres with premises and installations for medical treatment"; so from April 28th, 1948 onwards the hospital in Sremska Kamenica was registered as nationalised property, which, of course, Katherine had not known. Her house in which she had lived was also nationalised in 1948; however Katherine managed to have this house restored to her ownership. The regional People's Council in Novi Sad passed a resolution on October 15th, 1949, according to which this house was restored to her; she then immediately started negotiations to sell the house and its courtyard to the Ministry of Internal Affairs, which installed there its own employees who worked in the Police School which was just across the road. However this sale was not finally concluded until 1951, when the right of ownership was officially transferred to the Ministry of Internal Affairs in Belgrade, in fact to the headquarters of the national police force. Earlier in 1947, Katherine had sold her vineyard with its small gardener's cottage to Vasilj Skrjaga, who had been her chauffeur for many years; and so she finally settled all problems relating to her property in Yugoslavia, and then returned to her home in Scotland, with a heavy heart, full of sadness and painful impressions. Her niece, Elspeth Biggs, described the state she was in after this visit: "This really broke her heart, and she was relieved to go, before she saw any more deterioration in everything that she had built up over the years in Yugoslavia. I've never seen her in tears, but my sister Ann told me not long ago that when she went into our Aunt's house when they had moved, she found Aunt Kathie, sitting on the floor, arranging her books in a bookcase, and crying bitterly. She was never really happy again."

Katherine had always kept in close touch with her family, especially with her sisters; however, so far in her life she had had little opportunity to spend much time with them; but during the years after her return from Yugoslavia she did in some way make up for this. Her younger sister Isabel had spent some years in Serbia during the First World War, and after the Second World War she settled with her family in the small town of West Coker in Somerset, where her husband inherited a fine old house, dating from the fourteenth century, with a very valuable library and extensive grounds; during these years Katherine often made long visits there, enjoying the company of her sister and her family, whom she had not seen for so many years, ever since Isabel went to China in 1923. During the year 1950 Katherine's older sister Janet moved with her family to St Andrews, after her husband, Dr. James McFarlane, retired; and here she became in some way the centre of the family, around whom they all gathered. So as well as her sister Annie, with whom she shared the house, Katherine also had nearby another sister, Janet, and also some other relatives who had also settled in St Andrews; so she was indeed surrounded by her family, with whom she enjoyed cordial relations. "Wherever Aunt Kathie was, there was nothing but fun, and we all adored her," wrote her niece Elspeth Biggs later. And in addition she made friends with many people in St Andrews with whom she kept in close touch, and became a well-known and eminent member of the local community. Nor was Katherine forgotten in international circles; the *Union International de Protection de l'Enfance* showed its recognition of her work in the Near East and in Yugoslavia from 1944 to 1947 by awarding her the *Ordre de Mérite* (Order of Merit); a formal certificate of this recognition was bestowed on her at a meeting in Geneva on October 15th, 1950.

During the fifties, after the definite break with the Stalinist policies of the Soviet Union, there was a radical change in the attitude of the Yugoslav Government at that time towards the western, so-called capitalist countries. Although there was still a certain element of caution and suspicion because of ideological differences, these countries were no longer regarded as enemies, but rather as allies within the framework of global politics; this also led to a change of attitude towards certain individuals, former friends from these countries, who during recent years had been vilified and proclaimed as spies and foes. These included Dr. Katherine MacPhail, whose noble work and enormous services to this country were finally recognised; and the representatives of the new communist administration then tried in some way to rectify the very painful impression made by their former behaviour. So during these years the local People's Council in Sremska Kamenica proposed that there should be some special recognition of the work of Dr. Katherine MacPhail "for the foundation and maintenance of a children's sanatorium, and for other services to the people of Sremska Kamenica". The council elected her an honorary citizen of Sremska Kamenica, and decided that the street on Čardak Hill in which the children's hospital was situated should be called after her: "Dr. Katherine MacPhail Street." Furthermore it was proposed that she should be awarded a life pension and some form of public recognition in the form of suitable decoration; however Katherine refused both these offers, and suggested something that obviously meant more to her, namely that a memorial plaque should be placed on the wall near the main entrance to the hospital, on which it should be stated that she was the founder of the hospital, which represented a memorial to the friendship between Great Britain and Yugoslavia. This suggestion was accepted, and a memorial plaque was placed on the right-hand wall of the entrance hall of the hospital, where there was the mosaic of the Scottish lion on the floor; the dedication of this plaque was arranged for September 1954, when it was planned to celebrate the twentieth anniversary of the foundation of the hospital. Katherine was sent an official invitation from the Ministry of Health, the Yugoslav Red Cross, and the Belgrade Medical Faculty, asking her to be present at this celebration; Katherine accepted the invitation, and once more visited Yugoslavia and Sremska Kamenica.

The celebration took place on September 22nd, 1954, in the presence of over 100 guests, who greeted Katherine very cordially in the hospital. Alice Murphy, her inseparable colleague for many years, accompanied her; she also found there her old friend Flora Sandes, who was then visiting Yugoslavia as a guest of the War Veterans' Association. There were many speeches (Fig. 91) by representatives of the local authorities, the director of the Main Regional Hospital in Novi Sad, to which the sanatorium would shortly be attached, and Dr. Svetislav Stojanović, her friend and colleague for many years; the speakers stressed her merits, and full acknowledgment and gratitude was expressed to Dr. MacPhail for all she had done for this country. In his speech Dr. Svetislav Stojanović said: "The name and personality of Dr. Katherine MacPhail, this modest and generous, tenacious and resolute Scotswoman, as enduring as the granite of her beautiful land, have become part of the national and medical history of Serbia. By her 35 years' work in our country she has gained the appreciation of our highest authorities. She has been elected an honorary citizen of Sremska Kamenica and a life president of the Red Cross. Her work in the fields of medicine and sociology will remain the emblem of the sincere friendship between the British and Serbian peoples". Katherine was given a specially warm welcome, with presents and flowers, by the doctors and staff of the hospital; and after the dedication of the memorial plaque Katherine walked round the wards and visited the small patients (Fig. 92). As Katherine recollected later, she was particularly pleased and amused when she saw her photograph on the wall of the hospital office, placed between photographs of Lenin and Marshal Tito. Later this photograph was placed above the memorial plaque in the entrance hall. At the end of the celebration there was a festive lunch in the courtyard of the hospital (Fig. 93); then Katherine went to the village where she was solemnly proclaimed an honorary citizen of Sremska Kamenica by the local People's Council; then she was elected an honorary life president of the local Red Cross in the premises of that organisation.

This was Katherine's last visit to Yugoslavia and her beloved Kamenica. Then she was contented and happy, according to her niece Elspeth Biggs, who wrote on the occasion of this visit: "It was a wonderful time for her, and a fine tribute to her work and her personality, freely and gratefully given". Katherine was also given an album of photos of the occasion, which happened to be her last visit to Yugoslavia, her "second homeland", as she used to say.

After the visit to Sremska Kamenica, which clearly made a very favourable impression on Katherine, she returned to St Andrews and, now more at peace, continued her retirement life among her numerous friends and members of her family, whom she frequently visited. During 1955 she suffered a serious loss, when her younger sister Isabel died after a long illness. She and Isabel had much in common; as a young woman Isabel had followed in her footsteps, and taken part in the First World War as a nursing sister; for some years they had worked together on the Salonica Front and later in Belgrade. Although after this they were separated for many years, they remained close, understandably since they had shared so much of their life experience, and had common memories, which they enjoyed recalling, and about which they often talked.

Although the loss of Isabel was a heavy blow for Katherine, she continued to have a very active social life, and still collaborated in a variety of humanitarian projects concerned with the protection of children. As she was, unfortunately, no longer able to invest her money and energy in some projects in Yugoslavia, through the Save the Children Fund Katherine took part in the founding and construction of an international children's home in Hermagor in Austria. She invested in this project a considerable amount of money that, it seems, she received from the Yugoslav government as compensation for the nationalisation of her estate in Sremska Kamenica. At the end of 1940s and the beginning of 1950s Yugoslavia conducted negotiations with several west European countries, including Great Britain, to regulate their mutual financial claims. At the beginning of the Second World War Britain passed a law blocking all claims from countries under German occupation, including Yugoslavia. But after the war Britain made a list of all Yugoslav citizens who had money in their banks and this was returned to them. As a reciprocal measure Yugoslavia, among other things, compensated British subjects whose property had been nationalised. Katherine gave most of the money she obtained in this way as her contribution to the home in Hermagor, and conducted an intensive correspondence with Colonel Basil Gardner-McTaggart, who was the representative of the Save the Children Fund in Austria, and had his headquarters at Klagenfurt. Tireless as always, in 1956 Katherine visited this place. She travelled by car with one of her former colleagues, Beatrix McCartney, who had been one of her drivers in a team that came to Yugoslavia in 1945 under the wing of UNRRA. With them came the irreplaceable Alice Murphy; Katherine's niece Ann Davidson and her husband accompanied them in another car. Although this journey was quite tiring, it gave Katherine much pleasure and satisfaction.

As the years passed, Katherine kept in touch with friends from her younger days, with whom she corresponded and exchanged visits. Naturally, her most frequent guests were her old and faithful colleagues Agnes Hardie and Alice Murphy, who were greatly liked by Katherine's family and who till the end of their lives kept in touch with Katherine and her relatives. Agnes Hardie, who for many years had been the head sister in the hospitals in Belgrade and Sremska Kamenica, lived in her retirement in a small house on the south coast of England, from which she often came to visit Katherine and regularly spent some time with her. Later she gave up her house by the sea and settled in a home for retired nursing sisters in Tunbridge Wells, where she died in 1983. Another frequent visitor was Alice Murphy, who for several years acted as secretary to the hospital in Belgrade and then in Sremska Kamenica. Alice Murphy lived in south London, from which she often came to visit Katherine and her family, especially over public holidays. An anecdote about Alice Murphy from this time was vividly remembered in Katherine's family. On one occasion Alice Murphy and Beatrix McCartney, or Trix, as they called her, were visiting Katherine, and Trix took Katherine and Alice for a drive in the neighbourhood of St Andrews. During this drive Alice suddenly fell silent, and for a long time did not utter a single word, which surprised and puzzled Katherine. Then Trix explained that on the way they had seen a white horse grazing in a field; and according to Russian popular belief, on this occasion no word should be spoken until another white horse was seen. As Alice Murphy was half-Russian, and thus a little superstitious, she did not speak a word at that time, and as though out of spite no other white horse appeared anywhere. As it was already tea time, they returned home, and Alice still remained silent. Then Katherine, who was already worried, suggested that they should go to a nearby factory where there would be horses harnessed ready to transport goods; so all three of them once more sat in the car and went to the factory, where they did indeed notice a white horse; after this Alice Murphy did immediately begin to talk, to everybody's satisfaction, and all three of them went happily home to afternoon tea. Alice Murphy spent the rest of her life in London, and died in 1973. Another former colleague with whom Katherine kept in touch was Katherine Sokolović (née Ogilvy) who before her marriage to Dr. Milan Sokolović had been the head sister in the Children's Hospital in Belgrade. After the Second World War, during which Dr. Sokolović was killed, Katherine Sokolović settled in Britain and for the rest of her life she kept in touch with Dr. Katherine MacPhail and visited her.

One of Katherine's good friends over many years was Dana Stanković, the daughter of her old friend from the Salonica Front, Constance Dušmanić; they visited each other over a period of sixty years, about which Dana's husband, Ratko Stanković, wrote as follows: "I had the honour and pleasure of getting to know Dr. MacPhail; she was often a guest in our home during the sixties when we lived in London, and she was still able to travel. One unforgettable impression she left on me was her sincere love for our people, and a deep respect for their past....Her love for the Serbian people was deep and sincere, founded on sympathy for their sufferings and triumphs, a full and all-embracing love, without any personal interest – except for personal satisfaction and a feeling of the fullness of life, which is the regular reward for all charitable and self-sacrificing work. She remained the same even after the experience of cruel ingratitude which – as Dr. MacPhail knew very well – was not an expression of the Serbian national soul."

One of her old friends who visited her several times in St Andrews was Helen Gordon - Duff, with whom Katherine had kept in touch over several years. A less frequent but still welcome visitor was Draga Srdić, the sister of Vasa Srdić, Katherine's old and unforgettable friend from Sremska Kamenica; and especially Dr. Svetislav Stojanović with whom she had worked for many years, and who had been a friend both in Belgrade and in Sremska Kamenica. Her niece Elspeth Biggs wrote: "Aunt Kathie lived for those meetings with her old friends and colleagues, who came here as though on a pilgrimage. And when one of them died she was deeply sad and dejected for several days".

Katherine also kept in touch with some friends in Yugoslavia who kept her informed about the work of her hospital, and also other events in which she was clearly interested, and about which she wrote in one of her letters: "I am glad to say that the hospital is still working with tubercular children, and with Professor Svetislav Stojanović, who was our surgeon thirty years ago, and with a team of specialists from the orthopaedic clinic in Belgrade, and with Dr. Manojlović, all personal friends and veterans of this hospital. I know that a large institution for tuberculosis patients has been built in the immediate vicinity of the hospital, so that the work will increase during the coming years. The seed was sown in Sremska Kamenica in 1934".

During these years Katherine became a highly valued and honoured citizen of St Andrews, she was invited to a variety of festivities and celebrations that, understandably, she usually declined to attend. However, on one occasion, when the Queen Mother came to St Andrews, the Town Council did manage to persuade her to join the group of prominent citizens who would greet the Queen Mother on her arrival. In 1923, when the Queen Mother was the Duchess of York, she had visited the Anglo-Serbian hospital in Belgrade, and she immediately remembered Katherine, and talked to her for quite a long time as though to an old friend, to the general satisfaction of all the representatives of the city who were present.

During 1962 Katherine's niece Elspeth Biggs settled permanently in St Andrews, so that Katherine then had a faithful companion as well as her sisters, who was of great help to her in every way. However, in June 1966 Katherine suffered another serious loss, when her older sister Annie died, with whom she had lived in the same house in St Andrews. Katherine had got on very well with Annie during the last 19 years, and she was the one member of her family with whom she could talk intimately and in detail about the events of their youth, and also about her life in Yugoslavia, since Annie had spent some years there in humanitarian work, first in the "Villa Bravačić" in Dubrovnik, and then in the school at Vlasenica and in the hospital at Sremska Kamenica. Annie was cremated and her ashes scattered in St Andrews Western Cemetery, and on one wall of the cemetery a small plaque was placed in her memory, to which Katherine's name was later added (Figs. 96 and 97). After Annie's death Katherine began to feel extremely lonely; this was partly due to her increasing deafness, which made it necessary for her to use a hearing-aid, which she did not like and kept losing; because of this she broke a number of these gadgets. She also suffered from a serious form of chronic bronchitis, which caused her difficulty with breathing; so when there was a strong east wind blowing, which happened quite often in that district, she had to stay indoors. All these things affected her quite unpleasantly, but her spirits remained high; she had her memories, and was surrounded by many objects, which recalled them. Her house was full of things, pictures and photographs, which she had brought from Yugoslavia, and nearly every day she wore a very special Serbian jacket with embroidered cuffs and front which she also brought from Yugoslavia, and which reminded her of her other homeland. Above the bed in her bedroom there hung a large oil-painting of Kajmakčalan of which she was specially fond, and which was a constant reminder of days spent at the foot of this mountain on the Salonica Front.

Despite the passage of time and increasing infirmity Katherine's spirits remained high, and her mind clear; this was especially evident when Jean Bray, her former colleague from the Save the Children Fund and editor of its journal, began to research and write a biography of Dr. Katherine MacPhail (Fig. 94). During the years 1969 – 1972 she visited Katherine several times and had long conversations with her and wrote down her recollections; later she sent her completed chapters to read and correct, a task which Katherine performed efficiently, without any problems, according to her niece Elspeth Biggs, who gave her most help at that time and then typed and duplicated her manuscripts. That same year the Save the Children Fund celebrated the fiftieth anniversary of its foundation, and on this occasion prepared a "golden edition" of its journal, containing descriptions of its main activities and its organisation. At their request Katherine wrote a short description of her work in Serbia and later in Yugoslavia, between 1915 and 1947.[96] In November 1969 a BBC television team came from London to St Andrews to prepare a film about the missions of British women in Serbia during the First World War; and there they filmed the section devoted to Katherine, an experience which she bore very well; she was obviously in a very good mood, and spoke well and with pleasure about her experiences at that time. The film was shown on British television in March 1970, and aroused considerable interest among the public; at the request of the public it was repeated several times. Afterwards Katherine received a large pile of letters from all sides, from numerous friends and acquaintances, and also from complete strangers. "That really thrilled her", her niece Elspeth Biggs wrote later. Katherine was a little surprised at that time when, among others, she heard from her old friend John Nickolls, with whom she had worked in France in 1916, and who had then asked her to marry him. He now came to see her in St Andrews, and, according to her niece Elspeth Biggs, the announcement of his visit aroused in her considerable excitement, and the need for great preparations; the actual meeting of the two old friends was very warm and cordial. After some time John Nickolls visited Katherine again, and this time he brought his wife. These meetings obviously agitated Katherine, and caused her to reflect about her life and her youth, since she then felt some regret that, at the time when she could have married and had children of her own, she had then looked after other people's children; however she continued to be firmly convinced that this was what she was called to do, and this was the path her life had to follow.

During 1970 Katherine's third niece, Ann Davidson, finally settled in St Andrews, so Katherine had close to her three nieces, and their mother Janet. As early as 1968, during a short holiday in Scotland, Ann Davidson and her husband Alexander, who were then living in Aden, bought the house in which Katherine was living alone, after the death of her sister Annie, and which was now too big for her. However the Davidsons allowed Katherine to remain undisturbed in the house for the rest of her life without in any way disturbing the comfort she had experienced so far. Katherine continued to live on the ground floor, since it was by then difficult for her to go upstairs; she was also able to use the garden behind the house. The Davidsons then went to work abroad again until 1970, when they finally returned to St Andrews. Meanwhile, during their absence, a completely independent flat was arranged for them, into which they finally moved, so that Katherine was no longer alone in the house. This arrangement was obviously very convenient for Katherine, since she now always had someone close to her nearby who could help her, since by that time she had become much weaker and often fell ill. Her local doctor at this time was Dr. Ellen Orr from Glasgow, with whom she had studied, and later lived with while she was in Glasgow during the Second World War. Dr. Ellen Orr, who had had her practice in St Andrews for quite a long time, was of great help to Katherine during these years when she needed constant medical attention.

These peaceful days of Katherine's life were disturbed by the death of her oldest sister Janet, who died in 1973; after this, having lost the last of her sisters, Katherine remained alone, the only surviving member of her large family. Fortunately she had nearby three nieces who looked after her, and many friends who had not forgotten her.

And so Katherine, surrounded by the care of close relatives and friends, spent her retirement years quietly in St Andrews, without losing touch with her friends from Yugoslavia. At the beginning of 1972 Katherine sent to the Serbian Medical Association in Belgrade her collection of slides that she had gathered together over a long period, and of which she was very fond. During the many years she had spent working in Yugoslavia she had assembled a fine collection of photographs on glass plates, most of which she had taken herself. These slides contained details of her work in hospitals in Belgrade, Dubrovnik, Topčider and Sremska Kamenica, also her travels throughout the country, unusual houses and people, mainly peasants and their national costumes. On January 4th, 1972, Katherine sent this collection as a gift to the Serbian Medical Association in Belgrade where it is still preserved today.[97] And indeed she was not forgotten in Yugoslavia, her second homeland. In the autumn of 1973 the History of Medicine and Pharmacy Section of the Serbian Medical Association in Belgrade, held a special meeting in her honour, as an expression of gratitude for her work during the First World War and subsequently. At this conference Dr. Milorad Dragić, earlier president of this medical history society, gave a talk on her life and work, in which he said: "Today at this meeting of our society, we send our greetings to Dr. Katherine Stewart MacPhail, whom we remember with deep gratitude; we send her our best wishes for good health and happiness; for she herself remembers her work here, and our people, whom she helped in their difficult days of wartime suffering. We send our thanks to Dr. Katherine MacPhail, a noble benefactor of our people". It was then announced that, on the initiative of this society, Dr. Katherine MacPhail had been elected an honorary member of the Serbian Medical Association; Professor Vladimir Stanojević, who was then the actual president of the society, informed Katherine about this meeting in her honour, and her election as an honorary member of the Serbian Medical Association; she was deeply moved by this, and in reply wrote a letter to Professor Vladimir Stanojević (Fig. 95) and the Serbian Medical Association dated December 28th, 1973, in which she expressed her thanks for her election as an honorary member of this association, and said, among other things: "You have given me the greatest possible pleasure in electing me as an honorary member of your society. Nothing could have given me greater satisfaction as a recognition of the medical work which I did among your sick children with the help of both British and Serbian doctors and nurses, which I began during the First World War and during the years which followed on to the second war and after the war, until 1947. I am glad my work among your people is still remembered and that friends and colleagues in Belgrade still remember me. I considered it a privilege to work with your people first as Allies and later as friends and I can never forget the Serbian people. This gesture on your part has given me great happiness especially after so many years".

Some time later, in June 1974, Katherine sent to the Serbian Medical Association, through some friends who were travelling to Belgrade, a small bronze plaque with a carving of her face, made in 1920 by the well-known sculptor Vasa Pomorišac; this was then placed in the premises of the Serbian Medical Association in Belgrade. Professor Vladimir Stanojević thanked Katherine for this gift in a long letter dated September 25th, 1974. However this letter arrived too late, when Katherine was no longer alive.

One other medical organisation in Yugoslavia wished at that time to show its recognition of Dr. Katherine MacPhail's work; this was the Yugoslav Orthopaedic and Traumatologic Association. As the sanatorium in Sremska Kamenica was in fact the first orthopaedic establishment in Vojvodina, the

Vojvodina Section of that Association initiated proceedings in 1973 that Dr. Katherine MacPhail, the founder of the children's hospital at Sremska Kamenica, should be elected an honorary member of the Association; in addition, it was proposed by the Ministry of Foreign Affairs that Dr. Katherine MacPhail should receive the Order of the Yugoslav Flag with a Golden Star in recognition of her contribution to relieving the suffering caused by two brutal wars. The proposal that she should be elected an honorary member of the Yugoslav Orthopaedic and Traumatologic Association was accepted, and it was planned that the formal election should take place at the sixth congress of the association, which was to be held in Ohrid (Macedonia) in September 1974. The president of the Association informed Dr. Katherine MacPhail about this and invited her to the Congress; however she replied as follows on February 10th, 1974: "Two days ago I received your letter of January 28th, 1974. I was extremely pleased when I read that the Vojvodina Section of your Association of Orthopaedic Surgeons and Traumatologists honoured me by its proposal that I should become an honorary member. Please accept my own warm thanks for this gesture. I believe that it was a privilege for me to be able to work as a doctor with sick and crippled children, both in connection with the establishment of the Children's Hospital in Belgrade and the Children's Sanatorium in Kamenica. In these hospitals British and Yugoslav staff worked together in perfect harmony. And so, in addition to our work with sick children, we made a small contribution to friendship and mutual understanding between our two nations. It is with great pleasure that I recall my work among you over many years. I am extremely sorry that I shall not be able to attend the meeting of the Association of Orthopaedic Surgeons and Traumatolgists of Yugoslavia in Ohrid in 1974, and therefore will not be able to receive the award personally. It is no longer possible for me to undertake such a long journey. So I thank you once more for your kindness and for remembering me. As I look back on my work among your people I can say that I had the satisfaction of being among brave allies and true friends".

The meeting of the Yugoslav Orthopaedic and Traumatologic Association took place on September 26th, 1974, in Ohrid; and on that day, since the news of her death had not yet reached Yugoslavia, Dr. Katherine MacPhail was elected an honorary member of the Association.

In the summer of 1974 Katherine's health suddenly deteriorated, since she suffered two strokes; after this, because she needed intensive care, she was moved to a nursing home for disabled patients: Freeland House, Gateside, Fife, and here she died peacefully on September 21st, 1974, in her 87th year. Her body was cremated and her ashes scattered in St Andrews Western Cemetery, where her name was added to the memorial tablet placed there earlier for her sister Annie (Figs. 96 and 97).

A few days later the local paper in St Andrews published a detailed obituary of Dr. Katherine MacPhail, including the following passage: "By a sad coincidence, just a few hours after her death, a letter arrived from the Yugoslav ambassador in London, informing her that in recognition of her many years of devoted service to their country, the Yugoslav Orthopaedic and Traumatologic Association had proposed that she should be awarded the Order of the Yugoslav Flag with a Gold Star"

The Save the Children Fund also published in *The World's Children* in March 1975 an extensive obituary saying in conclusion: "We, in Save the Children are proud to have known her and to have supported her work".[98]

The news of Dr. Katherine MacPhail's death arrived in Yugoslavia a little later, and on October 14th, 1974, a memorial tribute to her was published in the leading Belgrade newspaper *Politika*, and then an obituary contributed by her old friends and colleagues: Professor Siniša Radojević, Professor Svetislav Stojanović, Professor Klimentije Krstić, and the medical sisters Vida, Anica, Tinka and Milka. Similarly, on October 16th, 1974, the Serbian Medical Association in Belgrade arranged a commemorative meeting in her honour.

So ended the rich life of this noble and courageous lady, who devoted her best years and all her energy to work in a distant and foreign land, in the service of another nation. She was often asked earlier in her life why she had done this, why she had not stayed in her native country which had also passed through difficult times, and which also needed help. Katherine explained this dilemma in the following words: "I was often asked why I went out there again and didn't stay and work for our own people. All I can say is that our own people had suffered a good deal in the war too. They had lost fathers and sons and husbands. But they had never had their country overrun, and they had no idea of the misery that these people were living in. And I think I spent about twenty-five years out in the country altogether, having undertaken to go out for six months. But I never regretted it. It was the most wonderful country to work in. The Serbs were the most lovable, hospitable, kindly people that I have ever met in Europe."

Although her noble and unselfish work in Yugoslavia had been rudely and irreversibly interrupted, Katherine felt that this did not represent the real wish of the nation and the ordinary people, and her attitude towards Yugoslavia remained friendly. It was always her greatest wish that the sanatorium in Sremska Kamenica should retain its identity as an Anglo-Yugoslav hospital, which would bear witness to the first humanitarian missions which gave so much unselfish help to the restoration of this country after the First World War; and also to the important role in all this of the Save the Children Fund; and that it would remain a lasting memorial to British-Yugoslav friendship. And, as regards her personal work, and that of many other men and women, known and unknown, who hastened to the aid of this ravaged and devastated country, and whose work and contribution were so soon forgotten – Katherine's old friend Dot Newhall, who also worked as a volunteer during the First World War, described and explained the situation simply in the following words: "It was an anonymous work, untrumpeted, unsung, forgotten. But it was very worthwhile I think!"

Fig. 90 The house at No. 4 Kinburn Place in St Andrews (with the front door open), in which Dr. K. MacPhail lived after her return to Scotland. (Photo by Ž. Mikić, Oct. 1989)

Fig. 91 A celebration in the courtyard of the hospital in Sremska Kamenica on September 22nd, 1954, to mark the 20th anniversary of the official opening of the hospital. Dr. K. MacPhail is sitting in the middle of the front row; the fourth person on her right is Miss Alice Murphy. (Courtesy of Mrs. M. Ćirić)

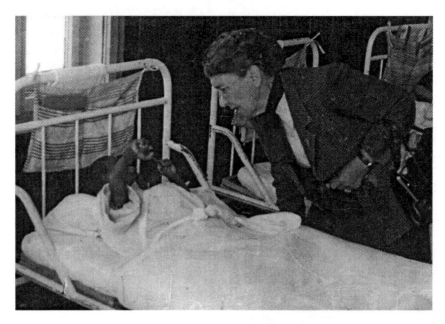

Fig. 92 Dr. K. MacPhail talking to a small patient during her last visit to the hospital in Sremska Kamenica in September, 1954.
(Courtesy of Mrs. M. Ćirić)

Fig. 93 An official celebratory lunch in the courtyard of the hospital in Sremska Kamenica in September, 1954.(Dr. K. MacPhail is sitting at the head of the table)
(Courtesy of Mrs. M. Ćirić)

Fig. 94 The last portrait of Dr. K. MacPhail, taken c. 1971-72.
(Courtesy of Mrs. E. Biggs)

Fig. 95 Facsimile of a letter from Dr. K. MacPhail to Dr. V. Stanojević, written on December 28th, 1973. (Courtesy of the SMA Museum)

Fig. 96 St Andrews Western Cemetery; (the memorial tablet to Annie and Katherine MacPhail is on the wall next to the white tombstone).
(Courtesy of Mr. Roland Keymer)

Fig. 97 The memorial tablet on the wall of St Andrews Western Cemetery, where the ashes of Dr. K. MacPhail and her sister Annie were scattered.
(Courtesy of Mr. Ronald Keymer)

Chapter 10

Epilogue

When the hospital at Sremska Kamenica was nationalised, and after Dr. Katherine MacPhail, Agnes Hardie and Alice Murphy finally left Yugoslavia in the summer of 1947, the sanatorium continued to work as it had done before, but under a different name; it was henceforward known as the State Sanatorium for Bone Tuberculosis. The only doctor in the hospital was Dr. Arthur Holländer, a surgeon from Novi Sad; however it is clear from a letter written to Dr. Katherine MacPhail, dated December 23rd, 1947, that he soon left the hospital and the country. The sanatorium was then attached to the Clinic for Orthopaedics in the Faculty of Medicine in Belgrade, established in 1947; and from then on Dr. Svetislav Stojanović, a member of that Clinic and a long-standing friend and associate of Katherine's, took charge of the Kamenica hospital. Mr. Branko Bugarski, the former administrative head of the sanatorium, also left at the end of February 1948. As the problem of tuberculosis of bones and joints in children was acute and widespread during that post-war period, the hospital continued to treat tubercular children according to the same principles as before, working as an annex of the Belgrade Orthopaedic Clinic. A report by Dr. Svetislav Stojanović from 1980 shows that 818 children up to the age of 14 were treated in the hospital between 1947 and 1957. The treatment of the young patients was brought up-to-date in 1947 by the use of a powerful new antibiotic drug, Streptomycin. This drug was discovered in 1943 but not widely used in the US Army until 1946; in the Kamenica hospital it had been sporadically used since 1947, and systematically used for all tubercular patients from 1950 onwards.

In 1955 the status of the Kamenica sanatorium was changed once more, when it was attached to the Main Regional Hospital in Novi Sad as the Department for Osteoarticular Tuberculosis (OAT), and Katherine's old friend and colleague Dr. Branko Manojlović from Sremska Kamenica, was appointed head of the hospital. As the problem of tuberculosis of the bones and joints in children still existed, the hospital continued to work as it had done previously, and Prof. Svetislav Stojanović continued his monthly visits and supervision. In one of his reports Dr. Branko Manojlović stated: "Between 1956 and 1959 there were always between 105 and 115 patients in the hospital, sometimes as many as 120. Since 1959 not a single doctor's request for admission was refused, and all the patients referred were immediately admitted."

In 1959 the hospital was repaired and renovated; and as it was the 25th anniversary of its foundation, the Vojvodina Medical Association journal *Medical Review* published a special issue on osteoarticular tuberculosis, to which several well-known experts, including Dr. Katherine MacPhail, contributed, and in which the work of the sanatorium in Sremska Kamenica was described in detail.[76]

In 1960 a large new, modern, well-equipped hospital, with 800 beds, named the Institute for Tuberculosis of Vojvodina, was built on a hill near the "English Hospital." Thus Dr. Katherine MacPhail's wish and hope that an appropriate institution for the treatment of all forms of tuberculosis should be built at Sremska Kamenica, as a very suitable place for this purpose, was finally fulfilled. When she heard about this, she remarked with satisfaction: "The seed was sown in Sremska Kamenica in 1934."

As the economic, social and public health situation in Yugoslavia improved considerably in the late fifties the number of children with bone tuberculosis declined significantly, and there was no longer any need for a special hospital in which to treat them; and on May 31st, 1963 the Department for Osteoarticular Tuberculosis at Sremska Kamenica was finally closed, and Dr. Branko Manojlović retired. After this the "English Hospital" changed its profile and became a Department of the Clinical Hospital attached to the newly established Medical Faculty in Novi Sad for the treatment of orthopaedic and traumatologic cases; it had 70 beds, and adult patients were admitted for long-term care, post-operative treatment and rehabilitation. Later it was known as the "Dr. Katherine MacPhail" Department of Orthopaedic Surgery and Traumatology and continued to function under this name until 1992, when this hospital was closed.

However the fame of the "English Hospital" still continues, and over the years many visitors have come to see it. Prof. Svetislav Stojanović visited the hospital for the last time in 1968 (Fig. 98); he died in 1977. In 1969 Mrs. Jean Bray and her husband visited the hospital and Katherine's former villa; she was then collecting the material for a book on the life of Dr. Katherine MacPhail, which, unfortunately, was never published. Monica Krippner, author of *The Quality of Mercy, Women at War, Serbia 1915-18* visited the hospital in 1977; this was one of several visits. In June 1985, on the occasion of 70th anniversary of the first allied missions to Serbia, a delegation of the Scottish Women's Medical Federation visited the hospital (Fig. 100), thus continuing the tradition of the Scottish Women's Hospitals. This delegation included Dr. Anne Shepherd, head of the organisation, Dr. Mary Keymer and her husband Mr. Ronald Keymer, Miss Margaret Shepherd, and Monica Krippner. The evening before the celebration they were the guests of the Medical Association of Vojvodina, where there was a meeting devoted to the allied missions to Serbia in 1915, and Jean Bray's documentary film *"Yesterday's Witness, Mission to Serbia"*, was shown; this was produced by the BBC in 1970, and in it Dr. Katherine MacPhail talked about her work. There were tears in the eyes of many of the audience.

In 1976 the Kamenica hospital was restored and modernised; central heating was installed, and a new plumbing system. In October 1985, on the 50th anniversary of the opening of the hospital, a new plaque was placed on the wall of the entrance hall (Fig. 100).

One of the dearest visitors to the hospital was Mrs. Elspeth Biggs, Dr. Katherine MacPhail's niece (see Appendix 1); she first came with Monica Krippner in September 1987. She visited Katherine's villa in the village, and then the hospital, and was obviously deeply moved and excited to see these places, which until then she had only heard about from her beloved Aunt Kathie (Fig. 101).

In order to keep alive the memory of Dr. Katherine MacPhail, in 1988 the Vojvodina Medical Association decided to erect a monument to her in the courtyard of the hospital, and to put a commemorative plaque on the wall of her villa in Sremska Kamenica. The monument with her bust was unveiled on June 15th, 1988 by her niece, Mrs. Elspeth Biggs, (Fig 103), in the presence of the British Ambassador, Mr. Andrew Wood, and the head of the British Council in Belgrade, Mr. Denis Ganton (Figs. 102 and 104), and many other guests. It was a beautiful sunny early summer day; though feelings were solemn, a festive mood prevailed among the many guests. The atmosphere was reminiscent of the "golden age" of Dr. Katherine MacPhail, about which we had only heard and read. It seemed as though her spirit was there above her hospital, and above all the people who had come to pay tribute to her, and to thank her once again for everything she had done for this country. Elspeth Biggs and the other members of Dr. Katherine MacPhail's family were very happy and pleased by this recognition and sign of gratitude. Elspeth Biggs later wrote in a letter: " It was the proudest day of my life."

Interest in Katherine MacPhail and her hospital has never ceased, and in 1989 the Belgrade Radio-Television made a documentary film about the foreign missions to Serbia during the Great War, in which the story of Dr. Katherine MacPhail played an important part. This film was shown several times on national television.

In September 1991, Mrs. Elspeth Biggs visited Yugoslavia for the last time (Fig. 105), since the dreadful war, which convulsed Yugoslavia had already started. Because of this war, and the many economic problems, which followed, the "English Hospital" had to be closed, for the second time in its history, on June 15th, 1992, to the great sorrow of all those who were familiar with the history and significance of that remarkable institution. Later, in October 1996, the Kamenica hospital became a centre for refugees from various parts of the former Yugoslavia, who still live there.

However, the memories of Dr. Katherine MacPhail and her hospital are still very much alive. On September 23rd, 2004, on the occasion of the 70th anniversary of the opening of the Kamenica sanatorium, the Vojvodina Medical History Society organised a commemorative meeting and a visit to the hospital at Sremska Kamenica, where bunches of flowers were left   beside the monument of Dr. Katherine MacPhail. In June 2005 a large group of members of the Norfolk and Norwich Novi Sad Association visited Novi Sad, and came to see the "English Hospital", as it continues to be called among the people here (Figs. 99, 106, 107 and 108).

It seems that the story still continues!

The authorities in Novi Sad and Vojvodina are planning to restore the hospital, as soon as the refugees have left, and to turn it into a memorial hospital, which would remain as a permanent witness to the friendship between the British and Serbian peoples, and also as a memorial to all heroic British women who came to the help of the Serbian people in the First World War, and with whom they made common cause during that War. This was always the wish of Dr. Katherine MacPhail herself.

Fig. 98 Prof. Svetislav Stojanović with the doctors and staff of the hospital in Sremska Kamenica during his last visit to the hospital in the spring of 1968.
(Photo by Ž. Mikić, 1968)

Fig. 99 An ancillary building of the hospital in Sremska Kamenica, where the communal dinning room was accomodated before the Second World War.
(Photo by Ž. Mikić, 1996)

Fig. 100 A visit from a delegation of the Scottish Women's Federation in June, 1980; left to right: Miss Monica Krippner, Dr. Ann Shepherd, and Dr. Mary Keymer, standing in front of the original memorial plaques to Dr. K. MacPhail (Translation, *right tablet*: "This children's hospital for bone tuberculosis was built in 1934, in the spirit of Anglo-Yugoslav friendship, by Dr. Katherine Stuart MacPhail, M.D. St. Andrews, Scotland a benefactor of our people. This memorial tablet was set in place on the 20th anniversary of the opening of the hospital", Srem.Kamenica, September 22nd, 1954"; *left tablet*: "On the 50th anniversary of the foundation of this institution, in memory of its founder, Dr. Katherine Stuart MacPhail (1881-1974), this memorial tablet was set in place, as a sign of gratitude, Sr. Kamenica, October 1984").
(Photo by Ž. Mikić, 1980)

Fig. 101 Mrs. Elspeth Biggs, a niece of Dr. K. MacPhail, during a visit to the hospital in Sremska Kamenica in September, 1987. (Photo by Ž. Mikić, 1987)

Fig. 102 Distinguished guests present at the formal opening of a memorial to Dr. K.MacPhail on June 15th, 1988; from left to right: Dr. Žarko Vuković, a well-known doctor, publicist and medical historian from Belgrade, Miss Monica Krippner, Mr. Denis Ganton, director of the British Council in Belgrade, Mr. Andrew Wood, British ambassador in Belgrade, and Prof. Želimir Mikić from Novi Sad as the host.
(Photo by B. Lučić)

228

Fig. 103 Mrs. Elspeth Biggs unveiling a memorial to Dr. K. MacPhail on June 15th, 1988, in the courtyard of the hospital in Sremska Kamenica.
(Photo by B. Lučić)

Fig. 104 Mr. Andrew Wood, the British ambassador, speaking at the official dedication of the memorial to Dr. K. MacPhail on June 15th, 1988. Beside him is Prof L. Lepšanović, president of the Vojvodina Medical Association.
(Photo by B. Lučić)

229

Fig. 105 Mrs. Elspeth Biggs, Dr. K. MacPhail's niece, during her last visit to the hospital in Sremska Kamenica in September, 1991.
(Photo by Ž. Mikić, 1991)

Fig. 106 The hospital in Sremska Kamenica, photographed from the inner courtyard, 1985.
(Photo by Ivan Knežević, 1985)

Fig. 107 The hospital in Sremska Kamenica as it was in 1990: the inner courtyard, with the statue, the central section with the main entrance, and the east wing of the building.
(Photo by Ž. Mikić, 1990)

Fig. 108 A monument to Dr. Katherine MacPhail, erected on June 15th, 1988, in the courtyard of her hospital.
(Photo by B. Lučić, 1988)

Notes

1. Shena Watson, the youngest granddaughter of Dr. James MacPhail described in 1948 the life and work of her grandfather in a booklet entitled *A Mission Hospital in India,* which unfortunately was never published. This very interesting manuscript has been kept in the family archives, and Elspeth Biggs gave a copy of it to me; much information from it was used in this book.

2. There has been some confusion about the date of birth of Dr. Katherine MacPhail; in various written documents relating to her, and even on the memorial plaque in the hospital in Sremska Kamenica, it is stated that she was born in 1881; this is a mistake, since she was in fact born on October 30th, 1887. This error has arisen because the written form of number 1 and 7 are very similar in English, so that it is often quite difficult to distinguish these numbers in hand-written documents.

3. Dr. Jean Scott's mother was Katherine's friend from early childhood; she was the source of stories about their games together, which Dr. Scott described in a letter written on September 3rd, 1986. I met Dr. Jean Scott (a pathologist who lives in Pitlochry in Scotland) during a visit to St Andrews in October 1989, when we talked on this subject, and she gave me some important photographs as well as valuable information. By chance she found in a bookshop in Ayr an old album of photographs taken in Serbia between 1915 and 1918; it was not known who had taken them. Some of these, connected with the Scottish Women's Hospital in Kragujevac, were passed on to me for inclusion in this book (Figs. 16-18 and 20).

4. These stories from Katherine's early childhood were related among members of the MacPhail family, and passed on to me by her niece Elspeth Biggs, from St Andrews, who has undoubtedly been the most valuable and reliable source of information about the life and work of Dr. Katherine MacPhail. When I wrote to her in March 1986, asking for her cooperation, she replied promptly and offered to help me as much as she could; she described "in instalments" (as she wittily expressed it) the life of her aunt Katherine, whom she greatly loved and valued; she also sent various documents, letters and photographs. This was the beginning of a wonderful friendship which developed between us. Elspeth Biggs visited Yugoslavia several times and loved it deeply; and when I visited Great Britain in October 1989, to collect material for this book, I was her guest in St Andrews. In this way, through personal contact, I learnt many details about Katherine MacPhail and her family, and had occasion to visit and photograph the house in which Dr. MacPhail lived, and the cemetery in which her remains were buried. Elspeth Biggs herself, who was a very charming and lovable person (Figs. 101, 103 and 105), and also exceptionally interesting, was in a sense a typical descendant of the MacPhail family, who inherited many of the characteristic qualities of the members of this clan (see Appendix 1).

5. From early childhood Katherine was called "Kath" or "Kathie", as a pet-name, and later her friends often used it as well. Her nieces, the younger generation, called her "Aunt Kathie", or "Aunt K." as I also did when communicating with Elspeth Biggs and her other relatives.

6. This information came from Dr. Katherine MacPhail herself, who gave it to her first biographer, Jean Bray.

Mrs. Jean Bray worked with the Save the Children Fund in London, and was one of the editors of their journal *The World's Children*; she wrote a biography of Dr. Katherine MacPhail entitled *The Extraordinary Ambassador: a Biography of Dr. Katherine Stewart MacPhail*. Unfortunately this was never published; the manuscript is in the archives of the Imperial War Museum in London. A BBC documentary film based on her ideas was made in 1970, about women's missions to Serbia during the First World War, entitled *Yesterday's Witness, Mission to Serbia*. Dr. Katherine MacPhail, Annie Christitch, Dorothy Newhall and Francesca Wilson all took part in this film, for which Jean Bray did the research. The evidence of those still living who had taken part in the wartime events in Serbia has been used in the present book. In connection with the research for the biography and the screening of the film, Jean Bray and her husband visited Novi Sad and the hospital in Sremska Kamenica in August, 1969, when I got to know her and showed her the hospital, and the villa in which Dr. Katherine MacPhail lived. After this visit I sent her several photographs of the hospital and the villa. In her letter of thanks for the photographs and the help given, dated September 6th, 1969, Jean Bray wrote: "I hope to see Dr. MacPhail next week, and I know she will also be very pleased to see these things " (i.e. the photographs, author's note). In fact Jean Bray had occasion to visit Dr. Katherine MacPhail several times between 1969 and 1972, and to have long conversations with her; on the basis of these meetings she wrote her biography, which she completed in 1972. Jean Bray sent the completed chapters to Dr. Katherine MacPhail for her to read and correct, and the manuscript contains numerous comments personally written by Dr. MacPhail herself. It is perhaps the most valuable aspect of this work, that its authenticity was personally confirmed by Dr. Katherine MacPhail, who, in a note in her own hand, written on January 1st, 1973, said that she had again read the manuscript and made a few corrections; after this it was finally typed, and the typescript completed on April 4th, 1973. Information from this manuscript, provided mainly by Dr. Katherine MacPhail herself, has been largely used in the writing of the present book, with appropriate acknowledgments.

7. See: Adams, J.T.: *Empire of the Seven Seas*; and Martin, G.R.: *Jennie*.

8. See: Buchan, H.: *Women in the University, Fifth Centenary of Glasgow University*.

9. The *Suffragettes* were supporters of the Women's Suffrage Societies in Great Britain and the USA, which campaigned for women's right to vote at the end of the 19th and at the beginning of the 20th century. When women in Britain gained the right to vote in 1918, and those in USA in 1920, the movement collapsed. Emmeline Pankhurst (1858-1928) was the leader of the movement in Britain. The term suffragette was sometimes used in a pejorative way, especially for militant feminists. At the beginning of the First World War Millicent Garrett Fawcett, president of the National Union of Women's Suffrage Societies (NUWSS), announced that the organisation would stop all its political activity, and would open in London a "Women's Service" bureau, which would organise women willing to perform useful war work. Before the end of 1914 this organisation had found work for more than 1300 women volunteers, many of whom completed First Aid courses or performed auxiliary tasks in hospitals.

10. The above quotations, and many facts about the First World War, are taken from Monica Krippner's book about women in Serbia during the First World War (see Appendix 3).

11. See: Balfour, F.: *Dr. Elsie Inglis*; and McLaren, E.S., ed., *A History of the Scottish Women's Hospitals;* and Anon.: *Elsie Inglis, A Heritage Trail.*

12. Annie Christitch, as she herself always wrote her name (Ana Hristić in Serbian), was born in Belgrade of a Serbian father and an Irish mother; she studied at Oxford, and became a journalist, one of the first women to work in Fleet Street. When the First World War broke out she was working for the London-based *Daily Express*, and played a considerable part in collecting help for the Serbs in Britain by writing articles and giving lectures on the history and culture of Serbia. She was attached as a translator to the first unit of the Scottish Women's Hospitals, with which she came to Serbia in 1915. Later she and her mother directed the relief organisation "Christitch Mission" at Valjevo (Serbia). She spent the greater part of her life in England, where she died in 1972.

13. Lady Paget, as everyone called her, or Leila Paget, was the wife of the British diplomat Sir Ralph Paget, formerly British Ambassador in Belgrade, who, during the First World War, was head of all the British missions in Serbia. Lady Paget, as early as the Balkan War of 1912, was an active worker in Serbian hospitals, where she acquired valuable experience. In the middle of November 1914 she came to Skopje (Macedonia) with the first hospital of the Serbian Relief Fund, with 600 beds; she worked there under difficult conditions, and fell ill herself with typhus. She refused to evacuate the hospital with its wounded patients, and was caught by the Bulgarian occupation on October 22nd, 1915. She continued to work with her hospital as a Bulgarian prisoner-of-war, but was repatriated on February 16th, 1916, and returned to Britain on April 3rd, 1916; after that she did not engage in any public work. She was awarded an OBE, and also the Serbian Order of St. Sava. There is a street in Belgrade, Lady Paget Street, called after her.

14. The Serbian Relief Fund (SRF) was set up in London by the end of September 1914, with its headquarters in Cromwell Road, under the patronage of Queen Mary, with Bertram Christian (a publisher, who had been active in relief work in Macedonia during the Balkan wars) as Chairman, R.W. Seton-Watson as

Honorary Secretary, and Sir Edward Boyle as Honorary Treasurer. An appeal was launched for funds, to which there was a rather generous response, and government funds were also contributed. By the end of the year teams of doctors and nurses had reached Serbia, and various supplies were sent. All this meant a great deal of work for Seton-Watson and May (Seton's wife), who spent much of her time on SRF work for the greater part of the war. A number of prominent people were members of the committees, e.g. Lloyd George, and Winston Churchill. This organisation was very energetic and successful in sending help to Serbia during the First World War, including some well-equipped hospitals, which were active in Serbia, Corfu, Corsica and the Salonica Front. In contrast to the Scottish Women's Hospitals, which employed only women, these hospitals accepted men and women, although women were usually in the majority, and the director of the hospital was always a woman. The SRF took on two other commitments in the spring of 1916: the regular supply of a minimum of food and clothing to 40,000 prisoners of war in Germany and Austria-Hungary, and the acceptance of responsibility for some of the refugee boys who had accompanied the Serbian army in its retreat to the Adriatic. Mme. Mabel Grujić (née Dunlop), an American married to Slavko Grujić, the Serbian ambassador in London, and later under-secretary in the Ministry of Foreign Affairs, rendered considerable services in setting up this Fund; after the outbreak of the war she worked tirelessly in Britain to secure help for the devastated country of Serbia. In addition she conducted a campaign in her native country, which contributed generously to the Red Cross Hospital in Serbia. The Serbian Relief Fund contributed about £ 1,000,000.00 in money and material help, and employed over 700 people (*Encyclopaedia Britannica*, Vol. 20 (1964), p. 350; Seton-Watson, H., Seton-Watson, C.: *The Making of a New Europe*)

15. Major Dr. Dimitrije Antić, later professor in the Faculty of Medicine in Belgrade, vividly described the dreadful situation in his hospital at Kragujevac, and indeed in Serbia, in 1915 during the horrible typhus fever epidemic, providing very reliable first-hand evidence of this difficult time. See: Antić, D.: *The Pockmarked Typhus Fever at the First Military Reserve Hospital at Kragujevac 1914–1915.*

16. Dr. Elizabeth Ross was born in Tain in Scotland, and graduated in medicine at the University of Glasgow. She worked for some time as a doctor in various places in Persia. After the outbreak of war she came as a volunteer to Serbia, where she worked devotedly, day and night, in the Infectious Diseases Hospital in Kragujevac (The First Military Reserve Hospital), right up until she herself fell ill with typhus. Her colleagues from the Scottish Women's Hospital, especially Dr. Frances Wakefield, with whom she had become friendly, looked after her; but in spite of their devoted care she died on February 14th, 1915. She was buried with full military honours; her grave is beside the church in the New Cemetery in Kragujevac, together with the graves of three medical sisters who also died of typhus. Today there is a street in Kragujevac called after her.

17. The quotes relating to the work of the SWH unit at Kragujevac are taken from Dr. K. MacPhail's manuscript of a lecture given at the Glasgow University in December 1915; this hand-written manuscript is currently in the Imperial War Museum in London. Mrs. Elspeth Biggs kindly deciphered and typed it for the purpose of this book.

18. The Scottish Women's Hospitals had very strict priciples with regard to their staff, and employed only women; so it is somewhat unusual that after arriving in Serbia they accepted Austrian prisoners-of-war as orderlies. It was probably the acute shortage of staff, together with the large influx of wounded men, that made them depart from their "feminist' principle.

19.   Dr. Frances Wakefield was one of the five doctors in the Scottish Women's Hospital in Kragujevac. Daisy, as she was called, was English by birth, a member of the well-known Wakefield family from Kendal, in the English Lake District. Before the First World War she worked as a medical missionary in Nigeria, but as soon as war was declared she came home and enrolled as a volunteer in the first unit of the Scottish Women's Hospitals in Serbia; she came with them to Kragujevac, where early in the spring of 1915 she fell ill with a serious form of typhus. Before that she had treated the unfortunate Dr. Elizabeth Ross, who   did not survive. After the expiry of her agreement with the Scottish Women's Hospital in the summer of 1915, she left Serbia and went to Cairo, where she learnt Arabic and travelled through remote parts of the Middle East, defending the cause of local nomadic tribes. She later settled in Tamenrasset, in the central Sahara, where she spent the rest of her life, studying the language of the Tuaregs from the Hoggar Mountains, and occupying herself in various other ways. Here she met Monica Krippner during her travels in Africa; it was from her that Monica Krippner first heard of the Scottish Women's Hospitals and other women who took part in the war in Serbia, about which she later wrote in her well-known book.

20.   General Dr. Vladimir Stanojević, later one of the most eminent Serbian medical historians, and professor of the Faculty of Medicine in Belgrade, wrote extensively about his war experience, and especially about the typhus fever epidemic in Serbia in 1915 in his book: *History of the Serbian Medical Corps*. He also wrote about Dr. Katherine MacPhail, of whom he had a very high opinion.

21.   There is an interesting story, related by Monica Krippner, in connection with this request for help. Since it was an urgent request, Dr. Eleanor Soltau, the head of the SWH unit at Kragujevac, had to send a telegram to their headquarters in Edinburgh. However, since the Serbian authorities for some reason wished to prevent spreading news of the typhus epidemic, the military censors did not allow any letters or telegrams to be sent in which typhus was mentioned; so Dr. Soltau sent a telegram in a kind of code, worded: "Dire necessity for fever nurses", reckoning that the censors would not understand the uncommon word "dire", and would not alter the wording of the telegram. She was right, the telegram reached the headquarters of the SWH in Edinburgh, and they understood it correctly.

22. At the request of the Serbian government, the Royal Army Medical Service (RAMC) sent a team of 30 epidemiologists, which arrived in Serbia in the early spring of 1915. The heads of the team were Colonel William Hunter and Lieutenant-Colonel Stammers; their task was to control the typhus epidemic. On their advice many defensive measures, sometimes draconian, but necessary, were introduced: all routes of infection between the troops and other parts of the country were cut off; strict quarantine rules were established behind the front lines, notification of the disease was compulsory; all army leave was stopped; railway transport was temporarily suspended, and a massive programme of disinfection was introduced, together with other measures. Since the means for such large-scale disinfection were not available, Lt. Col. Stammers had the idea of using an improvised wooden wine barrel or metal barrel to disinfect clothes, blankets and bedding; this proved very effective, and was later known as the "Serbian barrel", although it was Stammers who invented it, and under this name it passed into medical literature. Since the Partisans in the Second World War also used the same device, it came to be known as the "Partisan barrel". In any case the measures undertaken proved effective, and by the summer of 1915 the epidemic had been suppressed.

23. Sir Thomas Lipton, owner of the tea and coffee plantations in Ceylon, one of the "tea-kings" of Great Britain, owned a luxury motor yacht named "Erin", and loved sailing. He was a great humanist and generous benefactor, witty and fond of jokes. During the First World War he several times used his yacht to transport staff, medical supplies and good-will missions from Marseilles to Salonica, including large numbers of British Red Cross units, which were serving in Serbia and Salonica.

24. Zemun was an Austro-Hungarian frontier town a few miles from Belgrade, just across the river Sava. The rivers Sava and Danube were the frontier between Austria-Hungary and Serbia before the First World War. Today Zemun is a part of greater Belgrade.

25. Dr. Edward Ryan was head of an American Red Cross mission which left New York on September 13th, 1914 and arrived in Belgrade in October, 1914. It consisted of several doctors and 12 medical sisters. They took over the Military Hospital in Belgrade, where on November 2nd, 1914, they added the American flag to that of the Red Cross, in the hope that this would protect the hospital from bombardment, since the USA was still neutral. After the fall of Belgrade on December 2nd, 1914 the mission remained in Belgrade, and Dr. Ryan took over the duties of American consul. After the liberation of Belgrade, following thirteen days of occupation, they continued their regular work. During the typhus epidemic Dr. Ryan himself fell ill, and was awarded a Legion of Honour medal, bestowed by France, while in his hospital bed. When Dr.

Katherine MacPhail fell ill from typhus, Dr. Ryan looked after her personally in his hospital, after which they became close friends.

26. Admiral Ernest C. Thomas Troubridge, Vice-Admiral of the British Navy, was the commanding officer of the British Naval Mission in Serbia, which came to Belgrade in January 1915, and consisted of 68 British and 15 Serbian military personnel, who formed the crews of the four naval vessels on the Danube, and four artillery batteries with two cannon. He lived in Belgrade, and was also in charge of the British Fever Hospital in Belgrade in the summer of 1915. His unit withdrew across Albania with the Serbian army in the autumn of 1915, and was then reorganised in the Albanian town of Durrës (Durazzo), as the British Adriatic Mission. At the end of 1918 Admiral Troubridge and his unit, together with the Serbian army, returned to Belgrade and continued their service on the Danube. He was a great friend of Dr. Katherine MacPhail, and always came to her help. He was popular with her family, who called him "Kath's Admiral". Admiral Troubridge kept a "war diary", now preserved in the Imperial War Museum in London.

27. The copies of Dr. Elsie Inglis' letter of June 1st, 1915 to Miss Mair; then of Dr. K. MacPhail's letter of November 19th, 1915 to Miss Marris; and also of the minutes of the SWH Committee of December 3rd, 1915 were kindly provided by Mrs. Elspeth Biggs. The originals are preserved in the Scottish Women's Hospitals Collection, in the Mitchell Library in Glasgow.

28. The First World War began on July 28th, 1914 when Austria-Hungary declared war on Serbia, following the assassination of the Archduke Franz Ferdinand, heir to the Habsburg Empire, in Sarajevo on June 28th, 1914. The Serbian Army successfully repulsed three Austrian attacks on Serbia, although Belgrade, which at that time was actually a frontier town, was briefly occupied on December 2nd, 1914; it was soon retaken on December 15th. However, in October 1915, Serbia suffered a more serious attack, in which German and Bulgarian forces also took part. The Serbian army, now very seriously outnumbered, decided to retreat rather than surrender; the only escape route available was through the formidable mountains of Albania to the Adriatic coast, where, it was hoped, Allied ships would be available to take the refugee army to some place of safety. This mass exodus, or Great Retreat, also described as the "Serbian Golgotha", began at the end of November 1915 when more than 200,000 men, followed by some 50,000 civilians, mostly young boys, set off over some of the most inhospitable mountains of Europe, where there were few towns, no roads except narrow mule tracks, all covered with deep winter snow. Among the soldiers and officers was the elderly King Peter, so crippled with rheumatism that he had to be carried by his soldiers; and also Crown Prince Alexander who, during this epic exodus, had to be operated for acute appendicitis. Mrs. St. Clair Stobart, whose British unit also took part in the retreat, later described how "thousands of women and children and old men, driven from their homes, also swelled the procession. It was a retreat of some hundreds of miles over icy mountains, travelling an average of one kilometre an hour in a world of shadows and dreariness, of wet and cold." An American, Fortier Jones, who also witnessed the retreat, later wrote: "Forty British women made the march that day. They made it without food and without drink; most of them made it on foot and in clothing intended only for the Balkan summer. I think it can be said that the party of British women stood it better than the Serbian refugees and fully as well as the Serbian army." Once they reached the Adriatic coast, the bulk of the 150,000 surviving soldiers were taken by boat to Corfu, and about 10,000 to Bizerta. In 1916 the reconstituted Serbian Army sailed and joined the French and British forces at Salonica, where the famous "Salonica Front" had already been established. (Further reading: Krippner, M.: *The Quality of Mercy, Women at War, Serbia 1915-18;* Seton-Watson H. and C.: *The Making of a New Europe*)

29. During the First World War the Quakers organised as the *Society of Friends*, or just "Friends" as they were usually called, were active in many parts of Europe, including the Meuse and Marne regions in France behind the western front in 1915-1916; they also worked in Haute Savoie. They were also active in the Second World War, and after the war they continued to work within the framework of UNRRA, and at that time they were very active in Yugoslavia too.

30. Verdun in northern France was scene of one of the greatest battles of the First World War, which lasted from February to December, 1916.

31. The Quaker John Nickolls (1893-1986) met Dr. Katherine MacPhail when he was working with a Quaker unit in the Marne-Meuse area, and made her a proposal of marriage, which she refused. Soon after that their ways parted for a long time. Much later, in the 1970s, John Nickalls saw Katherine on television, got in touch and came to visit her in St Andrews; their meeting was very warm and friendly. After Katherine's death he kept in touch with her niece, Jessie McFarlane, until his death in November 1986. After his death his son Chris found among his papers a copy of a biography of Katherine by Jean Bray, from which he learnt that his father had been friendly with Katherine during the First World War. He then got in touch with Jessie McFarlane and then learnt the whole story. During the Second World War Chris also worked with the "Friends" in the Middle East and then he met Dr. Katherine MacPhail in Cairo; later he also worked with Quakers in Yugoslavia

32. See: Wilson, F., *In the Margins of Chaos*.

33. Anne McGlade, or Nan, as she was called, was the secretary of the Third SRF Hospital, which arrived in Kragujevac in April 1915. She took part in the "Great Retreat" through Albania in the autumn and winter of 1915, and then in 1917 became secretary of the SRF Hospital in Sorović (present-day Amindeon) on the Salonica Front in northern Greece. At the beginning of 1918 she organised the first voluntary canteen in Macedonia (part of the Sandes-Haversfield Canteens), with which she eventually reached Belgrade, with the Serbian army, travelling through Nish. In Belgrade she spent some time with Dr.

Katherine MacPhail, and then lived for several years in China. After an operation and serious illness she spent some time convalescing in Katherine's villa in Sremska Kamenica; however, as her illness got worse Katherine placed her in her hospital in Belgrade, where she was cared for during a long illness, until she died.

34. Dorothy ("Dot") Newhall worked as a health inspector in Beckenham until the outbreak of the First World War. After this she spent some time with the British army on the Western Front, until its retreat. She then joined the third hospital of the SRF, with which she arrived in Kragujevac in April 1915. Here she contracted typhus. In the autumn and winter of 1915 she took part in the "Great Retreat" through Albania; then in 1917 she worked in a SRF hospital in Sorović (Amindeon), in northern Greece, and later in Germian. After the break-through on the Salonica Front she arrived with her hospital in Nish, where the hospital remained for some time. She then worked in an orphanage established in Nish by the SRF. In 1915 she was awarded a medal for service and a Cross of Mercy, and later a medal for devoted service, a medal for courage and the Order of St Sava, third class.

35. Dr. Agnes Bennett (1872-1960) was an Australian, who studied medicine in Sydney, and also in Edinburgh, where she graduated in 1899, and was there when the First World War broke out. She immediately attached herself to the Australian and New Zealand forces in Egypt; then in 1916 she moved to the Scottish Women's Hospitals, where she was appointed head of the "America Unit", so called because the funds for its establishment and upkeep were mainly collected in America. Most of the staff were from Australia and New Zealand. This hospital also had a special transport section, with its own lorries and ambulances, which gave it a special advantage as regards mobility and the transport of the wounded. The head of this section was an Australian named Mary Bedford. This hospital was the main Serbian field and transit hospital during the battle for Kajmakčalan, which took place between September 18th, 1916, and October 4th. It played a very important part in these events, since it was the nearest hospital to the front, and nearly all the wounded from this severe battle were taken there. In the summer of 1917 the staff and patients of this hospital suffered from an epidemic of malaria, which Agnes Bennett caught too, so in November 1917 she had to return to Australia. After her recovery she continued her medical work in Australia and New Zealand, and worked for a time with the Flying Doctor Service in northern Queensland. Just before she died she founded a memorial laboratory in Sydney, in memory of her father, called the William and Agnes Bennett Laboratory. She died in 1960, in her 88th year.

36. *The Scottish Women's Hospitals Motor Ambulance Column*, usually called the "transport unit", was set up as a separate unit consisting of 18 members, which arrived at Salonica in the summer of 1916 and was stationed near Ostrovo (today Arnissa in Greece). During the battle for the mountain Kajmakčalan this unit played an important part, working day and night transporting wounded men to a nearby Scottish Women's Hospital. In December 1916 the transport department of the so-called "America Unit" of the SWH was merged with the ambulance unit, under the able command of Mary Bedford, known throughout the region as "Miss Spare Parts". In January 1917 this unit was transferred to a new base at Jelak, perched amid a pine forest 5,000 feet up on a shoulder of Kajmakčalan. During one year members of this unit drove some 63,000 miles and transported 8,477 wounded men. In the summer of 1917 Mary Bedford fell ill with malaria, and Kathleen Dillon took over the unit, and, advancing behind the Allied armies, followed the difficult route via Prilep, Veles, Kumanovo, Vranje and Nish, arrived in Belgrade and later Novi Sad, where, at the beginning of 1919, all members of the unit were decorated and demobilised.

37. Elsie Cameron Corbett, daughter of Lord Rowallan, volunteered for service as a VAD in May 1915. She was accepted by a British Red Cross unit, and sent with the famous steam yacht "Erin" to Salonica with a unit of 20 members. Here she met Kathleen Dillon, a member of a distinguished Oxfordshire family, who was also a volunteer nurse. The two young women immediately became close friends, sharing their fate in the difficult days that lay ahead. From Salonica they were sent to a British Red Cross hospital in Vrnjačka Banja, a famous spa in Serbia, where they were taken prisoners in November 1915; in February 1916 they were repatriated. In the summer of 1916 they joined the SWH "motor column unit" with which they reached the Salonica Front (see the note 36). After the war they returned to England and lived together in Kathleen's house in the village of Charlbury. In 1960 Elsie Corbett published her book *With the Red Cross in Serbia*, based on her recollections of the time she had spent there, and also on Kathleen Dillon's diary.

38. See: Corbett, E.C., *With the Red Cross in Serbia*.

39. The *slava* is a traditional Serbian religious celebration, characteristic only of the Serbian Orthodox Church. The word *slava* is derived from the verb *slaviti*, meaning to glorify or celebrate, and takes place on the saint's day on which the family ancestors were supposedly converted to Christianity. The celebration usually begins with a short service in front of the icon of that saint or festival, followed by a family feast; the rest of the day is spent in receiving guests, eating, drinking, and rejoicing.

40. The *kolo* is a traditional South Slav dance, thought to be a relic of sun-worship. The dancers join hands, usually in a ring and dance to appropriate music, either keeping in the ring, or forming a line or spiral. The *kolo* is usually danced on festive occasions, such as weddings or the celebrations of the family *slava*, and frequently at the performances of the various folklore societies. (See Fig. 28)

41. See: Lindsay, S., *Coatbridge and the Great War*.

42. The Briton mentioned here was Mr. Riddell, a priest from Manchester, who already had three sons. He was one of the many British people who adopted and educated children from war-devastated Serbia.

43. General Charles Fortescue was the head of the British Joint Supply Commission in Belgrade, who directed the distribution of British war material remaining in the country after the war. In July 1919, in co-operation with domestic organisations for the protection of children, he set up a joint committee for the care of children, whose task it was to co-ordinate the work of native and foreign organisations engaged in this activity. This committee included Dr. Katherine MacPhail and other heads of humanitarian missions; it held regular meetings at which money contributed in Britain was distributed. When General Fortescue returned to London he invited Dr. Katherine MacPhail, who then happened to be in Britain, to supper, and here she met his daughter Helen Gordon-Duff, who later became a close friend. Helen Gordon-Duff joined later as a driver of the Save the Children Fund unit led by Dr. Katherine MacPhail in Yugoslavia in 1945, and they remained close friends for many years. She died in 1991, in her 94th year.

44. See: MacPhail, K., *The Anglo-Serbian Children's Hospital Belgrade 1918-1921 (Report)*.

45. Major John Frothingham was a great American humanist and benefactor. Right from the beginning of the war he and his family sent help to war-devastated Serbia, which he visited several times with the American Red Cross. Among other things at the beginning of the war he sent a complete hospital that was set up in Skopje (Macedonia). He was married to Jelena Lozanić, the daughter of the well-known Serbian scientist Sima Lozanić, whom the Serbian Red Cross sent to the USA in November 1914, to collect funds. Later John Frothingham showed more concern for children and war orphans, and for many years supported two children's homes, one in the so-called "castle" in Sremska Kamenica and another in Vranje. His sister Elizabeth Frothingham was also a great friend and benefactor of these children's homes. He gave also financial help to the Anglo-Serbian Children's Hospital in Belgrade, where there was a "John Frothingham bed" which he supported with regular annual contributions. He was awarded two of the highest Serbian decorations: The Order of the Karadjordje Star and the Order of the White Eagle. (Translator's note: the white eagle is part of the official Serbian coat of arms). Major John Frothingham died in 1935 in France.

46. Annie Dickinson was the head of the London Branch of the Serbian Red Cross. She first came to Serbia at the beginning of 1915 with a British Red Cross hospital which was established in the "Therapy Hotel" in Vrnjačka Banja, a well-known spa in Serbia, and which was officially known as the Anglo-Serbian Hospital, but everybody called it "Berry's unit", after the surgeon Mr. James (later Sir) Berry. The hospital was under the joint command of Mr. James Berry and his physician wife Dr. May Dickinson Berry, both from the Royal

Free Hospital, London. Dr. May Dickinson Berry was Annie Dickinson's sister. Annie Dickinson and all members of her unit were imprisoned at the end of 1915, and repatriated at the end of January 1916. She later returned to Serbia as a representative of the Red Cross in order to distribute food and equipment of various kinds. She remained in Yugoslavia after the war and founded a home and School of Carpentry for Orphan Boys at Vlasenica, a small town in eastern Bosnia, which was later removed to Travnik, also in Bosnia. While the "Villa Bravačić" functioned in Dubrovnik the children from this home went there for convalescence, where they were taught by Annie MacPhail, Katherine's older sister. After the "Villa Bravačić" was closed, Annie MacPhail spent about a year working in this school at Vlasenica as a teacher. With her there were two well-known artists, Sydney Gausden and Bernard Rice, who instructed the children in decorative carpentry, and especially in making furniture. The fate of these children was very varied. When he returned to Britain Sydney Gausden brought one of the orphans with him, whom he adopted. In Britain this boy, Božidar, was trained as a decorative carpenter and helped his adoptive father; later he settled in Cornwall, married, and had a son called Peter and continued to live there happily with his family.

47. Vasa Srdić was clearly a very important person in the life of Katherine MacPhail; unfortunately there is very little accurate information available about him. He was the son of a mixed marriage, with a Scottish mother and a Serbian father; and had a sister called Draga, who, after the First World War had an embroidery shop in Sarajevo, and who was also a friend of Dr. Katherine MacPhail. He studied agronomy at the Frankfurt University before the First World War, and then joined the Serbian army as a volunteer on the Salonica Front. As an officer of the Serbian army serving in Boka Kotorska he helped Isabel MacPhail to set up the "Villa Bravačić" in Dubrovnik, and, it would seem, from then on became a friend of the MacPhail sisters. After the First World War he was given a small estate in Temerin, very near Novi Sad, which he cultivated until 1941 (Fig. 56). During this time he helped Dr. Katherine MacPhail in many ways, most of all with the building of the new hospital in Sremska Kamenica; at this time he was an invaluable friend. Because of his Scottish mother, and the fact that he spoke Serbian with a foreign accent, Katherine and her friends called him Mac Srdić. In the period between the wars he was a member of the Anglo-American Yugoslav Club in Novi Sad. After the outbreak of the Second World War he was driven out of Temerin and interned in a camp in Belgrade, where it seems he was killed in 1942.

48. See: MacPhail, K., *The Anglo-Serbian Children's Hospital in Belgrade 1921-1931 (Report)*.

49. See: Sandes, F., *British Magic*.

50. The Save the Children Fund (SCF) was established in London in 1919, founded by Eglantyne Jebb. It publishes its own journal, *The World's Children*, which has provided valuable material for this biography. Its emblem is the *Bambino* sculpture carved by the famous Italian sculptor Andrea Della Robbia, a copy of which is placed at the entrance of the children's sanatorium (now known as the "English hospital") at Sremska Kamenica (Fig. 66). (For further information see: Kathleen Freeman, *If Any Man Build*).

51. See: Anon., *Crippled Children*

52. The Faculty of Medicine in Belgrade was established in 1920: on February 20th the first staff meeting took place, consisting of three professors. The first generation of students enrolled in the academic year 1920-21, and on December 9th, 1920 Professor Niko Miljanić gave the first introductory lecture on anatomy and thus inaugurated the teaching programme of the newly established Medical Faculty. Dr. Niko Miljanić worked earlier for some time in the Anglo-Serbian Children's Hospital in Belgrade, and was a friend of Dr. Katherine MacPhail. He helped her to come to the new Yugoslavia in 1945. The Paediatric Clinic of this faculty began work in January 1925.

53. See: Vuković, Ž., *Allied Medical Missions in Serbia*.

54. Queen Maria Karadjordjević (1900-1961), or "Mignonne", as she was generally called, was the third daughter of the Rumanian Queen Maria (1875-1938), and King Ferdinand Hohenzollern (1865-1927) who reigned in Rumania from 1914-1927. His great-grandfather was Alfred, duke of Edinburgh, the second son of Queen Victoria. Princess Maria married King Alexander on June 8th, 1922. From 1938 onwards she lived in Britain, where she died on June 22nd, 1961, after a long illness, and where she was buried.

55. This incident early in the life of the Duchess of York, better known in England as "Queen Elizabeth the Queen Mother", is typical of the human warmth and interest in people which made her so enormously popular throughout her long life (Translator's note).

56. See: MacPhail, K., *Appeal for Funds*.

57. See: MacPhail, K., *For the Children of Serbia. A Little Hospital and a Great Work*.

58. See: Sandes, F., *Autobiography of a Woman Soldier*.

59. See: MacPhail, K., *''Community Singing''*.

60. *Yugoslavia* means "the land of the South Slavs". The union of all the South Slav peoples, which had been a long-standing dream among many Slovenes, Croats, Bosnians, Serbs, Montenegrins and Macedonians who lived under foreign domination before First World War, was accomplished after the end of that war, when the so-called *Kingdom of the Serbs, Croats and Slovenians* (abbreviated as SCS) was established on December 1st, 1918 under the rule of the Prince Regent, Alexander, later (after 1921), King Alexander. On   January 6th, 1929 he introduced a dictatorship (the so-called "January Sixth Dictatorship"), after which he ruled as an absolute monarch. At the end of 1929 the King changed the name of the state to the *Kingdom of Yugoslavia*, and at the same time introduced a new system of territorial organisation, by which the country was divided into a number of districts known as *banovine*. One of these was the

Dunavska Banovina or Danube District, of which Novi Sad was the centre. The *Banovina*, as a regional unit, was ruled by a *Ban*. *Ban* was originally a Persian word, introduced into Europe by the Avars, and later taken over by the Slavs. It originally signified the governor of a military district; today the term *Banat* signifies the eastern part of Vojvodina.

61. See: MacPhail, K., *The Children's Hospital at Belgrade*.

62. See: MacPhail, K., *The Anglo-Yugoslav Children's Hospital in Belgrade 1921- 1931 (Report)*.

63. See: MacPhail, K., *To Pastures New*.

64. The name *Fruška Gora* (lit. "Frankish hills") is used to describe a range of hills which stretches for some 48 miles along the southern bank of the River Danube. It is 7-9 miles wide, and 1768 feet high at its highest point. Its name is derived from the German tribes known as Franks, who conquered the area of present-day France in the 6th century A.D; later, in 805, under their famous ruler Charlemagne, they subdued the Avar tribes which had settled in the so-called Pannonian Plain between the Danube and Tisza rivers; the "Frankish hills" then formed the frontier of the extensive Frankish empire. The Slavs who had accompanied the Avars into the Balkan Peninsula called the Franks "Frunzi"; hence the region came to be known as "Fruška Gora" (lit. "Frunzi's Hills"). This beautiful mountainous region, which has been proclaimed a National Park, is covered with luxuriant woods and vineyards, some dating back to Roman times; these produce the well-known Fruška Gora vines. After the Turkish conquest of the Balkan Peninsula, many Serbs migrated from that area and settled in the Fruška Gora region; because of this many Orthodox monasteries were built there, in well-concealed places.

65. This road still exists today, but has been repaired and newly paved. Over the years many houses and "week-end homes" have been built alongside it, and from 1954 this road has been called "Dr. Katherine MacPhail Street".

66. *Petrovaradin*: Today this is part of the city of Novi Sad. Originally it was a small military town, situated just across the river from the centre of that city. It is well-known because of the large "Petrovaradin Fortress" built on the top of a massive rugged cliff above the Danube, which forms part of the Fruška Gora Hills. Because of its position this fortress is often called the "Gibraltar of the Danube". Traces of human settlement have been discovered, dating back as far as 45,000 years; during the pre-historic period, many tribes of Celts, Sarmatians and Pannonians roamed through this area. However the first fort, known as *Cusum* was built by the Romans during the second half of the first century A.D., when they built a series of defensive fortifications along the Danube, known as the Danubian frontier or *limes*. The enormous fortress still standing today was built between 1692 and 1780, when this region was part of the Habsburg Austro-Hungarian Empire, it was built according to the French "Vauban" system, and is still well preserved. Since 1950 the Fortress has been used as a tourist and recreation centre.

67. See: Anon., *Yugoslav Princes' Visit to Pioneer British Hospital.*

68. Vasilj Skrjaga (1898-1977), a Ukrainian by origin, came to Yugoslavia some time in 1920. He lived and worked in various places, even in France, and eventually came to Belgrade where he stayed longer and worked as a taxi driver. It was in Belgrade that he got to know Dr. Katherine MacPhail, whom he often drove in Belgrade and elsewhere. He then began to work for her, and the hospital, and moved to Sremska Kamenica in 1934, where he finally settled with his wife Julka Skrjaga. He worked as Katherine's chauffeur until the Second World War, and after the war until 1947. Then he worked for about a year as a driver for the Red Cross at Sremska Kamenica. In 1948 he was arrested and imprisoned for 9 months, where he was cross-examined and tortured and suspected of being a spy, having worked for Dr. Katherine MacPhail who was also regarded as a spy. He was questioned closely about all her movements, but dismissed without trial. After that he drove passengers from Sremska Kamenica to Novi Sad in his motor-boat. In 1966 he travelled to the Soviet Union to visit his family. He remained a faithful friend and devotee of Dr. Katherine MacPhail until his death in 1977.

69. The official name of the new hospital in Sremska Kamenica was: *The Anglo-Yugoslav Children's Hospital for Tuberculosis of the Bones and Joints*; however, it was rarely referred to by this title. Instead it was usually described as the Sanatorium, then the Anglo-Yugoslav Children's sanatorium and Anglo-Yugoslav Hospital, or sanatorium. However, among the people it was known and even today still is as the "English Hospital".

70. Queen Maria was unable to attend the official opening of the Sremska Kamenica sanatorium, as she was on her way to France, where a state visit had been arranged for King Alexander. The King was supposed to travel to France by boat from Dubrovnik to Marseilles; however the queen decided not to sail with the king, but to travel by rail, on account of the   rough seas and her state of health. That change of plan saved the queen's life, as King Alexander was assassinated in Marseilles. The queen heard about her husband's death in the train at Besançon, on her way to join him.

King Alexander (1888-1934) was a member of the Karadjordjevic dynasty, the younger son of the King Peter I and the Montenegrin Princess Jelena. He became Crown Prince in 1909, regent in 1914 and King in 1921. He ruled Yugoslavia from the First World War till 1934 as an absolute monarch, and in 1929 established an open dictatorship and dealt ruthlessly with all opposition, which made him unpopular, especially among the Non-Serbian population and the communists. In 1921, as he was leaving the parliament, a communist terrorist tried to assassinate him. On October 9th, 1934, during a state visit to Marseilles, while he was being driven in an open car with M. Berthou, the French Foreign Minister, a Macedonian terrorist jumped on the running board and opened fire, killing the King and mortally wounding Mr. M. Berthou.

King Alexander was succeeded by his son Peter, an eleven year old schoolboy, for whom Alexander's cousin, Prince Paul, acted as regent, actually as the head of a Regency Council. Two Ministers were also appointed regents or members of that Council, but ultimately Prince Paul assumed sole control. He was an artistic, cultivated man, educated in Great Britain, who had spent much of his life abroad. During his regency there was a return to a milder form of central government, and more democracy.

71. See: MacPhail, K., *The Anglo-Yugoslav Sanatorium.*

72. Lilian Vidaković, an Englishwoman married to the Serbian journalist Alexander Vidaković, was president of the Anglo-Yugoslav Club in Belgrade and later director of the British Council in Belgrade; she was a great friend of Katherine's, and a benefactor of the children's hospitals in Belgrade and Sremska Kamenica. She died in Belgrade on November 12th, 1979.

73. Princess Olga Karadjordjević (1903-1997) was the daughter of Prince Nicholas of Greece (1872-1938) and Helena Vladimirovna Romanov, grand-duchess of Russia (1882-1957); and grand-daughter of King George I of Greece (1845-1913). In October 1923 she married the Prince Paul Karadjordjević, by whom she had two sons, Prince Alexander (b. 1924) and Prince Nicholas (1928-1954), and a daughter, Princess Elizabeth (b. 1936). She had two sisters, Elizabeth (1904-1953), and Marina (1906-1968), who married Prince George, duke of Kent, younger brother of King George VI (1852-1942), and was known as the duchess of Kent. She, and Princess Olga, were the so-called "British connection" of Dr. Katherine MacPhail. (For further reading see: Balfour, N. and Mackay, S., *Prince Paul of Yugoslavia*).

74. See: MacPhail, K., *The Anglo-Yugoslav Children's Hospital for Tuberculosis of Bones and Joints, Report 1934-1936, Kamenica, Srem, Yugoslavia.*

75. See: Anon., *For the Children of Yugoslavia, Dr. Katherine MacPhail's Pioneer Work.*

76. See: Group of Authors, *Double Issue Dedicated to the Problem of the Bones and Joints Tuberculosis.*

77. *Pannonia* or *The Pannonian Plain* is a vast area of central Europe, situated between the Alps on the west, the Carpathian mountains on the north and east, and the Dinaric range and its adjacent mountains on the south. The term Pannonia dates from Roman times, as they called the region after the *Illyrian* tribe of *Pannons (*Pannonians*)* who lived there on the banks of the Sava, Drava and Danube rivers, before the Roman occupation. As its name implies, it is a predominantly lowland area, through which several rivers flow, of which the Danube is the largest. It is believed that about two million years ago this plain was a sea, the so-called Pannonian Sea. Today four countries occupy the largest part of this plain: Hungary, Croatia, Serbia and Rumania. This region has a continental climate, with hot summers and cold winters; because of its fertile soil it is a mainly agricultural area.

78. See: MacPhail, K., *Heliotherapy in the Osteo-Articular Tuberculosis in Children*.

79. Professor Čižek, an Austrian of Czech origin, was a professor of the History of Art in Vienna before and after the First World War; he developed original methods of teaching art to the youth of Vienna, which became known as "Čižek's school". (For further information, see Francesca Wilson, *In the Margins of Chaos*).

80. Constance Dušmanić (1889-?), "Con" as she was usually called, born Constance Miller, was of Scottish origin, and as a young woman volunteered to work in one of the Scottish Women's Hospitals on the Salonica Front, and there she met Katherine MacPhail; this was the beginning of a friendship that lasted nearly 50 years. When Constance was smoking a forbidden cigarette in the hospital laundry, she met Vladimir Dušmanić, an artillery officer in the Serbian army, whom she later married, and by whom she had four children. She helped Katherine MacPhail to collect money for the children's hospital in Belgrade, and later frequently visited the hospital in Sremska Kamenica with her children, where they often spent Christmas. When Yugoslavia was attacked in 1941 she fled with her children to Palestine, which was then a British protectorate. Her children immediately volunteered for war service, and her daughter Dana, following her mother's example, became an ambulance driver with the British Eighth Army in Egypt where she met again Dr. Katherine MacPhail. She then joined Dr. MacPhail's unit under the auspices of UNRRA and with them went to Yugoslavia. After the war Dana returned to England to complete her studies, and later married Ratko Stanković, with whom she settled in England. She remained in contact with Dr. Katherine MacPhail till the end of Katherine's life. Ratko Stanković wrote me several useful letters about the Dušmanić family, which were used in the preparation of this book.

81. The Anglo-American Yugoslav Club was founded in Novi Sad on October 28th, 1934, with premises in the Park Hotel. Darinka Grujić Radović was elected the first president, and Vasa Srdić was among the first members.

82. See: MacPhail, K., *Farewell to Yugoslavia*

83. .See: MacPhail, K., *"Of Other Days"*

84. The *Tripartite Pact*, between Germany, Italy and Japan was signed in Berlin on September 27th, 1940. Yugoslavia, then under the rule of the Regent, Prince Paul and his Regency Council, was under enormous pressure from the so-called Axis powers to join this pact, because of its strategic geographical position; however, the Yugoslav Government was reluctant to take this step. But by the end of 1940 the country's position had become increasingly precarious. The Italians, already in control in Albania, had invaded Greece, and the Germans had overrun Hungary, Rumania and Bulgaria, so that Yugoslavia was surrounded on all sides. In a desperate attempt to keep Yugoslavia out of the war, the Tripartite Pact was signed on March 25th, 1941. According to this pact Yugoslavia was not expected to take an active part in the war activities of the

Axis powers, but only to allow safe passage on her main railway lines for German war material, and to suppress all anti-Axis activities within her borders. The railway line was particularly important to the Germans, because of the projected conquest of Greece and ultimate attack on the Allied forces in Egypt. However, there was a violent reaction to the signing of the pact, resulting in the *coup d'état* of March 27th, 1941.

85. The *coup d'état* of March 27th, 1941, proved to be a legendary event in Yugoslav history. It was carried out by a group of young Airforce officers under General Dušan Simović, with the support of the Royal Guards and other army units; it was bloodless and effective. The young Crown Prince Peter, then 17 years old, was proclaimed King, and the Regents were arrested and expelled from the country. Many thousands of excited demonstrators marched through Belgrade and other major towns shouting the famous slogans: *"Bolje rat nego pakt!"* ("Better war than the pact!"), and *"Bolje grob nego rob"* ("Better grave than the slave"). When the news of this event spread round the world, Winston Churchill declared: "The Yugoslav nation has found its soul." Perhaps this was so, but the price was enormous and horrifying. Within three weeks Yugoslavia had been ruthlessly bombed, and invaded from all sides. Generally unprepared, the Yugoslav Army tried to confront the much more powerful Axis troops; but, although help had been promised, none came, and many thousands were killed and wounded. On April 17th, 1941, an unconditional capitulation was signed, after which Germany and her allies tore the country to pieces. Germany kept part of Slovenia and Banat (the eastern part of Vojvodina), and gave the southern part of Slovenia, including Ljubljana, and the Adriatic coast to Italy. Macedonia was given to Bulgaria, Bačka (part of Vojvodina) to Hungary, and puppet states with quisling governments were established in Croatia and Serbia. Meanwhile, on April 14th, 1941, the young King Peter II and his government fled to Greece, and subsequently to Britain, where they stayed during the war. Peter II Karadjordjević (born on September 6th, 1923 in Belgrade), married Princess Alexandra of Greece in 1944, and died on November 3rd, 1970, in Los Angeles. He ruled Yugoslavia only for a few weeks in 1941 as its last king, before the communist government abolished the monarchy in 1945.

86. Milan Gavrilović before the Second World War was the leader of the Serbian Agricultural Party, and in 1940 became the first ambassador of the Kingdom of Yugoslavia to the USSR. After the coup d'état of March 27th, 1941, he joined the government of General Simović as minister without portfolio, and was later a member of the refugee government in London.

87. UNRRA (The United Nations Relief and Rehabilitation Administration) was a body temporarily set up by the United Nations Organisation on August 8th, 1943, in order to provide help with the provision of food, clothing, and medical supplies, the repatriation of exiles and the general restoration of liberated countries devastated by war. In contrast to the situation after the First World War, when the assistance offered to such countries was spontaneous and sometimes chaotic (see Francesca Wilson, *In the Margins of Chaos*), UNRRA, which was sponsored and financed by 44 member states of the United Nations, was a highly professional international organisation, which organised and co-ordinated help for the liberated countries in a very professional way. Its activity ended in 1947, and the organisation was officially wound up in September 1948 (For further information, see Wilson F.: *Aftermath*).

88: See: Wilson, F., *Aftermath*

89. See: Anon., *Relief for Yugoslavia*.

90. *Trieste,* known from the Roman times as *Tergeste*, is the biggest and the most developed town on the northern shore of the Adriatic Sea. It is inhabited mostly by Italians, also by Slovenians and Croats. It was the main port of the Austro-Hungarian Empire until 1918, from 1918 till 1943 it was under Italian control, and from 1943 till 1945 the Third Reich occupied it. In May 1945 the Yugoslav National Liberation Army under the command of Marshal Tito liberated Trieste and, because of the significant South Slav population there, and because it was a major Slovenian cultural centre, the new communist authorities of Yugoslavia wanted to incorporate Trieste and its surroundings in the new Yugoslavia. However the Allies were fervently against that solution, and an acute tension between the new Yugoslavia and Western Allies, especially Great Britain, broke out in 1945 and lasted for several years. From 1947 till 1954 Trieste had the status of the Free Territory, and finally in 1954, according to the London Agreement, Trieste was integrated into Italy.

91. *Vojvodina* (spelt "Voivodina" in English) is an autonomous province of former Yugoslavia and present-day Serbia. It occupies the south-eastern part of the Pannonian Plain and the northern part of Serbia, beyond the Danube and Sava rivers, and is bordered by Hungary and Rumania on the north and east, and Croatia on the west; it occupies an area of 13,363 square miles. The rivers Danube, Tisza and Sava mark the boundaries of the three districts of Vojvodina: Bačka lies to the west, between the Danube and the Tisza; Banat to the east, between the Tisza and the Rumanian frontier, and Srem to the south, between the Danube and Sava rivers. Before the First World War this region formed part of the Austro-Hungarian Empire; however, because of its large Slav population (mainly Serbs, but including some Croats and Slovaks), part of this region was granted a measure of autonomy by the Habsburg Empire, and a leader known as *vojvoda* (lit. "Duke") was recognised, and the region came to be known as *Vojvodina* (lit. "Duchy"). This autonomy was not approved in the former Kingdom of Yugoslavia, and it was only after the Second World War, under communist Yugoslavia, that the region of Vojvodina gained its autonomy. It is a multi-national and multi-cultural area, in which 24 different nationalities live, mostly Serbs and Hungarians, also Croats, Slovaks, Rumanians and others. It is the most highly-developed and richest part of the country. The capital of Vojvodina is Novi Sad.

92. See: Anon., *Hospitals in Yugoslavia*.

93. See: Tew, M., *Anglo-Yugoslav Hospital*.

94. See: Anon., *Dr. Katherine MacPhail's Work*.

95. See: Anon., *News from Yugoslavia*.

96. See: MacPhail, K., *Yugoslavia 1919 – 1969*.

97. In the accompanying letter Dr. Katherine MacPhail sent her collection of 120 slides, mostly of photographs taken by herself, to the Serbian Medical Association in Belgrade. The slides relate to the Anglo-Yugoslav Children's Hospital in Belgrade, the dependencies in Topčider and Dubrovnik, and the Anglo-Yugoslav Children's sanatorium in Sremska Kamenica. They include photographs of patients, various places in Yugoslavia, and national costume. Explanations of most of the photographs are included in an accompanying letter. Photographs were made from these slides during 1988, and an exhibition organised on December 6th, 1988 in the premises of *Matica Srpska* in Novi Sad. Many of these photographs have been included in the present book, and the collection of slides is preserved in the museum of the Serbian Medical Association in Belgrade. (Translator's note: *Matica Srpska*, the *Serbian Queen Bee*, is a prestigious literary and cultural society, with its own publishing house, founded in 1826).

98. See: Anon., *Katherine Stewart MacPhail OBE*.

Appendices

Biographical Information

Appendix 1. Elspeth Carrick Biggs (née McFarlane) (1919–2006), from St Andrews, was born in 1919 in Hamilton, Lanarkshire, near Glasgow, the second child of Janet and Dr. James McFarlane; her mother Janet was Katherine MacPhail's eldest sister. She went to Hamilton Academy Junior and Senior school, and then studied economics and political science at the University of St Andrews, where she graduated in 1947; during the war, when she was a student, she volunteered for the Women's Royal Naval Service (WRNS) where she spent five years. First she spent three and a half years in a bunker of the Atlantic command in Liverpool, and was then transferred to Egypt. During the so-called "Battle of the Atlantic", the longest battle of the Second World War, this was the most dangerous place in Great Britain, from which the entire battle was controlled. These were, according to Elspeth's recollection, extremely difficult and laborious days, when they had to work day and night, with a rest day only once every 10 days. Elspeth was twice decorated for this war service. She was demobilised in 1946, and then completed her studies and worked as a secretary in Oxford. In 1951 she married Henry Charles Biggs (1908-1977), whom she met in 1945 while she was working in the Near East, actually in Jerusalem, where she was on leave. Henry Biggs was then an artillery officer, a major in the British Army. Elspeth and Henry Biggs lived first in the London area, and then in 1955 they went to the West Indies, and made homes in Barbados, Jamaica and Trinidad. They had a daughter Alison (b. 1958), who in 1984 married Guy Thomson, with whom she lives in Ceres, Fife. After returning to Great Britain Elspeth retired and settled in St Andrews with her family. Her husband died in 1977. After she moved to St Andrews, Mrs. Biggs and her sister were a great support to Dr. Katherine MacPhail, with whom she spent much time, and helped in many ways; among other things she helped her with the preparation and proof-reading of the manuscript of her biography, written by Jean Bray, and personally typed and made three copies of the manuscript, and thus learnt many details about the life and work of Dr. Katherine MacPhail. When the Imperial War Museum in London prepared an exhibition of "Women at War 1914-1915" in 1977, a copy of this manuscript, together with many photographs, letters and other documents, which until then had remained in the family archives, was handed over to this museum, at their request, for the purpose of this exhibition. It was officially opened in March 1977 by Princess Anne in the premises of the museum, afterwards it was taken to the major cities of Great Britain, including Glasgow, until October that year. Since then all the material has remained in the possession of the museum. When I was researching material for this book in October 1989, I spent several days in this impressive museum, where I had the opportunity to examine and study all the material that has been incorporated into this book. Elspeth Biggs died peacefully on March 1st, 2006 in St Andrews.

Appendix 2. Dr. Elsie Inglis (1864-1917), one of the greatest heroines of the First World War, was founder and driving force behind the Scottish Women's Hospitals for Foreign Service, which were a great help to Serbia during the First World War. She was born in India on August 16th, 1864, into the family of a high-ranking colonial official. After her birth her family moved to Tasmania, where Elsie attended school until she was fourteen; then in 1878 her family settled in Edinburgh. She studied medicine in Glasgow and Edinburgh, and graduated from the University of Edinburgh in 1899. She began working as a doctor in various places, and then in 1904 opened in Edinburgh a small surgical and gynecological hospital for poor women, known as the *Hospice*, staffed entirely by women. In addition to her regular medical work, she was involved in activities of social interest, and made a considerable contribution to the suffragette movement in Scotland. In 1914 she became honorary secretary of the Scottish Federation of Women's Suffrage Societies, which had its headquarters in Edinburgh, and was for many years vice-president of the Edinburgh Women's Liberal Association. This society did not employ militant tactics and struggled to secure the rights of women by legitimate means. "The ordinary male disbelief in women's capacity cannot be argued away – it can only be worked away", said Dr. Elsie Inglis once; and so she acted. Immediately after the outbreak of the war she occupied herself fully in organising the Scottish Women's Hospitals. During 1915 she came to Serbia in order to supervise the work of these hospitals personally; in the face of an enemy offensive they withdrew to Kruševac, where she was taken prisoner. After a few months she was repatriated; immediately after her return home, although not in good health, she began to prepare a larger hospital, with which she travelled to Russia in September 1916; here, on the Dobrudja front, her hospital joined the Southern Slav Volunteer Division formed mainly by Serbs. In November 1917, when Dr. Elsie Inglis herself was already ill, the remnants of her hospital and the Serbian division were evacuated and the day after the ship had docked at Newcastle, on November 26th, 1917, Dr. Elsie Inglis died. After a magnificent funeral with full military honours she was buried at Edinburgh's Dean Cemetery. The recognition of women's achievements during the wartime hastened progress for women on the domestic front. Shortly before her death Elsie Inglis had learned that women over thirty were to be granted the Vote – a right she herself was never to exercise. Soon afterwards, the Elsie Inglis Memorial Maternity Hospital was established in Edinburgh, and a little later a memorial hospital in Belgrade, with a memorial plaque to Dr. Elsie Inglis. She was posthumously awarded the Order of the White Eagle, the highest order in Serbia, and there is a bust of her in the Scottish National Portrait Gallery in Edinburgh, carved by famous Croatian sculptor Ivan Meštrović and given to the Scottish nation by the Serbian people. There is also a memorial plaque in honour of Dr. Elsie Inglis in the Physiological Institute of the Medical Faculty in Belgrade, and a memorial drinking water fountain, erected in 1915, in Mladenovac (Serbia), in the memory of the Scottish Women's Hospitals and Dr. Elsie Inglis. For further details of the life and work of this brave Scotswoman, see *Dr. Elsie Inglis* by Frances Balfour, published by Hodder and Stoughton, London, 1918.

Appendix 3. Monica Krippner was born and educated in Australia, and came to Great Britain in 1947. She then began her career as a traveller and writer, travelling through Africa from Cape Town to Algeria in the course of ten months; this provided the subject matter for her first book. After this she did a year of postgraduate study, and then spent two years travelling through Yugoslavia and Greece, and writing books and articles.

During her travels through Africa she had an interesting encounter (see note 19) about which she later wrote: "Many years ago, when travelling in north Africa, I met Dr. Frances ('Daisy') Wakefield in Tamanrasset (Fort Lapperine), where she had lived for many years. During the days that followed I listened entranced as she related her experiences as a doctor, missionary and linguist among the nomadic peoples of the Middle East and the Tuaregs of the Hoggar mountains in central Sahara. Then one day she spoke about her service as a young doctor with a Scottish Women's Hospital unit in Serbia during World War I. This was the first time I had heard of such units and it was a revelation to learn of the extraordinary wartime medical service of so many women-surgeons, nurses, VADS and drivers - in front-line hospitals and field stations". Fascinated by stories about British women who had taken part in the First World War in Serbia, she began to collect material about them.

During 1960 she became a special correspondent for the *Daily Herald* and the *Guardian*, based in Vienna; she then obtained a post with the Atomic Energy Agency of the United Nations in Vienna, and worked as an editor in their publications department until her retirement, after which she continued to live in Vienna and in Retz (Austria). Monica Krippner was a great friend of the Serbs, and later visited Serbia several times (Figs. 100 and 102).

After several years of preparatory work, in 1980 her exceptionally interesting book entitled *The Quality of Mercy, Women at War, Serbia 1915-18* came out, about the many British women who came to the devastated land of Serbia during the First World War with different medical missions. A Serbian translation of this book, by Prof. Dr. Veselin Kostić, came out in 1986, with a preface by Dr. Žarko Vuković. I personally met Monica Krippner in 1987 when she visited Novi Sad; after that we corresponded for many years, and she helped me a great deal in preparing material for this biography of Dr. Katherine MacPhail, and by her advice on a number of points.

Appendix 4. Annie MacPhail, Katherine's sister (1886-1966), usually called Nan, studied at Glasgow University and then at a missionary college, which she left. She lived with her parents, first in Coatbridge and later in Hamilton, to which they moved after Dr. Donald MacPhail's retirement. She spent some time in Yugoslavia after the First World War, and helped Katherine with the work of the "Villa Bravačić" sanatorium established in Dubrovnik in 1920-21 (see Figs. 35-37), and later worked as a teacher in a home for orphans in Vlasenica established by Annie Dickinson. Later, in 1923, she had to return to Scotland in order to look after her elderly parents. After their death she moved to St Andrews, where she bought a house, (No. 4, Kinburn Place), for herself and Katherine, where she lived with Katherine until her death. During 1932 she again helped Katherine for a short time in running the temporary hospital in Sremska Kamenica. She died on July 13th, 1966, and was cremated and her ashes scattered in the Western Cemetery in St Andrews; on one wall in this cemetery there is a memorial tablet dedicated to her and to Dr. Katherine MacPhail (Figs. 96 and 97).

Appendix 5. Isabel MacPhail (1889-1955) was Katherine's youngest sister. She studied modern languages at Glasgow University from 1907 to 1910, and graduated in November 1910. At the beginning of 1915 she completed a nursing course, and immediately joined a unit of the Scottish Women's Hospitals as a VAD; she was then sent to France, where she spent almost two years. Between September and December 1916, her hospital was stationed in North Africa (*Hôpital Aux. 301, Armée d'Orient*), and when the French Eastern Army was transferred to the Salonica Front, this Scottish Women's Hospital unit, including Isabel, was also transferred to Salonica. After the arrival of Dr. Katherine MacPhail at the Salonica Front, Isabel left this hospital and joined Katherine, with whom she worked for some time behind the front line in the Bitola area (today in Macedonia). Later she worked as a surgical sister in the Prince Regent Alexander's Serbian Hospital in Salonica; she stayed there until August 1918, when she and Katherine went on leave to Scotland. She returned in the winter of 1918, as a worker in a voluntary canteen run by the YWCA with which, as the front advanced, she reached Vranje, a small town in southern Serbia, where she remained for some time, then in 1919 she moved to Belgrade, where she again met Katherine. She worked for a time with the British Joint Supply Commission in Belgrade, and then helped Katherine with her work in the hospitals in Belgrade and Dubrovnik. When their parents visited Yugoslavia in the summer of 1920, she accompanied them after which she herself returned to Scotland. She then completed a secretarial course in London, where she worked for some time, and then in 1923 she obtained a post as a secretary in the British Embassy in Peking. In 1926 she married Edward Nathan (1887-1963), who was manager of the Kailan Mining Company in Tientsin (China); they lived there until the Second World War and the arrival of the Japanese. They had two daughters, Joan (b. 1927), and Ann (1930-1965). During the war Edward Nathan was interned by the Japanese Army, but Isabel and her daughters managed to escape to Canada where they settled in Nova Scotia. After the war the family once more settled in England, where Edward inherited a fine, large house, built in the 14th century, with a very valuable library and an enormous park; this was called the Manor House situated in West Coker in Somerset, near Yeovil, where the family then settled. Their daughters graduated at St Andrews University. Joan, the oldest, who lives in Crieff in Perthshire, married Cecil Longden (1919-1969), by whom she had a son, Crispin (b.1959), who lives in Edinburgh, and a daughter, Gabrielle (b.1962), who lived with her two daughters in London. Sadly, about 1950, Isabel became seriously ill with a rare neurological disease, and was placed in a nursing home in Gloucestershire, where she died in 1955 and was cremated in Bristol. In the course of her work on different wartime fronts, Isabel wrote many interesting letters home, which have been used as a source for this biography, and most of which remain in family archives.

Appendix 6. Janet MacPhail (1884-1973), Katherine's oldest sister, studied French and German at Glasgow University, and spent her last year partly at the Sorbonne and partly at Grenoble. After this she worked as a language teacher until her marriage to Dr. James McFarlane (1886-1955) in 1913. They moved to Hamilton, some 15 miles from Glasgow, where their three daughters were born: Jessie (1917-2006), Elspeth (1919-2006) and Ann (1922-2005). In 1925 Dr. McFarlane bought a country practice in Chapelhall, about 3 miles from Coatbridge, where the family lived until Dr. McFarlane's retirement in 1950, when they moved to St Andrews. Jessie, the oldest daughter, did not marry, Ann, the youngest daughter, studied English Language and Literature at St Andrews and later married Alexander Davidson (1919-1981), a senior colonial official with whom she lived for many years in Africa, about which she wrote an interesting book: Ann M. Davidson, *The Real Paradise, Memories of Africa 1950-1963*. She had no children, and from 1970 onwards lived in St Andrews, until her death in August 2005. She inherited most of Dr. Katherine MacPhail's papers.

Appendix 7. Flora Sandes (1876-1956) was one of the legendary heroines of the First World War in Serbia. She was born and spent her childhood in Suffolk. She was very well-educated, and loved riding, motoring and archery, and attended a number of first-aid courses. Before the First World War she worked as a secretary in London. When the war broke out she volunteered for service with the British Red Cross and in August 1914 arrived in Kragujevac, where she spent three months working in the First Reserve Military Hospital. In December 1914 she returned to Britain and worked to raise help for Serbia, to which she returned in January 1915, with 110 tons of medical equipment and supplies and worked as a VAD in Valjevo. In April 1915 she fell ill with typhus, from which she recovered after a period of convalescence in England. She returned to Serbia, later joined the Serbian army as a regular soldier, and shared with them the retreat through Albania; she achieved the rank of corporal and was decorated with the Order of St Sava, and also the Karadjordje Star for bravery. She later went to the Salonica Front where she met Dr. Katherine MacPhail with whom she became a life-long friend. Flora Sandes was later promoted to captain and demobilised in 1921. (For further information, see: Monica Krippner, op.cit; Flora Sands, *Autobiography of a Woman Soldier* (1927); and idem, *An English Woman Sergeant in the Serbian Army* (1916).

Appendix 8. Mabel St Clair Stobart was born into a wealthy and aristocratic family, the daughter of Sir Samuel Bulton of Forderbridge in Hertfordshire. She lived for some time in South Africa, with her first husband, Colonel Stobart, engaging in agriculture and trade, until his death during a journey through South Africa. She married John Greenhalgh as her second husband, but retained her surname from her first marriage. In 1912 she founded the Women's Sick and Wounded Convoy Corps, a medical unit in which all the members, including doctors, were women. The only exception was her husband, John Greenhalgh, who looked after the financial affairs. She took the unit to Bulgaria, where, during the First Balkan War against the Turks, under very difficult conditions, she set up and managed a surgical hospital in Kirklarelija, near the front line. She also took part in the suffragette movement in London. After the outbreak of the First World War she founded the Women's Imperial Service Hospital, which worked behind the front line near Antwerp; she was the director of the hospital, and her husband was the treasurer. When the Germans captured Antwerp, she narrowly escaped being shot as a spy, but was in fact pardoned and repatriated. After this she ran an Anglo-French hospital near Cherbourg. On hearing about the difficult situation in Serbia, and the appeal for volunteers, she left the Cherbourg Hospital and offered her services to the Serbian Relief Fund in London, where, in view of her experience, she was put in charge of the third SRF hospital (the first two were in Skopje), which had a staff of 50, including 7 doctors; her husband, John Greenhalgh, acted as treasurer. At the end of April 1915, this very well - equipped hospital arrived in Kragujevac and was set up on a former race -track. At the beginning of October 1915, on the order of Colonel Lazar Genčić, head of the medical services, the hospital was divided. The main hospital remained in Kragujevac, but a smaller section, with 18 beds and 60 Serbian soldiers, working as drivers or medical orderlies under Mabel Stobart's direction, known as "Stobart's Flying Unit", was handed over to the Šumadija Division and officially known as the First Anglo-Serbian Field Hospital. Mabel Stobart was the director of this hospital, and was given the rank of temporary major in the Serbian army. Prior to her departure from Kragujevac Colonel Terzić, the commanding officer of the Šumadija Division, sent her a horse, so that she could ride at the head of the unit; and from then on, as Monica

Krippner relates, she rarely descended from the saddle, since, as she herself asserted, on horseback she had "better mobility to command". The hospital was sent to Pirot, and when the general retreat began, Mabel Stobart's unit withdrew across Albania with the Serbian army, then continued their journey in an Italian boat; at the end of December 1915, they disembarked at Brindisi. After her return to England Mabel Stobart organised a journey through America where she gave a series of lectures; all the money earned from these was given to the Serbian Red Cross. After this she withdrew from public life.

Bibliography

1. Adams, J.T., *Empire on the Seven Seas*, Scribner's, New York, 1940.
2. Anon., *A Hospital Moves to New Site at Kamenica, Dr. MacPhail talks to the "Herald"*, South Slav Herald, Belgrade, Sept. 16th, 1933, pp. 2 and 5.
3. Anon., *The Anglo-Yugoslav Children's Sanatorium*, Save the Children Fund Annual Report, The World's Children, London, 1938 - 39, pp. 11-13.
4. Anon., *Belgrade Calling*, The World's Children, London, November 1927, p. 24.
5. Anon., *Crippled Children in Yugoslavia, Anglo-Yugoslav Children's Hospital begins a New Effort, Queen Mary's Interest*, The World's Children, London, October 1934, pp. 5-6.
6. Anon., *Distinguished Medical Service in Two Wars*, St Andrews Citizen, St. Andrews, September 28th, 1974, p. 1.
7. Anon., *Dr. Katherine MacPhail's Work*, The World's Children, London, August 1946, p. 153.
8. Anon., *Elsie Inglis, Heritage Trail*, Hermiston Publications Ltd, Edinburgh, 1989.
9. Anon., *For the Children of Yugoslavia, Dr. Katherine MacPhail's Work*, The World's Children, London, February 1938, pp. 69-70.
10. Anon., *H.R.H. Crown Prince Alexander's Visit to the "Crown Prince Alexander's Serbian Hospital in Salonica" in July 1917*, Vojno-sanitetski glasnik (Military Corps Herald), Belgrade, 1934, Vol. 5, No. 3, p. 17.
11. Anon., *Hospitals in Yugoslavia*, The World's Children, London, December 1945, p. 196.
12. Anon., *Minutes of the Annual Meeting of the Yugoslav Orthopaedic and Traumatologic Association held at Ohrid on September 26th, 1974*, Acta Orthopaedica Iugoslavica, Belgrade, 1975, Vol. 6, pp. 247-255.
13. Anon., *News from Yugoslavia, World's Children Report*, The World's Children, London, August 1947, p. 14.
14. Anon., *News: Katherine Stewart MacPhail, OBE*, The World's Children, London, March 1975, p.16.
15. Anon., *Opening of the Children's Sanatorium at Sremska Kamenica*, Politika, Belgrade, September 21st, 1934, p. 21.
16. Anon., *Our Property in Swiss Banks*, Dnevnik, Novi Sad, November 30th, 1996, p. 9.
17. Anon., *Relief for Yugoslavia, King Peter Hands a £ 5000 Gift to the Save the Children Fund*, The World's Children, London, May 1945, pp. 84-86.

18. Anon., *The Anglo-Serbian Children's Hospital*, The World's Children, London, October 1925, p. 22.
19. Anon., *The Children's Hospital at Belgrade*, The World's Children, London, March 1931, p. 109.
20. Anon., *The Unveiling of Dr. Katherine MacPhail's Monument*, Eliksir, Novi Sad, No. 201, August 5th, 1988, p. 63.
21. Anon., *The Unveiling of the Monument in the Former Anglo-Yugoslav Hospital*, Lekar, (Physician) Serbian Medical Association, Belgrade, No. 96, June 1988, p. 6.
22. Anon., *Yugoslav Mothers' Faith in British Doctors*, The World's Children, London, May 1931, p. 153.
23. Anon., *Yugoslav Princes Visit to Pioneer British Hospital*, The World's Children, London, June 1933, p. 137.
24. Antić, D., *Pockmarked Typhus Fever in the First Reserve Military Hospital at Kragujevac in 1914-15*, in the book: *History of the Serbian Military Corps, Our War Medical Experience*, ed. and publ. by Vladimir Stanojević, Belgrade 1925, pp. 314-328.
25. Balfour, F., *Dr. Elsie Inglis*, Hodder & Stoughton, London, 1919.
26. Balfour, N., Mackay, S., *Prince Paul of Yugoslavia*, Hamish Hamilton, London, 1980.
27. Berić, B., Miškov, D., *Survey of the History of the Novi Sad Hospital (1730-1980)*, Medicinski pregled (Medical Review). Novi Sad, 1981,Vol. 34, pp. 259-265.
28. Blair, D.M., *Alexander MacPhail, In Memoriam*, The Times, September 2nd, 1938.
29. Bray, J., *Yesterday's Witness, Mission to Serbia*, Documentary Film, BBC Production, London, 1970.
30. Buchan H., *Women in the University, Fifth Centenary of Glasgow University*, Glasgow Herald, Glasgow, Outram & Co. Ltd. Glasgow, 1951.
31. Corbett, E., *With the Red Cross in Serbia*, Cheney, 1960.
32. Dautović, R., *The First Time after the Second World War. A Padlock on the "English Hospital"*, Dnevnik, Novi Sad, November 8th, 1992, p. 15.
33. Davidson, A., M., *The Real Paradise, Memories of Africa 1950 – 1963*, The Pentland Press Ltd, Edinburgh - Cambridge – Durham, 1993.
34. Djordjević, D. *The Opening of the Sanatorium for the Treatment of the Bones and Joints Tuberculosis at Sremska Kamenica*, Politika, Belgrade, September 24th, 1934, p. 9.
35. Dragić, M., *Dr. Katherine Stewart MacPhail, In Memoriam*, Politika, Belgrade, October 14th, 1974, p. 10.

36. Dragić, M., *Dr. Katherine Stewart MacPhail*, Proceedings of the Section for History of Medicine and Pharmacy of the Serbian Medical Association, Belgrade 1973, Vol. 8, pp. 255-262.

37. Freeman, K., *If Any Man Build*, Hodder and Stoughton, London, 1965.

38. Group of Authors, *Double Issue Dedicated to the Problem of the Bones and Joints Tuberculosis*, Medicinski pregled (Medical Review), Medical Association of Vojvodina, Novi Sad, 1960, Vol. 13, No. 1-2.

39. Gusman, D.J., *A Short History of Orthopaedic Surgery and Traumatology in Novi Sad*, Medical Association of Vojvodina, Novi Sad, 1979.

40. Hložan, B., *Dr. Katherine MacPhail's Bust Unveiled*, Dnevnik, Novi Sad, June 16th, 1988, p. 164.

41. Krippner, M., *The Quality of Mercy, Women at War, Serbia 1915-18*, David & Charles, Newton Abbot - London, 1980.

42. Lindsay, S., *Coatbridge and the Great War*, Hay Nisbet & Co. Ltd, Glasgow, 1919.

43. MacPhail, K., *Appeal for Funds for the Anglo-Serb Children's Hospital in Belgrade,* Belgrade, May 1923.

44. MacPhail, K., *"Community Singing" in the Belgrade Children's Hospital*, The World's Children, London, May 1919, p.159.

45. MacPhail, K., *Farewell to Yugoslavia, How War Came to the Anglo-Yugoslav Children's Hospital*, The World's Children, London, Winter 1941-42, pp. 48-51.

46. MacPhail, K., *For the Children of Serbia. A Little Hospital and a Great Work*, The World's Children, London, December 1925-January 1926, pp. 46-48.

47. MacPhail, K., *Heliotherapy in Osteo-Articular Tuberculosis in Children*, Medicinski pregled (Medical Review), Novi Sad, 1960, Vol. 13, pp. 5-8.

48. MacPhail, K., *"Of Other Days", A Memory of the Anglo-Yugoslav Chldren's Hospital,* The World's Children, London, Winter 1942, pp. 85-86.

49. MacPhail, K., *The Anglo-Serbian Children's Hospital Belgrade, 1918-1921 (Report),* Alex. Pettigrew Ltd, Coatbridge, 1921.

50. MacPhail, K., *The Anglo-Yugoslav Children's Hospital Belgrade, 1921-1931*, The Weardale Press Ltd, London & Bedford, 1931.

51. MacPhail, K., *The Anglo-Yugoslav Children's Hospital for Tuberculosis of Bones and Joints, Report 1934-1936*, Djordje Ivković, Novi Sad, 1936.

52. MacPhail, K., *The Anglo-Yugoslav Sanatorium, Dr. Katherine MacPhail describes her Child-saving Work*, The World's Children, London, February 1935, p. 69.

53. MacPhail, K., *To Pastures New, Dr. Katherine MacPhail describes the New Scheme for the Belgrade Children's Hospital*, The World's Children, London, October 1933, pp.9-10.

54. MacPhail, K., *Yugoslavia 1919-1969, Golden Jubilee Issue*, The World's Children, London, 1969, pp. 29-31.

55. McLaren, E.S., ed., *A History of the Scottish Women's Hospitals*, Hodder & Stoughton, London, 1919.

56. Manojlović, B., *One Important Medical and Social Institution, The Anglo-Yugoslav Children's Hospital at Sremska Kamenica fulfills its Important Mission for a Whole Year Now, H.M. the Queen Maria is the Patron of the Hospital*, Dan, Novi Sad, October 27th, 1935, p. 6.

57. Martin, G.R., *Jennie, The Life of Lady Randolph Churchill, The Dramatic Years 1895-1921*, Vol. 2, Signet Book, The New American Library, Inc., New York, 1972.

58. Mikić, Ž., *Development of Orthopaedics and Foundation of the Clinic for Orthopaedic Surgery and Traumatology in Novi Sad*, Medicinski pregled (Medical Review), Novi Sad, 1998, Vol. 51, pp. 457-468.

59. Mikić, Ž., *Dr. Katherine MacPhail's Monument has been Unveiled*, Medicinski pregled (Medical Review), Novi Sad, 1988, Vol. 41, pp. 345-346.

60. Mikić, Ž., Lazić, D., *Dr Miloš Ćirić, Pulmonologist 1893-1979*, Medicinski pregled (Medical Review), Novi Sad 1986, Vol. 39, pp. 277-282.

61. Mikić, Ž., *History of Orthopaedic Surgery and Traumatology in Vojvodina*, Suppl. 50 Years of JUOT, Acta Orthopaedica Iugoslavica, Belgrade 1982, pp. 65-68.

62. Mikić, Ž., *Scottish Women's Hospitals, Tthe Ninetieth Anniversary of their Work in Serbia*, Medicinski Pregled (Medical Review), Novi Sad, 2005, Vol. 58, pp. 597-608.

63. Mikić, Ž., Lešić, A., *Seventy Years from the Founding of the Anglo-Yugoslav Children's Hospital for Tuberculosis of Bones and Joints at Sremska Kamenica*, Srpski arhiv (Serbian Archives for Medicine), Belgrade, 2004, Vol 132, pp.469-473

64. Mikić, Ž., *Seventy Years of the Anglo-Yugoslav Children's Hospital for Tuberculosis of Bones and Joints at Sremska Kamenica*, Medicinski Pregled (Medical Review), Novi Sad, 2004, Vol.57, pp.627-630.

65. Mikić, Ž., *Visit to the Former "Anglo-Yugoslav Children's Hospital for Tuberculosis of Bones and Joints" at Sremska Kamenica*, Lekar (Physician), Serbian Medical Association, Belgrade, March 1986, No. 84-85, p. 5.

66. Miller, M., *Hospital Life in Serbia, Impressions of the Anglo-Serbian Children's Hospital*, The World's Children' London, November 1930, pp.84-86.

67. Milovanović, B., Vuković, Ž., *Good Fairies of the Serbian People*, Documentary TV Film, Belgrade Television, Belgrade, May 1990.

68. Mitrović, A., *Serbia in the First World War*, Srpska književna zadruga (Serbian Literary Society), Belgrade, 1984, pp.188-194.

69. Mitrović, M., *Katherine MacPhail, In Memoriam*, Acta Orthopaedica Iugoslavica, Belgrade, 1975, Vol. 6, pp.3-5.

70. Moreton, A. L., *Alexander MacPhail, M.D.,C.M.(Glasgow), F.R.F.P.S. (Glasgow), 1872-1938, In Memoriam*, Saint Bartholomew's Hospital Reports, London, 1938, Vol.72, pp.7-9.

71. Obradović, S., *Celebration at Sremska Kamenica, Half of the Century of the Hospital*, Dnevnik, Novi Sad, October 29th, 1984, p. 9.

72. Obradović, S., *In Memory of Our Friends, Foundation of Doctor Katherine,* Dnevnik, Novi Sad, November 4th, 1984, p. 9.

73. Parsons, F.G., *Alexander MacPhail, In Memoriam*, The British Medical Journal, London, September 10th, 1938.

74. Petranović, B., *UNRRA's Help to Yugoslavia*, History of the Twentieth Century, Proceedings 2, Belgrade, 1961, pp. 163-225.

75. Rakić, C., *Work and Schooling in the Treatment of the Osteo-Articular Tuberculosis,* Medicinski pregled (Medical Review), Novi Sad, 1960, Vol. 13, pp. 127-130.

76. Sandes, F., *An English Woman-Sergeant in the Serbian Army*, Hodder & Stoughton, London, 1916.

77. Sandes, F., *Autobiography of a Woman Soldier*, Witherby, London, 1927.

78. Sandes, F., *British Magic, A Glimpse of the Anglo-Serbian Children's Hospital*, The World's Children, London, January 1927, pp. 57-59

79. Seton-Watson, H., Seton-Watson, C., *The Making of a New Europe*, Methuen, London, 1986.

80. Shepherd, A., *British Medical Women in Serbia*, Medical Woman, London, 1986, Vol. 5, No. 2, pp. 15-17.

81. Shepherd, A., *The Yugoslavian Connection*, Edinburgh Medicine, August 19th, 1987, Vol. 45, p. 11.

82. Stanulović, D., (ed.) et al., *A Commemorative Volume of the Faculty of Medicine in Novi Sad, 1960-1980*, Faculty of Medicine, Novi Sad, 1980.

83. Stefanović, S. (ed.) et al., *50 Years of the Faculty of Medicine in Belgrade, 1920-1970*, Galenika, Belgrade, 1970.

84. Stanojević, V., Dragić, M., *Dr. Katherine Stewart MacPhail*, Medicinska revija (Medical Review) Belgrade, 1974, Vol. 24, pp. 75-83.

85. Stanojević, V., *Pockmarked Typhus Fever in the Serbian Army 1914-1915*, In the book: *History of the Serbian Military Medical Corps, Our*

War Medical Experience, ed. and publ. by Vlad(imir) Stanojević, Belgrade, 1925, pp. 329-335.

86. Stojanović, S., Simić, P., Došen, M., *Clinical and Statistical Data of the Department of Osteo-Articular Tuberculosis at Sremska Kamenica 1934-1958*, Medicinski pregled (Medical Review), Novi Sad, 1960, Vol. 13, pp. 131-137.

87. Tew, M., *The Anglo-Yugoslav Hospital*, The World's Children, London, September 1946, p. 164.

88. Vuković, Ž., *Allied Medical Missions in Serbia 1914-1918*, Politika, Belgrade, August 2nd – 12th, 1984.

89. Vuković, Ž., *Lest we Forget, Allied Medical Missions in Serbia 1915*, Plato, Belgrade, 2004.

90. Vuković, Ž., *Roses from Edinburgh*, Politika, Belgrade, January 6th, 1986, p. 14.

91. Wilson, F., *In the Margins of Chaos, recollections of Relief Work in and between Three Wars*, John Murray, London, 1944.

92. Wilson, F., *Aftermath*, Penguin Books, West Drayton, England & New York, 1947.

93. Wilson, F., *Relief Work in Yugoslavia*, The World's Children, London, February 1947, pp. 38-40.

Pronunciation Key

a	pronounced as in *father* (Novi Sad)
c	pronounced *ts* as in *bats* (Mladenovac)
č	pronounced *ch* as in *church* (Čardak, Čiča)
ć	pronounced as č but softer, usually appears at the end of surnames (Mikić)
dž	pronunced as *j* in *jazz* (džez = jazz)
đ or dj	pronunced similar to dž but softer (Đorđević or Djordjević)
e	pronounced as in *bed* (Petar, Pero)
i	pronounced as *e* in *we* (Niš, Nikola)
j	pronunced *y* as in *yet* (Jugoslavija, Jelak)
lj	pronunced as *l* but softer as *j* usually softens a preceding consonant (Valjevo)
nj	pronounced as softened *n* as in *new* (Vranje)
o	pronounced as in *not* and *ought* (Olga)
r	pronunced as *r* in Rome (Ružičić)
š	pronunced *sh* as in *ship* (Fruška Gora)
u	pronounced as *oo* in *room* (Ulcinj)
ž	pronounced as *s* in *pleasure* (Želimir)

Abreviations

ASCH	Anglo-Serbian Chidren's Hospital
IWM	Imperial War Museum
JUOT	Yugoslav Orthopaedic and Traumatologic Association
OAT	Osteo-Articular Tuberculosis (Tuberculosis of Bones and Joints)
OBE	Order of the British Empire
RAMC	Royal Army Medical Corps
SCF	Save the Children Fund
SMA	Serbian Medical Association
SRF	Serbian Relief Fund
SWH	Scottish Women's Hospitals
UNRRA	United Nations Relief and Rehabilitation Administration
VAD	Voluntary Aid Detachment
WRNS	Women's Royal Naval Service
YWCA	Young Women's Christian Association

Printed in the United Kingdom
by Lightning Source UK Ltd.
121373UK00001B/11-54/A

9 781905 399277